The Scottish Office

THE NEW WHITEHALL SERIES

is prepared under the auspices of

THE ROYAL INSTITUTE OF PUBLIC ADMINISTRATION

and is edited on its behalf by Sir Robert Fraser, O.B.E.
The purpose of the series is to provide
authoritative descriptions of the present work
of the major Departments of Central Government

Already published

THE HOME OFFICE (*reprinted*)

THE FOREIGN OFFICE (*reprinted*)

THE COLONIAL OFFICE

THE MINISTRY OF WORKS

THE SCOTTISH OFFICE

In preparation

THE MINISTRY OF LABOUR AND
NATIONAL SERVICE

THE MINISTRY OF PENSIONS AND
NATIONAL INSURANCE

THE MINISTRY OF TRANSPORT AND
CIVIL AVIATION

THE MINISTRY OF SUPPLY

THE NEW WHITEHALL SERIES

The Scottish Office

And Other Scottish Government Departments

SIR DAVID MILNE
K.C.B.

LONDON · GEORGE ALLEN & UNWIN LTD
NEW YORK · OXFORD UNIVERSITY PRESS INC

PRINTED IN GREAT BRITAIN
in 10 point Times Roman type
BY R. & R. CLARK, LTD
EDINBURGH

Preface

IN this book an attempt is made to give a comprehensive account of the scope and variety of the work performed by Scottish Government departments, or, more accurately, by departments which are responsible to Scottish Ministers. It will be seen that the book does not deal with the affairs of departments of other Ministers of the Crown whose responsibilities extend throughout the whole of Great Britain. Their arrangements and work in relation to Scotland have already been outlined in the Scottish Office publication *A Handbook on Scottish Administration* (Revised Edition, H.M.S.O., 1956).

It will be apparent from even a cursory perusal of this book that in all the diverse duties which the Scottish Office has to fulfil, its members work together as a team. The production of the book has been no exception. In its general layout and the settlement of its contents I have had the benefit of the assistance and advice of my senior colleagues, to whom I am in this, as in other matters, deeply indebted. But, more particularly, I should like to record my thanks to Mr. I. M. Robertson, a former Principal Private Secretary to the Secretary of State for Scotland, for the help he has given in the co-ordination and presentation of the material provided by the departments, and for the historical research which he has undertaken.

D. M.

Contents

PREFACE   *page* V

PART ONE: THE SECRETARY OF STATE
AND HIS FUNCTIONS

Chapter

  I. *Introduction*   3

 II. *Development of the Office of Secretary of State*   8

III. *The Scottish Office*   22

PART TWO: THE DEPARTMENT OF
AGRICULTURE FOR SCOTLAND

 IV. *The Land of Scotland*   35

  V. *Agricultural Production*   46

 VI. *The Agricultural Guarantee System*   58

PART THREE: THE SCOTTISH EDUCA-
TION DEPARTMENT

 VII. *Education in Scotland*   67

VIII. *Schools*   72

  IX. *H.M. Inspectorate and the Scottish Leaving
       Certificate Examination*   81

   X. *Teachers*   86

  XI. *Further Education*   91

 XII. *The Financing of Public Education in Scotland*   94

PART FOUR: THE DEPARTMENT OF
HEALTH FOR SCOTLAND

 XIII. *The National Health Service*   105

 XIV. *The Care of the Aged and Infirm and the
        Welfare of the Handicapped*   116

  XV. *Town and Country Planning*   121

 XVI. *Housing, Water Supplies and General Sani-
        tation*   132

PART FIVE: THE SCOTTISH HOME
DEPARTMENT

Chapter

XVII.   *Public Order, the Care of Children and Miscellaneous Services*   *page* 145

XVIII.   *Local Government*   161

XIX.   *Industry and Transport*   165

XX.   *Scotland's Minister*   175

PART SIX: OTHER RESPONSIBILITIES OF
THE SECRETARY OF STATE

XXI.   *Joint   Ministerial   Responsibilities: The
Forestry Commission and the Crown Estate
Commissioners*   181

XXII.   *The Smaller Scottish Departments and Offices*   188

PART SEVEN: THE LAW OFFICERS AND
THE LORD ADVOCATE'S DEPARTMENTS

XXIII.   *The Law Officers and the Lord Advocate's Departments*   203

XXIV.   *Conclusion*   210

APPENDIX I: *The Scottish Boards*   212

APPENDIX II: *Holders of the Offices of Secretary of
State, Minister of State and Permanent Under-
Secretary of State; Joint Parliamentary Under-
Secretaries of State and Secretaries of the Four
Departments*   216

*Holders of the Offices of Lord Advocate and
Solicitor-General for Scotland*   218

INDEX   225

PART ONE

The Secretary of State
and his Functions

CHAPTER I

Introduction

EVERY day at St. Andrew's House in Edinburgh and at Dover House in Whitehall, bundles of letters are delivered addressed to the Secretary of State for Scotland, as well as to his Scottish ministerial colleagues and the Scottish departments. On a typical day, there will be letters from Members of Parliament and from patients in mental hospitals, from Peers and from prisoners; there will certainly be formally expressed letters from lawyers and local authorities; and there may be informal and even abusive communications, scrawled on a postcard. There will be letters on hand-made paper with embossed letter-headings, and letters written on scraps torn from an old notebook. The subject matter of all these letters will be almost inconceivably diverse. On the same morning, the Secretary of State may be asked to consider appeals against the proposed erection of a large power station in the south of Scotland and of a fish-meal factory in the north; for remission of a sentence imposed by the courts, or against the closing of a rural school. The same post that brings him the considered views of the Convention of Royal Burghs on a Bill may also bring a pathetic letter from someone who wants a house, representations about employment prospects from the local branch of a Trade Union, and a request from a lady in America for a set of bagpipes.

The only feature that these letters have in common is that they all deal with some aspect of Scottish life, and their number and variety are a fair indication of the extent to which the Secretary of State is popularly regarded as the Minister responsible for anything that happens in Scotland. Most other Ministers are responsible for one or more specific aspects of the nation's affairs—for Trade or Labour or the Royal Navy—but the Secretary of State's responsibilities, broadly speaking, are determined geographically rather than functionally. South of the Border, he has his share in the collective responsibility of all members of the Government for its decisions and actions; north of the Border, not only is he the Scottish equivalent of a number of English Ministers but he is regarded as 'Scotland's Minister', who must see that the Cabinet are made aware of the impact on Scotland of whatever they are discussing, and will indeed be failing in his duty if he does not do so.

The later chapters of this book will show how this heavy and rather unusual burden came to be borne by the Secretary of State, what the principal functions of the Scottish departments are and how they perform them. But it may be convenient at this point to say very briefly what the Scottish Office is and to sketch roughly the nature of the Secretary of State's work.

The Scottish Office, in one sense, denotes the headquarters of the Secretary of State. It includes, on the Ministerial side, a Minister of State and three Parliamentary Under-Secretaries of State, and on the official side, the Secretary of State's chief permanent adviser (the Permanent Under-Secretary of State), the Assistant Under-Secretary of State, and of course the various private secretaries. All these lead a nomadic life between Edinburgh and London, but the majority of them will be for the most part in London while Parliament is sitting and in Scotland when it is not. (The two Scottish law officers, the Lord Advocate and the Solicitor-General for Scotland, are *not* part of the Scottish Office, but have their own departments—the Lord Advocate's Department in London and the Crown Office in Edinburgh. Although these departments are entirely separate and independent, their contacts with the Scottish Office are necessarily close and frequent and no account of Scottish administration would be complete that did not deal with them. See therefore Part VII of this book.)

In the more general sense with which this book is concerned, the Scottish Office includes four separate departments, each located in Scotland with its headquarters at St. Andrew's House, Edinburgh, and each with only a small liaison staff in London. These departments —Agriculture, Education, Health and Home—are the instruments with which the Secretary of State administers in Scotland, matters which in England are the concern of eight separate Ministers. The main functions of the departments may be summarised as follows:

Function	Scottish Department	Corresponding English Minister
Agriculture	Department of Agriculture for Scotland	Minister of Agriculture, Fisheries and Food
Food	Primarily Department of Agriculture for Scotland but also Department of Health for Scotland and Scottish Home Department	Minister of Agriculture, Fisheries and Food Minister of Health
Education	Scottish Education Department	Minister of Education
Health and Welfare Services	Department of Health for Scotland	Minister of Health
Housing and General Sanitation		Minister of Housing and Local Government
Town and Country Planning		

Public Order (Police, fire, prisons, civil defence), Criminal Justice and miscellaneous social services		Home Secretary
Local Government		Minister of Housing and Local Government
Fisheries	Scottish Home Department	Minister of Agriculture, Fisheries and Food
Electricity		Minister of Power
Roads		Minister of Transport and Civil Aviation
Legal Services		Lord Chancellor

The four Scottish departments have no legal existence independent of the Secretary of State, for whom they act, although the Secretary of each, like the head of an English department, is responsible to Parliament as Accounting Officer for the money spent by his department. Therefore when the functions of the Department of Agriculture for Scotland, for example, are discussed later in this book, they are simply the functions of the Secretary of State wearing his agricultural hat. Indeed it would be more helpful to an understanding of Scottish administration if the six symbolic figures which decorate the outside of St. Andrew's House could be replaced by statues showing the same man clad symbolically in different ways.

The identity of the Secretary of State with his departments is perhaps not yet fully understood, although it has been a constitutional fact since 1939. There is still prevalent in Scotland a vague belief that the departments can act on their own authority and make decisions against which there is an appeal to the Secretary of State. In fact, of course, the departments act only by authority of the Secretary of State, express or implied, and it is in recognition of this that their formal letters begin 'I am directed by the Secretary of State to . . .' The use of this formula does not mean that every letter where it is used has been seen personally by the Minister; but he, or the Government, has settled the policy and the responsibility is his. The formula is an acknowledgment of the constitutional position, though its validity does not go without question. Mr. T. A. Critchley, for instance, wrote in 1951 in his book on the Civil Service, in the course of a plea for simpler, less official forms of correspondence:

Absurdity is reached when [the Civil Servant] writes to the Town Clerk declaring that he is directed by the Secretary of State to request that a toddler's lavatory should be installed at Muddlecombe-on-Sea. Everybody knows that Secretaries of State cannot with the best will in the world concern themselves with toddler's lavatories, and when the civil servant pretends that they do he is lying, the public knows he is lying, and he knows the public knows he is lying.[1]

The problem is not as simple as that, because of the Minister's responsibility to Parliament. Many matters must be handled by officials, but it is on behalf of their Minister that they act, and if what seems at first sight a comparatively trivial local matter raises difficult issues, or becomes the subject of strong public feeling—as often happens—the Minister will *have* to concern himself with it. (Oddly enough, the Secretary of State for Scotland answered two parliamentary questions on the subject of 'toddlers' lavatories' during 1955.[2]) As compared with the formal official communication sent in the name of the Secretary of State, the informal semi-official letter has its uses, but a town clerk does not want to know that Mr. X of the Scottish Home Department has agreed to give the town council a grant; he wants the authority of the Secretary of State. The uninformed may think of the departments or their officers as bureaucrats exercising arbitrary powers; but it really is not so. Each officer knows, and must never forget, that every official action he takes commits the Secretary of State, who may have to answer for it in Parliament or in the courts. If he is not confident that the Secretary of State would agree with the line he is taking, he must seek ministerial approval first.

The tendency to regard the Scottish departments as something separate from the Secretary of State is probably a survival of the days when a great deal of Scottish administration was carried on by Boards or departments with an independent legal existence. As the following chapters will show, once the office of Secretary for Scotland had been created in 1885, the new Minister was regarded as the natural spokesman of these Boards in Parliament. It was clearly an awkward arrangement for the Secretary for Scotland (or Secretary of State for Scotland, as he became in 1926) to have to answer in Parliament for Boards for which he had only partial responsibility as a Minister, and with whose actions he might not even agree. Gradually, therefore, the Boards were abolished and their functions were transferred to the Secretary of State.

Once the office of Secretary for Scotland had been created, it also tended to exercise a sort of magnetic attraction on other administrative organisations concerned with Scotland. Because a Minister existed who had very substantial responsibilities in Scotland and was indeed the chief representative of the Government in Scotland, it was a natural step for Parliament to give him other important duties. Some of these are discharged through the St. Andrew's House depart-

---

[1] *The Civil Service Today* (Gollancz, 1951), page 89.
[2] *Hansard* for 25th January (cols. 12-13) and 3rd March (written answers, col. 307), 1955.

ments, and others not through those departments at all but through such bodies as the Forestry Commission and the Office of the Crown Estate Commissioners. Thus, although the four Scottish departments have no existence independent of the Secretary of State, the reverse is not true. This book would obviously be incomplete if it did not deal with all the duties and functions of the Secretary of State, and chapters will therefore be found in Part VI which describe briefly the operation in Scotland of the Forestry Commission, the Crown Estate Commissioners and a number of smaller but nevertheless important departments and offices.

All these matters have been imposed specifically on the Secretary of State by Parliament; the field has been carefully surveyed and the boundary fence set up. But outside is a much more dubious area, a sort of no-man's-land into which the Secretary of State may have to venture because, as has been noted above, he is popularly regarded as 'Scotland's Minister'. As long ago as 1937 the Gilmour Committee[1] noted this 'increasing tendency to appeal to him on all matters that have a Scottish aspect, even if on a strict view they are outside the province of his duties as statutorily defined' and the tendency has certainly become more marked since. A no-man's-land is usually a source of trouble and this one is no exception. A Secretary of State for Scotland—whatever his political complexion—may often find that the sector on which he is most violently assailed in Parliament or in the Scottish press is one which he has no direct duty to defend. If there is a gap in the line it must be manned, but what if one of his colleagues has charge of the defences? The traditional excuse of the civil servant, 'Sorry, that's not my pigeon', is seldom available in the Scottish Office and both the Secretary of State and his departments have to go delicately between two extremes. If they seek to intervene unduly in matters for which other Ministers are directly responsible, they will be an intolerable nuisance to their colleagues; if they fail to intervene when their close acquaintance with Scottish conditions makes intervention seem desirable, they will be blamed, and probably justly.

[1] *Report of Committee on Scottish Administration*, Cmd. 5563.

CHAPTER II

Development of the Office of Secretary of State

PEOPLE tend to think of a Government department as a piece of administrative machinery; but a machine has no power to develop to meet changing circumstances. When it has ceased to be useful it is scrapped; it can be described, but it has no history. A department is in a curious way more like a living organism that has evolved to meet the requirements of its environment from beginnings that may be hard to trace. For that reason, although the main purpose of this book is to show how the Scottish Office is composed and works at present, it is worth while—and indeed necessary—to describe briefly the stages of its development.

The Scottish Office in its present form goes back only to 1939, and the name 'Scottish Office' will not be found before 1885. But the office of Secretary of State is very much older, although the Minister responsible for Scottish affairs has, in modern times, been a Secretary of State only since 1926. His Seal, which consists of the Royal Arms in their Scottish form—that is, with the Scottish lion in the first and fourth quarters, the English leopards in the second and the Irish harp in the third—bears the words 'Secretary of State for Scotland' and by this name he is usually known. There are at present seven Secretaries of State in the Government, and all of them in strict constitutional theory hold one office[1] deriving, as Sir Frank Newsam shows in his book on *The Home Office*,[2] from the ancient one of King's Secretary. Any one of them can constitutionally exercise the functions of any of the others. Therefore, when the Secretary of State for Scotland is out of the country or for some other reason not available to discharge business, Scottish documents which require the signature of a Secretary of State (e.g. Warrants and submissions to the Queen) are signed by one of his colleagues; and in the same way he can and does act for them.

EARLY HISTORY

Before the Union of the Parliaments of Scotland and England in 1707, Scottish affairs were administered for the King by a Privy

---

[1] For this reason, references in Statutes are, in general, simply to 'The Secretary of State'. But there have been recent exceptions to this practice and, for example, Section 13 of the White Fish and Herring Industry Act, 1951, refers to 'the Secretary of State concerned with fisheries or agriculture in Scotland' and Section 17(6) of the Transport Act, 1953, to 'The Secretary of State for Scotland'.

[2] Pages 19 ff.

Council in Scotland of which the Officers of State were influential members. The Secretary was one of them and the office can be traced back to the 'King's Secretary' who appears in the reign of David II (1329–71). This office—although Sir George Mackenzie in his *Memoirs of the Affairs of Scotland* comments that 'the office of Secretary was not of old esteemed much in Scotland'—had a regular place in Parliament and in the Privy Council from the fifteenth century. Some distinguished men like Maitland of Lethington held it and it became one of some influence and patronage after 1660, when, too, the official style of 'Secretary of State' began to be used. Some of the other offices, also of very great antiquity, such as the Lord Advocate, Lord Clerk Register and Lord Justice Clerk, still survive in rather altered form. To follow the course of their history, and outline the nature and alteration of their powers, would be an interesting subject of historical research but one quite beyond the scope of this book. It may be noted, however, that the Officers of State sat and voted *ex officio* in the Estates (the Scottish Parliament) and in the powerful executive committee of Parliament known as the Lords of the Articles; they were appointed by the King, although for a period in mid-seventeenth century Parliament succeeded in establishing that its consent to the appointments was necessary.

Under William III and Anne, in the last years of its existence, the Scots Parliament, although still not democratically elected, shook itself free of the Lords of the Articles and began to function vigorously. As a result, the task of the Secretary or Secretaries (for there were sometimes two of them) and the other Great Officers became very difficult. Lord Seafield's[1] correspondence shows him as travelling frequently between Edinburgh and London (it took him eight days by coach from London to Newcastle in August, 1700, when it was too hot to ride post) in his endeavours to reconcile the policy and wishes of the Sovereign in London with what it was practicable to get through the Estates in Edinburgh. He sometimes took refuge in obscurity and the Duke of Hamilton complained to him:

> You great men gett a way of wrytting soe mystically that plain countrie gentilmen like myself will need plainer langwag before I can understand you.

At the time of the Union in 1707 there were two Scottish Secretaries in office, the Earls of Mar and Loudoun. The Office of Secretary of State in (or for) Scotland was not explicitly preserved by the Treaty of Union, however, and neither indeed was any of the administrative structure which had existed in Scotland before 1707. In 1708 the Scottish Privy Council was abolished, Mar was dismissed and

---

[1] James Ogilvy, fourth Earl of Findlater and first Earl of Seafield, one of the astutest of the pre-Union Secretaries of State, who is remembered for his half-sad, half-humorous reference to the Union as 'the end of an auld sang'. See his correspondence, edited by James Grant for the Scottish History Society.

B

Loudoun resigned. In the following year the Duke of Queensberry was added to the two United Kingdom Secretaries of State already in office in London and given special responsibility for Scottish affairs.

As early as July, 1711, only a week after the conclusion of Queensberry's two years as Secretary of State for Scotland, Daniel Defoe expressed himself strongly in a memorandum to Harley against the appointment of a third Secretary. He complained that the office had already become 'The Center of The Hungry Sollicitations Naturall to . . . a poor Craveing and Importunate people' and would prevent the Union from becoming a reality by preserving the separateness of Scotland. 'Scotland No More Requires a Secretary Than Yorkshire or Wales, Nor (the Clamour of Petitions Excepted) can it Supply bussiness for an Office with Two Clarks.'

Further objections to the appointment of a Scots Secretary were summarised by Defoe as follows:

It keeps up a Faction in Scotland . . . He Constitutes himself a kind of a Governor of Scotland, Since he becomes quietly and Gradually (Whether with or without Design) the Medium of all Transactions between her Majtie and The people of Scotland, and Makes those people More Depending on him than perhaps is fit for any particular person on that Side to boast of.

It Seems to lay a foundation of a Custome which in Time will plead prescription and be Claim'd by Posterity as a Right, and No Time can be so proper to Crush it as while (The Thing being young) No Such Claim can be made.

It Layes The Crown Under a Constant and Needless Expense.[1]

No historian has claimed for the office of Secretary of State for Scotland in the period between 1707 and 1745 that it was a great success. Those who held it found it necessary to spend much of their time in London (where the Court and the Parliament were) and tended to rely a good deal on remote control. It is noticeable, too, that the office was dispensed with in times of difficulty; Montrose was dismissed at the time of the '15 Rebellion and Roxburghe was dropped by Walpole in 1725, probably because he had been intriguing against him and fomenting disturbances in Scotland over the Malt Tax.

Walpole is said to have described the Scottish Secretary as 'a public nuisance' and Duncan Forbes of Culloden, the Lord Advocate of the time, wrote in a letter after Roxburghe's dismissal:

It yields a prospect that for some time at least we shall not be troubled with that nuisance, which we long have complained of, a Scots Secretary, either at full length or in miniature. If any one Scotsman had absolute power we are in the same slavery as ever, whether that person be a fair man or a black man, a peer or a commoner, six foot or five foot high, and

[1] *Letters of Daniel Defoe*, edited by G. H. Healey (Oxford, 1955), pages 336-337.

the dependence of his country will be on that man and not on those that made him.[1]

The Secretaryship was briefly revived on the fall of Walpole in 1741 and lasted until the '45 Rebellion, during which the Marquess of Tweeddale resigned it. He had done little to assist the Government forces in Scotland (three weeks after Charles Edward had landed in Eriskay he wrote from London to the Lord Advocate that he thought it 'very doubtful if the Pretender's son be himself actually landed in Scotland') and no new Secretary of State for Scotland was appointed.

THE LORD ADVOCATE AND THE 'SCOTTISH MANAGER'

As a result of the administrative changes that followed the Union, the Lord Advocate emerged as the principal Officer of State in Scotland. As an Officer of State he had traditionally been not simply a law officer but one of the King's advisers in Scotland on all matters, and it was therefore natural that whichever Secretary of State in London had responsibility for Scottish affairs should correspond regularly with him and rely largely on his advice. This practice became firmly established during the tenure of office of Duncan Forbes of Culloden—a man of strong personality, great public spirit and ability, and wide interests. For the period from 1745 to 1827, the conduct of Government business in Scotland was formally the concern of one of the Secretaries of State (after 1782, the Secretary of State for the Home Department) while the real power was shared in varying proportions between the Lord Advocate and unofficial 'Scottish Managers' who happened to enjoy great influence both in the Cabinet and in Scotland.[2] The informal nature of the arrangements does not seem to have worried anyone, least of all the Prime Minister, for in June, 1748, during the Pelham administration a Mr. Dupplin wrote to Craigie, the ex-Lord Advocate:

Who the Scottish Minister is at present Mr. Pelham is at a loss to know. He cannot tell but that character may be as applicable to yourself as to any other person.[3]

If not formally defined, the power of the Scottish Manager was no doubt well enough understood, as it was by the uncontrolled exercise of patronage that the families of Argyle and Bute and then of Dundas held this dominant position. The most famous of them all was the great Henry Dundas, a man of considerable administrative capacity as well as influence, who towered over Scotland as his statue on its

[1] Burton's *Lives of Lovat and Forbes*, page 333.
[2] The 'Scottish Manager' was a Scot who held some ministerial office unconnected with Scotland which gave him a seat in the Cabinet, where he acted as an informal adviser in Scottish affairs.
[3] Glendoick MSS. quoted by Omond in *The Lord Advocates of Scotland*, vol. ii, page 44.

pillar now towers over St. Andrew Square, Edinburgh. He was appointed Solicitor-General in 1766, at the age of 24, but his great influence began when he became Lord Advocate in 1775; in 1782 he was appointed in addition Keeper of the Scottish Signet for life, with patronage of all places in Scotland. Later Ministerial responsibility for India, the Home Office and the War Office added to his opportunities for patronage and, by 1802, 43 of the 45 Scottish members returned at the General Election were his nominees[1] and he also prepared the list of Scottish representative peers.

Early in the nineteenth century the extent of the Lord Advocate's powers began to attract attention. Lord Advocate Hope's handling of certain matters was criticised in the House of Commons in 1804 by Whitbread and in his reply the Lord Advocate drew attention, perhaps unwisely, to the endless succession of his duties. He declared that the functions shared before 1707 by a number of Great Officers of State and even the military arrangements for the defence of Scotland now devolved on him, and he claimed to have 'the whole of the executive government of Scotland under his particular care'. This speech of Hope's led to the English newspaper paragraph quoted by Lord Cockburn:

> Arrived at Edinburgh—the Lord High Chancellor of Scotland, the Lord Justice General, the Lord Privy Seal, the Privy Council and the Lord Advocate, all in one post chaise, containing only a single person.[2]

A little later a series of articles by Cockburn appeared in the *Edinburgh Review*, which suggested that the Lord Advocate's political duties should be transferred to the Home Secretary. Cockburn said in one of the articles (as Defoe had over 100 years before) that there was no more need of a separate Secretary for Scotland than for Yorkshire, Northumberland or Wales, but by 1836, after he had had experience of office as Solicitor-General for Scotland, he had modified this view and advocated the appointment of a Scottish Secretary.[3]

THE HOME SECRETARY AND THE LORD ADVOCATE

In 1827 the system of Government by 'Scottish Manager' came to an end when the second Lord Melville, who had succeeded to a great deal of his father's influence, refused to take office under Canning. Thereafter until 1885 the Home Secretary (who had been formally responsible since 1782) took over Scottish affairs, acting with the advice and help of the Lord Advocate. A 'Scotch Lord of the Treasury' was also appointed to assist in handling Scottish affairs in that department and in the House of Commons.

[1] Hume Brown's *History of Scotland*, vol. iii, page 310.
[2] *Memorials of his Time*, chapter iii.
[3] *Journal*, 12th August, 1836.

The disappearance of the Scottish Manager (who, however un-democratically selected, was at least a Scot with influence in the Cabinet) did not improve the administration of Scottish affairs and by the middle of the nineteenth century there was increasing dis-satisfaction. W. C. Smith, writing in 1885 of the circumstances which led to the creation of the office of Secretary for Scotland, says:

A feeling grew up in Scotland that national interests were neglected in Parliament; that the actual wants of the country were not understood by London departments; that necessary legislation was abandoned or delayed; that injustice was done in the matter of imperial grants.[1]

The Convention of Royal Burghs presented a memorial to Parlia-ment in 1851 on the neglect of Scottish affairs and a Society for the Vindication of Scottish Rights was founded, under the Presidency of Lord Eglinton, in 1853. There were debates on the same subject in Parliament in 1858, 1864, 1867 and 1877. The first of these may be taken as typical; the House of Commons rejected by 174 votes to 47 a motion by Mr. Baxter, the member for Dundee, 'that in the opinion of this House an Under-Secretary of State for Scotland should be appointed to perform the political duties at present attached to the office of Lord Advocate'. Those who supported the motion argued that the Lord Advocate's powers, both political and legal, were too great and his duties too numerous for any one person, however able, to carry out. His legal duties often required him to be in Edinburgh when Parliament was sitting and as a result Scottish business in the House was neglected. The opponents argued rather inconsistently (a) that the appointment of a Scottish Minister would transfer the administration of Scotland to London, and (b) that it would, as Disraeli put it, 'bring us back to a state of provincial administration'. The Home Secretary (Palmerston) and the Lord Advocate claimed that the latter acted merely as a law officer and that all non-legal Scottish business was settled by the Home Secretary.

In 1867, when Mr. Baxter tried again, the Lord Advocate was not even a member of the House, and no Minister replied for the Govern-ment.

In 1869 a letter was sent to Mr. Gladstone on behalf of a majority of the Scottish Members of Parliament asking for the appointment of a Chief Secretary for Scotland. It argued that the system of administration by Scottish Boards in Edinburgh[2] was unsatisfactory because they were not directly responsible to Parliament; and—once again—that the Lord Advocate had too much to do and that the Government of Scotland should not be a monopoly held by the legal profession. Mr. Gladstone took refuge in the customary enquiry, which was held by Lord Camperdown and Sir William Clerk.

---

[1] *The Secretary for Scotland*, 1885, page xii.
[2] See page 17 and Appendix I.

The Camperdown Commission, acting with commendable speed, reported on 11th March, 1870,[1] after taking evidence from representatives of the various Boards and many other witnesses. Although they found the Scottish Boards economical and efficient, they admitted, with some apparent reluctance, that most of their witnesses had found the ministerial arrangements not wholly satisfactory. The dissatisfaction came, they thought, more from Members of Parliament than from the Scottish people, 'who, we agree with some of the witnesses in thinking, have had no opportunity or means of forming an opinion on the subject'. They recommended, without enthusiasm, that the Home Secretary should be 'in fact, as he already is in theory, Minister for Scotland, having two advisers—the Lord Advocate and a Civil Parliamentary Officer attached to the Home Department'.

No immediate action was taken on this recommendation and Scottish M.P.s continued, as they had done for years, to discuss Scottish administrative matters with the Lord Advocate. In 1877, however, the Conservative Home Secretary, Mr. Cross, decided to bring Scottish matters more closely under his control and had the Lord Advocate moved from his separate office in Spring Gardens into the Home Office. Mr. Dalrymple, one of the Lords of the Treasury, speaking on the Secretary for Scotland Bill in 1885, said of this change:

Anyone who had seen the room at the Home Office in which the Lord Advocate sat would not doubt for a moment that his condition had of late years been of a provisional kind. It was a small and dark apartment and he doubted if it was even wholesome.[2]

In 1878 Mr. Cross introduced a Bill providing for the appointment of an additional Under-Secretary for Home Affairs to deal with Scottish business, but after the Bill had had its Second Reading in the middle of the night without Government explanation, no more was heard of it. In 1881 Lord Fife raised in the Lords the question of the Government's handling of Scottish business. The debate was notable for the mastery of the subject shown by Lord Rosebery who not only sketched the history of Scottish administration and summarised the often-repeated arguments but added a weighty new one:

For every other part of the country and every other Department of the Government there is a permanent staff and when a new Minister comes into one of these Departments he finds the traditions and arrangements of the office working on, whatever political changes occur. But there is no such Department and no such tradition in Scotland. Everything has to begin again *de novo* on the accession of the Lord Advocate.[3]

It was becoming increasingly difficult for a Government of either party to ignore the matter, and in 1883 the Liberal Home Secretary,

---

[1] C. 64.
[2] *Hansard*, 3rd August, 1885, cols. 953-954.
[3] *Hansard*, 13th June, 1881, col. 319.

Sir William Harcourt, introduced a Bill to provide for the creation of a Local Government Board for Scotland, the President of which would have a seat in Parliament and would be responsible for a great variety of Scottish business. Harcourt made a curious speech on First Reading in which he seemed to suggest that the proposed new Minister would in fact have very little to do because (a last echo from the age of *laissez-faire*):

> Scotchmen do their own business so well that the questions that come up for solution by the Central Government are singularly few.[1]

The Bill passed the Commons, but was thrown out by the Lords, and this aroused such indignation in Scotland that a mass meeting, representative of all classes and all shades of religious and political opinion, was held in Edinburgh in January, 1884, under the presidency of Lord Lothian. The resolutions adopted at this meeting demanded unconditionally the appointment of a Secretary of State for Scotland and were conveyed to Mr. Gladstone by a strong deputation. Shortly afterwards, in May of the same year, Lord Dalhousie introduced a Bill for the appointment of a Secretary for Scotland. A quarrel between the Houses led to the withdrawal of the Bill after it had received a unanimous Second Reading, but in 1885 it was reintroduced by Lord Rosebery, who had had experience of Scottish administration as a junior Minister at the Home Office and indeed, after persuading Gladstone that a full Secretaryship was necessary for Scotland, had been asked by him to take the new office if it was created. Gladstone's Government had now been succeeded by a Conservative one under Lord Salisbury, but Lord Rosebery's Bill was treated as a non-political one and with Government support became law.

It is curious to record that the general principle that there should be a Scottish Secretary, which had been generally regarded in 1853 as a romantic extravagance of Lord Eglinton's Society, was accepted in 1885 virtually without debate. Discussion centred mainly on whether education should be included among the new Secretary's manifold functions, and the view that it should not was expressed picturesquely by Sir Lyon Playfair:

> But Scotland alone, which above all other countries is essentially educational, is in future to have a Minister made up of a large variety of heterogeneous materials mixed up like a Scotch haggis and then salted with education to give it a flavour.[2]

CREATION OF THE SCOTTISH OFFICE

The Secretary for Scotland Act of 1885 transferred to the new Minister a list of duties in Scotland previously carried out under

[1] *Hansard*, 29th June, 1883, col. 1990.
[2] *Hansard*, 3rd August, 1885, cols. 936 and 937.

various statutory powers by the Home Secretary, the Privy Council, the Treasury and the Local Government Board. The list of functions transferred, which was so miscellaneous as to lead to some witticisms when the Bill was going through, ranged from police to fisheries, and from wild birds' protection to prisons.[1] The Duke of Richmond and Gordon was immediately appointed as the new Minister and set up his office in Dover House, Whitehall, which continued to be the Scottish Ministerial headquarters until damaged by enemy action in 1941, and to which the Scottish Office has recently returned. The Duke's tenure of the newly created post was brief and that of his immediate successors briefer still. When the Secretary for Scotland Act of 1887—which increased the powers and duties of the office— was before Parliament, Lord Rosebery complained that it was not so much new powers as continuity of administration that was required, and he pointed out that there had been five Secretaries for Scotland within 16 months. He was also insistent that the Minister responsible for Scottish administration should have the prestige conferred by membership of the Cabinet. In the Commons, Members complained of the inconvenience of having the Scottish Secretary in the Lords. Several more Peers were to hold the post but after 1892 the Scottish Secretary was always a member of the Cabinet, except during the periods of the War Cabinets.

The Secretary for Scotland remained in sole charge of Scottish affairs—with assistance of course from the two Law Officers, the Lord Advocate and the Solicitor-General for Scotland—until 1919, when the office of Parliamentary Under-Secretary for Health was created by the Scottish Board of Health Act. In 1926 the office of Secretary for Scotland was abolished by the Secretaries of State Act and the functions hitherto exercised by its holder were transferred to one of His Majesty's Principal Secretaries of State—the roundabout but constitutionally correct method of making the principal Scottish Minister a full Secretary of State. As a result of the change, the Parliamentary Under-Secretary for Health became a Parliamentary Under-Secretary of State. The increasing volume of work in the Scottish Office was reflected in the appointment of a second Parliamentary Under-Secretary of State in 1940,[2] and of a third in 1952.[3] A Minister of State, Scottish Office, was also added,[4] towards the end of 1951, to assist the Secretary of State.

To sum up the Ministerial story, from 1707 to 1725 and from 1741 to 1745 there was a Secretary of State mainly responsible for Scotland; from 1745 to 1885 there was no special Scottish Minister, other than the Lord Advocate, concerned with Scottish administration;

[1] W. C. Smith (op. cit.) deals in detail with them all.
[2] Under the Defence (Parliamentary Under-Secretaries) Regulations, 1940.
[3] Under the Ministers of the Crown (Parliamentary Under-Secretaries) Act, 1951.
[4] Under the authority conferred by the Re-Election of Ministers Act, 1919.

from 1885 to 1926 there was an office of Secretary for Scotland; and from 1926 onwards the Ministerial responsibility for Scottish business has been carried by one of the Principal Secretaries of State, who is now assisted by a team of four Ministers—the Minister of State and three Parliamentary Under-Secretaries of State—and who also continues to rely on the advice and assistance of the Lord Advocate and the Solicitor-General for Scotland.

THE SCOTTISH BOARDS

One part of the ancestry of the Scottish Office and its Secretary of State has now been traced—the side from which the name derives. On the other side a great many of the present functions of the Secretary of State were taken over by him from once independent Boards located in Edinburgh. The duties of the present Department of Agriculture for Scotland and Department of Health for Scotland, for example, were performed as late as 1928 by the Board of Agriculture for Scotland and the Scottish Board of Health respectively, and the duties of the Scottish Home Department in relation to fisheries and prisons were also formerly carried out by Boards. Something more is said of these various Boards in Appendix I but this account of the history of the Scottish Office would not be complete without some mention of them.

There were perhaps three main factors which made the development of the system of Boards an important feature of Scottish administration in the nineteenth century. First, there was no one Minister between 1745 and 1885 whose main concern was Scottish administration; the Lord Advocate was primarily a legal officer—or in Henry Dundas's case, primarily a politician—and the Home Secretary had enough to do without concerning himself over the details of Scotland's domestic affairs. Secondly, the distance between Edinburgh and London and the consequent delays in communication made it desirable to have a high degree of administrative independence in Edinburgh. Thirdly, in the first half of the nineteenth century, in both Scotland and England, there were what Dr. F. M. G. Willson[1] has called 'strong ideological objections to any permanent intervention by the State in economic affairs and intense local opposition to centralised administration'.

The majority of the Boards in existence before 1885 were responsible to the Home Secretary and either he or the Lord Advocate on his behalf would answer in Parliament any questions or complaints about their actions. (The Fishery Board, however, was responsible to the Treasury.) Sir William Harcourt went so far as to say that he could count upon his fingers the questions of great importance

[1] 'Ministries v. Boards: Some Aspects of Administrative Development since 1832' in *Public Administration*, Spring, 1955.

that came to him from Scotland while he was Home Secretary.[1] The statement is so exaggerated as to be suspect, but it is undoubtedly true that the greater part of the Boards' work was done without troubling Ministers. The evidence given to Lord Camperdown's Committee in 1870 suggests that the Chairmen and Secretaries of the Boards usually kept their Minister at pen's length and were rarely summoned to London.

The Boards selected their own staff—or, to use a phrase less commonly heard today, exercised their own patronage—but it was already general by 1870 for those chosen to have to pass the examination of the Civil Service Commissioners. In their last days the Boards were in fact served by civil servants, and this made the transition from Board to Government department relatively simple.

The Royal Commission on the Civil Service (1914)[2] and the Haldane Committee on the Machinery of Government (1918)[3] both reported against the Scottish system of administration by Boards because it offended against the doctrine of Ministerial responsibility and also because, as the Royal Commission put it, 'the system affords no room for that type of selected and trained permanent official represented by the administrative class'. Instead there were Board members appointed by patronage, who came in at the top from outside and had to learn while they administered. No immediate action to replace the Boards was taken. Indeed the Scottish Board of Health was formed as late as 1919, to take over from three earlier Boards. But it became increasingly recognised that Boards were an anachronism, and in 1928 the Scottish Boards of Agriculture and Health and the Prisons Commission for Scotland were abolished and their work was assigned to statutory departments.

INCREASING RESPONSIBILITIES OF THE SECRETARY OF STATE

The tendency in the twentieth century had in fact been to increase the direct responsibility of the Scottish Secretary for Scottish administration and this culminated in the reorganisation of 1939. Up to that year there had been, since 1707, various separate Scottish Boards, Commissions and departments, established from time to time for varying purposes, modified or superseded as new needs arose and—after 1885—responsible in varying degrees to the Secretary for Scotland or, from 1926, the Secretary of State. In 1939, as a result of a general review of Scottish administration by a Committee under the chairmanship of Sir John Gilmour, the Secretary of State's responsibility was made almost complete when the functions of the Depart-

[1] *Hansard*, 29th June, 1883, col. 1990.
[2] Fourth Report. Cd. 7338.
[3] Cd. 9320.

ments of Agriculture, Education,[1] Health and Prisons and the Fishery Board for Scotland were vested directly in the Secretary of State by the Reorganisation of Offices (Scotland) Act, 1939. Only the Trustees of the National Galleries, the Keeper of the Registers and Records, the Registrar General and the General Board of Control for Scotland remained separate entities after 1939 and the last two were brought into closer association with the Secretary of State's departments. Everything else of importance became the direct responsibility of the Secretary of State in the same way as the functions he had acquired by statute in and since 1885 and had hitherto administered through the Scottish Office in Dover House, Whitehall. Those functions, as well as those of the Prisons Department and the Fishery Board for Scotland, were allocated to a new department which was named the Scottish Home Department.

Since 1939 the Scottish Office has taken the form suggested by the Gilmour Committee and outlined in Chapter I. In London, there is the Ministerial and Parliamentary headquarters and a liaison office for each of the four departments. In Edinburgh, there are the departments themselves—no longer statutory bodies each with a separate legal identity but organisations existing to aid the Secretary of State in discharging his functions. There is in addition the Permanent Under-Secretary of State, who acts as a general adviser to the Secretary of State over the whole range of his duties. The Secretary of State can alter the allocation of functions between the departments as circumstances from time to time may require.

The concentration of powers in the hands of the Secretary of State in 1939 was symbolised by a physical change in the same year when the major departments—or as much of them as could be got in—were brought under one roof in a new Government building at St. Andrew's House, Edinburgh.

While the administrative pattern drawn by the Gilmour Committee did not change in outline between 1939 and 1957, it was altered in detail by transfers of further work to the Secretary of State since the former date, as well as by some transfers in other directions. The statutory duties of the office were multiplied during and after the war by legislation giving it additional responsibilities for assisting agriculture and promoting agricultural production; for the National Health Service; for town and country planning and development; for rebuilding the fishing fleets and supporting the fishing industry; for hydro-electricity; and for much else. The Secretary of State became a Commissioner of Crown Lands under the Crown Lands Act, 1943;[2]

---

[1] The Scottish Education Department was formed in 1872, formally as a Committee of the Privy Council, but in practice as a separate Government department.

[2] Under the Crown Estate Act, 1956, he is still the Minister responsible for the Crown Estate in Scotland, but ceases to be a Commissioner (see Chapter XXI).

and he assumed responsibility for forestry in Scotland under the Forestry Act, 1945. By administrative arrangement, he took over from the Home Office most of their work in connection with civil defence in Scotland, and in 1953 the Transfer of Functions (Ministry of Pensions) Order gave him responsibility for the medical care of war pensioners. It would be misleading to suggest that the transfers were all in one direction. Before 1939 there were examples of transfers to other Ministers and departments—to the Electricity Commission, the Forestry Commission, the Minister of Transport and the Unemployment Assistance Board. Between 1939 and 1955, the most important transfer was that of the Secretary of State's insurance responsibilities to the Minister of National Insurance. But for the most part, both before and after 1939, the gains have vastly exceeded the losses.

Some of the most recent additions to the Secretary of State's duties are the result of an exhaustive review of Scottish administration by a Royal Commission presided over by Lord Balfour. Their report, published in 1954,[1] endorsed the general conclusions of the Gilmour Committee but recommended certain transfers of functions. As a result, the Secretary of State has acquired the Lord Chancellor's responsibilities for the appointment of justices of the peace in Scotland,[2] and (with one qualification) the Minister of Agriculture's responsibility for animal health;[3] thirdly, the responsibility for roads and bridges, which passed from the Secretary for Scotland to the Minister of Transport in 1919, returned to him in augmented form on 1st April, 1956.[4]

Even that is not the end of the story. The Electricity Reorganisation (Scotland) Act, 1954, transferred to the Secretary of State the Minister of Fuel and Power's responsibilities for electricity in Scotland; and on the disappearance of the Ministry of Food in 1955[5] he was given most of the Scottish duties of that Minister.

At each major change that has been made in the Secretary of State for Scotland's official interests and responsibilities, there have been impatient critics who said that it did not matter who did the work provided it was well done; but to balance that, there were always others to whom it mattered passionately and who feared that the ruin of the country would result from what might appear to be a minor constitutional change. In this book one can only chronicle the development as it happened. Some of the alterations may have been made for political reasons, others out of a desire for administrative tidiness; the river may have flowed erratically, but its main course has

[1] Cmd. 9212.
[2] Transfer of Functions (Justices of the Peace) (Scotland) Order, 1955.
[3] Transfer of Functions (Animal Health) Order, 1955.
[4] Transfer of Functions (Roads, Bridges and Ferries) Order, 1955.
[5] Transfer of Functions (Ministry of Food) Order, 1955.

been clear. There has been a definite and increasing tendency to assign to a Scottish minister matters in which there is a distinctive Scottish tradition or body of law or where Scottish conditions are notably different from those in England and Wales. The present administrative structure is not the result of design, but of constant change and adjustment over a period of 250 years. It is unlikely that it is complete but no one can say what the future changes will be. Time finds its own solutions.

CHAPTER III

The Scottish Office

IN the account which has so far been given of the Scottish Office, the Secretary of State may perhaps seem to resemble a rider in a circus, who at each circuit of the ring has another horse under his control until finally he thunders round standing perilously on two and guiding several more. Like most analogies, this one is not perfect, but it does help to emphasise that the Secretary of State must be able to control quickly and directly each of the departments for which he is responsible, and that although they move separately, they move in unison, under his guidance.

Unity in diversity is in fact one of the characteristic features of the Scottish Office. The diversity is mainly one of function, as will be apparent enough when we come to examine what each of the departments does; but each has retained its independence in financial and establishment matters, and there are still minor differences in custom and practice, as is natural in a federation of four bodies of varying ancestry. For example, while Health and Home file their papers so that the latest is always at the top, Agriculture and Education remain firmly convinced of the merits of their traditional practice by which the file reads like a book and the newest paper is at the back. These are *minutiae*, however, and if there are any deeper differences they are rapidly dying out. What is more important to remember is the unity —the ways in which the four departments act together as the Scottish Office, and what they have in common.

It is perhaps worth mentioning here that the overwhelming majority of civil servants in the Scottish Office are Scots—born and educated in Scotland and working in Edinburgh. An Englishman once expressed surprise that his first official contact with the Scottish Office had been a voice on the telephone saying ''oskins 'ere', but no one walking along the corridors of St. Andrew's House would doubt what country he was in. Moreover, the importance of the decision to concentrate the four departments in one building should not be underestimated. As we shall see later in this chapter, there are various formal means of securing that they act in unison but undoubtedly the machinery of administration runs all the more smoothly for the countless informal discussions that take place in the rooms, in the corridors or in the canteen (or, as it is rather grandly called, the dining club) of St. Andrew's House. These things having been said to fill in the background, we may turn to the main subject of this chapter and discuss the Scottish Office proper, the Ministers and the Permanent Under-Secretary of State, and the relationships which the four departments have in common with Parliament and other Government departments in London and with the town and county councils and other local bodies in Scotland.

THE MINISTERS

As we have seen, the Secretary of State is responsible for all the actions of the Scottish Office departments; this is not simply a formality. In the course of a year he will have considered many papers from each department submitting for his decision both matters of policy and difficult individual cases. He will also have been subjected to question and supplementary question in the House of Commons on most of the important aspects of his work, he will have taken part in debates on the floor of the House and in Committee, and he will have written personally to M.P.s and others on a wide range of subjects. During the parliamentary session, he will probably have attended on an average two Cabinet meetings a week and several other meetings of Ministers, and before each meeting he will have had to study a number of memoranda. He will also have had to spend a considerable part of his time in Scotland, to meet deputations and to attend important ceremonial occasions, and he will probably have carried out an extensive tour in some part of the country. In what time remains to him, he will have eaten, slept and read the newspapers.

Much of this is, of course, the fate of any senior Minister but the Scottish Office presents certain peculiar problems. In most Government departments the Minister has his main body of staff close at hand in London; when a question suddenly becomes important, the papers and the officials who are familiar with them can be brought to his room very quickly. In the Scottish Office, the Secretary of State will generally have to be in London while Parliament is sitting, but the bulk of his departmental advisers and their papers are 400 miles away in Edinburgh. Many a Secretary of State, striving to follow the usually lucid thought-processes of one of his senior officers through the corrupt and garbled text of a teleprinter message, has experienced this physical handicap.

There must always be many matters with which only the Secretary of State can deal. Where the responsibility rests, there the major decisions must be taken. In any important matter, Members of Parliament and deputations often feel that they ought to plead their case before the responsible Minister himself. And there are many duties —such as the signing of regulations and warrants—which other Scottish Office Ministers cannot perform for him. Nevertheless, the fact that the Secretary of State is now assisted by a Minister of State of Cabinet rank and by three Parliamentary Under-Secretaries makes possible a much more detailed ministerial supervision of the varied activities of the office than he himself could undertake under modern conditions.

There is, of course, nothing final about the present ministerial arrangements, and as there has not been a Labour Government in office since a Minister of State and a third Parliamentary Secretary were added to the team, those arrangements are not, as it were, endorsed by both sides. But it may be useful to record what they are. The Minister of State, who acts as the Secretary of State's deputy, has up to now been a member of the House of Lords and has acted there as Government spokesman on Scottish affairs. His lighter parliamentary duties have enabled him to attend meetings and carry out engagements in various parts of Scotland and to discuss urgent matters with officials in Edinburgh on days when Cabinet business or the demands of the Whips would have made it difficult for the Secretary of State to leave London. Like the Secretary of State, he has dealings with all four departments; and he has up to now been specially concerned with questions affecting development, industry, the general aspects of local government, and the special problems of the Highlands and Islands. It seems likely that the relationship between the two senior Scottish Ministers will remain a flexible one and that the Minister of State will continue to form that 'mass of manœuvre' beloved of Sir Winston Churchill, i.e. a force not wholly committed which can be employed wherever the pressure is greatest. But much will obviously depend on the experience, the inclinations and above all the personalities of the holders of the two posts.

The work of the Scottish Office has been subdivided into three parts, each allotted to one of the three Joint Parliamentary Under-Secretaries. Each of the three will normally see all submissions that are made to Ministers by the departments for which he is responsible and with a number of such submissions senior Ministers will not have to be troubled at all. The Parliamentary Under-Secretaries share with the Secretary of State the handling of Scottish legislation in the House of Commons and the duty of answering parliamentary questions, and they frequently represent the Scottish Office at meetings with outside organisations and with their ministerial colleagues in other departments. The present allocation of subjects among them is as follows:

(i) Agriculture and Food   Department of Agriculture for Scotland
    Fisheries and Food   Scottish Home Department
    Forestry   Forestry Commission

(ii) Housing and allied subjects ⎫
     Health   ⎬ Department of Health for Scotland
     Town and Country Planning   ⎭
     Local Government   Scottish Home Department

(iii) Education   Scottish Education Department
      Police, Fire and Civil Defence ⎫
      Criminal Justice   ⎪
      Children and miscellaneous   ⎪
            social services   ⎬ Scottish Home Department
      Industry and Development   ⎪
      Electricity   ⎪
      Roads   ⎭

The two law officers, the Lord Advocate and the Solicitor-General, have, as we have seen, always taken an interest in policy as well as in purely legal matters and, as they are responsible for the drafting of Scottish legislation and take their share in piloting it through the House of Commons, it is natural that they should continue to do so.

The Secretary of State may call meetings of Scottish Ministers (including the law officers) to discuss major issues, and Ministers regularly talk over the problems of the moment, so that at the ministerial level there is a useful informal means of co-ordinating the activities of the various departments.

THE PERMANENT UNDER-SECRETARY OF STATE

The Scottish Office in its present form is the creation of the Gilmour Committee and it is clear from their Report that one aspect of their proposals exercised them particularly. What would happen if the four departments (each of which *is* the Secretary of State) gave him different advice—if, to return to our original analogy, the horses ran in different directions or one of them became larger and stronger than the others? The Committee's solution was to recommend the appointment of a Permanent Secretary, senior in rank to the heads of the four Scottish departments—and equal in rank to the heads of the major Whitehall departments. When the Committee's recommendations were put into effect in the Reorganisation of Offices (Scotland) Act, 1939, the proposed creation of a Permanent Secretary attracted as much comment as any part of the Bill. Members of Parliament, showing an unexpected but gratifying concern for the four departments, were anxious that the new senior official should not have power to exercise control over them; but if he was not going to exercise control over them, what was he going to do?

In practice, the office has operated much as the Gilmour Committee envisaged that it would, and the Royal Commission on Scottish Affairs in 1954 endorsed the arrangements, emphasising again 'the necessity for the Secretary of State having the advice and assistance of a senior officer who is not burdened with the charge of a particular Department'. The Permanent Under-Secretary of State,[1] then, acts as a personal adviser and assistant to the Secretary of State

[1] As the Permanent Secretary is called in a Government department which is in the charge of a Secretary of State.

C

over the whole area of the latter's responsibilities, but this in no way cuts across the direct responsibility of the heads of the four Scottish departments for the administration of their offices. While Parliament is sitting and the Secretary of State is mainly in London, he too has to spend a good deal of time there. But it is important that he should not become a London Scot, in touch with Scottish affairs and the Scottish departments only through newspapers and official minutes. He therefore spends much of his time at St. Andrew's House, where he is in close touch with the Minister of State and the Scottish departments and where he holds periodic conferences of the heads of the departments at which matters of common interest to them all are discussed. The departmental heads have direct access to the Secretary of State and the Minister of State personally or by minute, but the Permanent Under-Secretary of State sees copies of submissions to Ministers by the heads of the four departments and, without becoming a 'bottleneck', is thus automatically kept informed of what is going on throughout the Scottish Office. He is, in general, concerned with the smooth working of the Office as a whole and in the allocation of responsibilities between the various departments. He is likely to be brought in particularly where a current problem concerns more than one department or where the Secretary of State as 'Scotland's Minister' is involved in something which may have very little official connection with any of the Scottish departments.

The Permanent Under-Secretary of State is assisted by an officer of under secretary rank, who works principally in London. There are many important official committees meeting in London with which no one Scottish department is primarily concerned but where it is desirable that a senior official should represent Scottish interests and the Scottish Office as a whole. Attendance at all such committees would tie the Permanent Under-Secretary unduly to London and would also take up too much of his time. The Assistant Under-Secretary of State attends a number of such meetings and also helps the Permanent Under-Secretary in co-ordinating matters of joint interest to all the departments. He has the special duty of acting as a liaison officer between the Scottish Office and the Forestry Commission, the Crown Estate Office, the Nature Conservancy, etc.

THE PRIVATE OFFICE

The Secretary of State has a principal and an assistant private secretary and the Minister of State and Parliamentary Under-Secretaries of State have one private secretary each. Their work is not basically different from that of private secretaries in other Government departments. Their principal function is, in essence, to ensure that the Ministers' views are fully understood in the departments and equally that the Ministers are fully aware of the advice of their officials. But in the Scottish Office their work, and especially that of the principal private secretary, is coloured by the special features of the office which have already been noted. The principal private secretary, as Mr. Herbert Morrison observes, is 'the continuous link between the Minister and the Permanent Secretary',[1] but in the Scottish Office he must also act as a link between the Secretary of State and the four departmental heads, and the latter may well be 400 miles away in Edinburgh when a sudden parliamentary squall blows up. By reason of his position, the private secretary is often the first to hear of some potentially difficult situation.

THE SCOTTISH OFFICE AND PARLIAMENT

It is at its narrowest point, at the apex of the pyramid, that the Scottish Office is in contact with Parliament, through the Ministers who move in both the official world and the political one. Ministers in other Government departments are likely to come into official contact with any one of the 630 Members of Parliament. The Scottish Ministers, and therefore the Scottish departments, deal on the whole with a restricted group. The bulk of their parliamentary correspondence, and of the parliamentary questions that have to be answered by them, will come from the members for Scottish constituencies—grown in number to 71 from the 'chosen five and forty' whom Burns addressed in rather irreverent terms about the whisky duty. These 71 members, together with a small number of members for other seats, 'press-ganged' for the occasion to keep the same political balance as in the House itself, form the Scottish Standing Committee, which discusses exclusively Scottish Bills in principle, and examines Scottish Bills in detail at the Committee stage; the Committee may also be empowered to consider some or all of the Estimates of the Departments for which the Secretary of State is responsible. The Scottish members have always tended to form a group (at least one nineteenth-century Lord Advocate used to have regular meetings with them in the tea-room in the House to discuss matters of common interest) and the Scottish Standing Committee has accentuated this tendency, so that all the Scottish members are well known to the Ministers and *vice versa*. Quite a number of them will also know the senior officials and private secretaries, and these informal contacts help the transaction of Scottish business. The Parliamentary Private Secretary, whose main function is to act as a link between his Minister and the back-benchers,[2] may also be very valuable in preventing friction at the point where the Scottish Office is geared to Parliament.

One peculiar difficulty must be mentioned from which the Scottish Ministers (and the Scottish Office) suffer in their relations with

---

[1] *Government and Parliament*, page 313.
[2] See Herbert Morrison, *Government and Parliament*, pages 115-116.

Parliament. Because of the extraordinary diversity of the Secretary of State's interests and the number of English ministers of whom he is the Scottish equivalent, it is extremely difficult to know when a Scottish Minister may not be required on the Front Bench to deal with points raised by a Scottish member. The Secretary of State may certainly be fairly confident that he will not be called upon to intervene in a debate on foreign affairs or on, say, Colonial unrest, but the discussion of a Great Britain Bill or any general debate on, for example, the economic situation, trade and industry, employment, fuel and power or civil aviation may start a Scottish hare. And he must watch carefully when any of his colleagues—the Minister of Education, perhaps, or the Minister of Health—is making a statement, even on a purely English matter. 'Will the Rt. Hon. Gentleman tell the House what the Scottish position is?' or, still worse, 'Where is the Secretary of State for Scotland? He is treating Scottish members with scant courtesy . . .', etc.—Scottish Secretaries, of whatever political complexion, are well accustomed to these interjections, which present a very real problem both to them and to the Scottish Office officials. If briefs were written and Ministers prepared to meet every possible parliamentary contingency, there would be very little time left for anything else. It is the old problem of defending a long coast line with few troops; one must try to know where the landing will be and hope one guesses right. A good intelligence service—that is, close liaison at every level, ministerial, private secretarial and official, with the English departments—will do a good deal to guard against surprise.

LIAISON

The difficulties that result from the 400 miles that separate Edinburgh and London have already been referred to and it is obvious that the efficiency of the Scottish Office will to some extent depend on the arrangements made to overcome them. The Gilmour Committee was particularly asked to enquire into 'the arrangements under which liaison is maintained between Edinburgh and London in the conduct of public business', and it devoted a chapter of its report to the subject. The Committee found that the methods adopted by the Scottish Agriculture, Education, Health and minor departments at that time (1936–37) to keep in touch with London presented 'considerable variety'; the then Scottish Office had the reverse problem and had only as recently as 1935 opened an office in Edinburgh. After hearing a good deal of conflicting evidence, the Committee made a recommendation which in fact describes the present arrangements— that each of the four Scottish departments should have its own liaison staff in London, borne on its own establishment and with a composition varying according to its requirements. The four liaison staffs have in fact varied in numbers and rank from time to time.

The Department of Agriculture and Home Department at present have assistant secretaries as their senior liaison officers, and the Education and Health departments, principals. The liaison staffs not only maintain routine contacts with the London ministries and act as collectors and transmitters of information in both directions; they also represent their departments at many committee and other meetings. Their efforts do not, of course, make it unnecessary for officers from Scotland to visit London but, supplemented by private telephone lines and a teleprinter service installed in accordance with another recommendation of the Gilmour Committee, they have done a good deal to link the two capitals administratively. It may be significant that the word 'liaison' does not appear in the index to the Report of the Royal Commission on Scottish Affairs (1954).

COMMON SERVICES

Rather as federal states may act through one central body for such matters as foreign affairs and defence, there are certain services which the Secretary of State's departments share in common because it is more efficient and more economical to do so. If the greater part of the work of a group of professional or technical officers is done for one department, it is obviously sensible that they should belong to that department and that the others should 'borrow' them when they require their advice. Thus, for example, the architectural staff of the Department of Health for Scotland provide any architectural advice that the Education Department or the Home Department may need; and the engineers of the same Department advise the Home Department on coast protection and harbour engineering. There are, however, certain services—such as the Solicitor's Office, the Scottish Information Office and the Statistician—of which it cannot be said that the interest of any one department is predominant, and it is perhaps appropriate to mention such services here, although for establishment purposes they come under the wing of the Scottish Home Department.

The Solicitor in St. Andrew's House, then, acts as Solicitor to the Secretary of State's departments. The work of his office includes the drafting of orders, regulations and other subordinate legislation, the provision of legal advice to the Department of Agriculture and Department of Health on questions arising in their work,[1] and other duties more closely akin to what is done in the office of a lawyer in private practice, such as conveyancing and the handling of claims, litigation, etc. The Solicitor also acts in Scotland for the Treasury and certain other Great Britain ministries.

[1] The Scottish Education Department and the Scottish Home Department receive legal advice from the Lord Advocate's Department. See Chapter XXIII, page 205.

The Scottish Information Office, also in St. Andrew's House, is both a press relations office and, as its name suggests, a clearing house for Scottish information. It conducts publicity campaigns for the departments; it keeps Ministers and officials informed of the press comment on any action they have taken or announcement they have made; and it enables newspapermen, when they want to ask some question about the work of the Scottish departments, to deal regularly with a press officer instead of with a large number of ultra-cautious or over-expansive departmental officers. Each of the press officers works as a rule with one or other of the departments, but the Director of the Information Office himself must watch the whole area of the Secretary of State's responsibilities. One of the press officers is stationed in London and acts as a liaison officer with the London press and, in particular, with the parliamentary lobby correspondents of the Scottish newspapers. The Scottish Information Office also acts in Scotland as an agent for the Central Office of Information.

The Statistician's principal duty is to prepare economic and other statistics relating to Scottish affairs, which would not otherwise be available and which are likely to be useful to Scottish Ministers and the various Government departments concerned with Scotland, or to be of general interest. Some fruits of his labours are to be seen in the *Digest of Scottish Statistics* which is published half-yearly. He is an officer of the Scottish Office and not of the Central Statistical Office but his work naturally leads him to keep in close touch with the latter.

THE SCOTTISH OFFICE AND THE LOCAL AUTHORITIES

So far this chapter has been concerned mainly with the London or parliamentary end of the Scottish Office. What is done at the Edinburgh end is rather a matter for the separate chapters on the work of the various departments, but since three of the four (the exception being Agriculture) are closely concerned in their day-to-day activities with the local authorities, it is perhaps appropriate here to make some general remarks—for the benefit of the non-Scottish reader— about Scottish local government.

Since the structure of Scottish local government was simplified and reformed by the Local Government (Scotland) Act, 1929, there have been three types of local authority—county councils, town councils and district councils. In what is called the 'landward area' of the county—which can most easily be defined negatively as the part of the county that is left if the burghs are excluded—the county council is responsible for all the main work of local government; the landward area may be divided into districts, within which a district council carries out certain duties. The powers of the town councils vary according to their size. In Edinburgh, Glasgow, Dundee and Aberdeen, the town council, like the council of an English county borough, is responsible for the whole work of local government; each is a 'county of a city'. In the twenty 'large burghs' (which, in general, are towns with a population of over 20,000) the town council is statutorily responsible for all local government services, except education and, in some cases, police, which are the responsibility of the county council; in the 173 'small burghs' (which extend from towns of some 20,000 people to the Royal Burgh of New Galloway with just over 300) many important functions such as housing, water supply, sewerage and scavenging are the responsibility of the town council, but a considerable block of the work, including again education and police, is entrusted to the county council. The county council, when dealing with a subject in which its jurisdiction extends to the burghs, includes representatives of the town councils. Within this general system, there are many permutations and combinations, since local authorities have power to act jointly where this seems the most convenient and efficient way to carry out any of their functions. The pattern is, in fact, continually changing, within the boundaries drawn by the Act of 1929.

All these local bodies are connected by innumerable invisible threads of correspondence to the various branches of the Secretary of State's departments. 'St. Andrew's House' has already, in less than 20 years, become widely used throughout Scotland and the Scottish press with all the connotations (favourable or unfavourable) that attach in England to 'Whitehall'; the words 'They ought to do something about it at St. Andrew's House' must often be heard at council meetings. St. Andrew's House is not regarded, however, as an impossibly remote place; the ivory tower of bureaucracy can be taken by assault, and a county clerk or town clerk who feels that he is not getting anywhere by correspondence or that 'they' are being unreasonable, will not hesitate to come to Edinburgh, either alone or accompanied by a deputation of councillors, to say so. Officials from St. Andrew's House may themselves pay local visits and, in particular, technical or general inspectors from St. Andrew's House do valuable liaison work. Both the civil servants and the local authority representatives may occasionally feel, in moments of despair, that, like the official described by Scott in *Old Mortality*, they spend their days 'in controlling petulance, exciting indifference to action, striving to enlighten stupidity and labouring to soften obstinacy'. Nevertheless, these personal contacts between central and local government are extremely valuable. Not only do they make administration a good deal easier; they also provide a very salutary practical check to prevent it from becoming too theoretical. Formal consultations with the main local authority associations[1] or other interested bodies are of

---

[1] E.g. the Association of County Councils in Scotland, the Convention of Royal Burghs (which represents all the burghs, large and small) and the Association of Counties of Cities in Scotland.

course frequent; but these informal discussions with people from all over Scotland are in their way just as useful, and on balance the advantages of maintaining these close contacts in Scotland more than outweigh the administrative difficulties caused by the geographical separation of the Scottish departments from Parliament, and other Government departments in London. 'The ear of the Secretary of State', it was once said, 'is very close to the handle of the parish pump'; it sounds an uncomfortable position but it is good for a central administration to be fully aware of how its actions are regarded locally.

PART TWO

The Department of Agriculture
for Scotland

CHAPTER IV

The Land of Scotland

STANDING on the threshold of St. Andrew's House, it is not easy to decide what to look at first. The Secretary of State's departments are rather like a large departmental store, where a very large number of commodities are handled between which it is not easy to find any very close or logical connection except that there is a demand for them. A man may write to the Secretary of State about the drainage of his land, about the education of his child or about the treatment of his wife in hospital—just as he may go to the store and buy anything from a bath to a budgerigar. The various duties that the Secretary of State carries out have accumulated gradually, as we have seen, imposed by Acts passed by successive Parliaments. The resulting system is probably not what anyone starting from scratch would invent—in this it resembles many other British institutions—but the fact that ministerial responsibility for so many aspects of Scottish life lies with the Secretary of State does enable him to take a comprehensive view of the condition of Scotland.

Let us start then on the ground floor, with the land of Scotland, which lies all around the cities in which the majority of us live, and which, in spite of continual invasion by the requirements of modern urban civilisation, still includes nearly $4\frac{1}{2}$ million acres of cultivated land and a further 11 million acres of mountain and heathland which provide rough grazing for cattle and sheep. From the number of people employed and the value of the product, agriculture is Scotland's major industry, and the Secretary of State exercises, through the Department of Agriculture for Scotland, a very wide range of powers and responsibilities for its conduct.

The Secretary of State's concern with agriculture is twofold. First, he has a general responsibility, as 'guardian' of Scottish farming, for keeping the industry stable and prosperous; and secondly, to meet the conditions of the post-war world, he and the Minister of Agriculture, Fisheries and Food have a particular concern that the part of the nation's food supplies produced at home should be produced as economically as possible. The object of this and the two succeeding chapters is to show in some detail the work that is done by the Department of Agriculture for Scotland on the Secretary of State's behalf.

In relation to the land itself, the Department has a variety of duties, all of which are considered later in this chapter. It advises the Secretary of State from the agricultural standpoint, in the decisions

he has to take on questions of land use; it has work to do in promoting land improvement and under the statutes that govern the
various forms of tenure of agricultural land; and it manages on the
Secretary of State's behalf a considerable acreage of agricultural
property. Chapter V describes the various ways in which the Department, working in conjunction with the agricultural executive committees, is concerned with improving the quality, and increasing the
quantity, of agricultural production, by inspection and control, and
by the encouragement of research. Then in Chapter VI some account
is given of agricultural policy and of the way the agricultural departments have sought to aid and guide production by price guarantees
and production grants.

The Secretary of the Department is assisted by two under
secretaries, one of whom acts as his deputy, and below them the
Department is organised into ten divisions, each in the charge of
an assistant secretary. There is also an assistant secretary in London,
with a small liaison staff. The organisation of the Department is
shown in more detail on page 64. Its present staff amounts to 2,516,
of whom 1,105 are at headquarters.

Sir Francis Floud, who wrote a book in the original *Whitehall
Series* on the Ministry of Agriculture and Fisheries in 1927, dedicated
it to his colleagues in 'the most human of all Departments'. It is
beyond the purpose of this book to assess the relative humanity of
Government departments but it is perhaps fair to say that the Department of Agriculture has more frequent dealings with the general
public than the other Scottish departments; much of its correspondence comes direct from farmers and smallholders and not through
the medium of an insulating band of town clerks, county clerks,
directors of education, secretaries of Boards and the like. Yet these
wide contacts with the farming public have been made in a comparatively short space of time. Up to 1912, when the Board (later the
Department) of Agriculture for Scotland was established,[1] it had been
largely an era of *laissez-faire* for agriculture, and there had been comparatively little constructive legislation affecting Scottish farming.
There were no subsidies or guaranteed prices to help Robert Burns at
Mossgiel—nor any agricultural inspectorate to offer him an alternative to employment as a gauger with the Excise. There was a period
of high agricultural prosperity in the mid-nineteenth century, but
this gave place to falling prices and agricultural depression which
lasted until the early 1900s. A time of moderate prosperity from
1906 onwards developed into a boom during and immediately after
the First World War, but this in turn was followed by the severe
depression of the late 1920s and early 1930s. The efforts that the
State found it necessary to make to alleviate this depression caused it
to assume a much more active rôle in agricultural affairs than it had

[1] See Appendix I.

ever played before. Legislation was passed to improve marketing, to regulate imports and to give financial assistance to particular sections of the industry, such as the producers of fat cattle, wheat and sugar beet. After the outbreak of war in 1939, the need to increase home food production led to a further strengthening of Government influence. To get more crops grown on individual farms, the Department of Agriculture had to have closer connections with every part of Scotland than had hitherto been necessary, and a regional organisation of agricultural executive committees was therefore set up. The war-time food production campaign was so successful that the net Scottish agricultural output in 1943–44 was 36 per cent. above that of the years immediately preceding the war. Generally speaking, it can be said that, since 1939, Scottish agriculture has enjoyed a period of expansion, technical development and economic well-being which contrasts markedly with its relatively depressed condition during much of the preceding 60 years.

THE SECRETARY OF STATE AS ARBITER OF LAND USE

The widest of the Secretary of State's responsibilities for the land is that, as planning Minister, the ultimate decision on most questions of land use lies with him. As will be seen in Chapter XV, proposals to use agricultural land for other purposes come to him under the Town and Country Planning Acts, either on an appeal against a decision of a local planning authority or when he has to approve the development plan of one of the authorities. In such cases, the Secretary of State's interests, as planning Minister and as agricultural Minister, are not quite the same. The Department's function is to act as a watch-dog of the agricultural interest, and to make sure that when the Secretary of State reaches a decision, he has had all the evidence on the agricultural side put fairly before him.

The issues that are referred to him are seldom easy to decide, if only because the considerations that have to be put on each side of the balance are hard to compare. On the one side, there is the monetary value of the food production lost, the fact that food may have to be imported to replace it, the loss of open country, and perhaps reluctance to displace a farmer whose family have occupied the land in question for generations. On the other, it may be argued that the houses, the schools, the factories or the hospitals have to be built somewhere, and that development of the sites available on poor or non-agricultural land would be too costly in terms of manpower or materials or simply of inconvenience to the community at large.

Before decisions are taken on developments involving the use of agricultural land, there is usually consultation both locally and, if agreement is not reached, within St. Andrew's House. The agricultural executive committees are consulted by the local authorities on their housing proposals and by the local planning authorities on their development plans. The committees, through their members and through the Department's Lands Officers who assist them in this work, know personally the land involved. The Department's contacts with the agricultural executive committees are close, and when planning questions come to the Secretary of State, he will be fully aware of the views of the appropriate committee. The Department itself discusses with the various other Government departments and national bodies their proposals for development. With the Forestry Commission, for example, there is a standing arrangement that the Department will be consulted on each planting proposal before the land is actually bought. The North of Scotland Hydro-Electric Board's draft constructional schemes, which come to the Secretary of State for confirmation, are also referred to the Department for its observations on the agricultural implications of what is proposed. The Department is, in addition, consulted about the land requirements of the Service departments.[1]

In all its work on problems of land use the Department is aided by two sets of maps which it has had prepared as a result of surveys of Scotland. One shows the quality of the land, classified in seven categories, and the other the type of farming practised on each individual holding.

It will serve to indicate the magnitude of the problem of conflicting uses for land that during the 11 years 1944–54 the amount of land used for local authority housing (the biggest single 'urban' demand) was 31,500 acres. Other 'urban' needs, such as factories, schools, roads and playing-fields, bring the total annual demand for land in Scotland up to something approaching 4,000 acres. Most of the area used is cultivated land—unavoidably, since for these requirements what is needed is mostly fairly flat ground in the near neighbourhood of the towns. The activities of the Forestry Commission, the Hydro-Electric Board and the Services, on the other hand, involve in the main the higher-lying areas with a large proportion of rough grazings. Since the end of the war the Forestry Commission has planted over 200,000 acres (including the replanting of some 60,000 acres of cut woodland) and about 100,000 acres have been taken for the other purposes mentioned.

Disused airfields no longer required for flying purposes are handed over to the Department so that they can be put back into agricultural use—usually by being let in sections to neighbouring farmers—until they are resold. Another rather specialised function of the Department is to advise the Secretary of State on proposals for using agricultural land for opencast coal operations. All proposals of the Ministry of Fuel and the National Coal Board are very closely examined. The Department is also responsible for carrying out the

[1] See Chapter XV.

restoration of the worked-out sites when the soil has been replaced. (The normal process involves reseeding with grass, controlled manuring and grazing for up to five years, and finally the installation of a permanent drainage system.)

LAND IMPROVEMENT

The acreage of cultivated land and rough grazing referred to at the beginning of this chapter supports some 32,000 'full-time' farms and there are almost as many holdings and crofts which normally provide only a part-time job for the man who works them. (The crofter has traditionally supplemented his income by other forms of work such as fishing, weaving and knitting.) Numerous as they are, these 'part-time farms' account for only some 15 per cent. of the total agricultural acreage. About two-thirds of the 'full-time farms' are worked by tenants but a rising proportion of farmers are acquiring the properties they occupy.

The land of Scotland has not always known the present high standards of fertility, as the accounts of travellers in the eighteenth century will show. Indeed, it is to the almost superhuman efforts of many generations of their forbears that Scottish farmers today owe the existence of their cultivated land. Most of it has had to be laboriously carved out of scrub or moor, or won from a hard, stony sub-soil. The process of reclamation and improvement still goes on, although now less spectacularly, and it is supported by a number of Government schemes.

Marginal Agricultural Production

The marginal production schemes, originally introduced during the Second World War in Scotland, as in England and Wales, are intended to increase the productiveness of the marginal or in-between land which lies between the true hill-farming land (on which only hardy hill sheep and a few cattle can be maintained) and the rich lowland farms (which produce fat stock, milk and arable crops). The difficulties that beset the farmers of such land include poor soil, an exposed and elevated situation and a severe climate, and the improvement of the land would usually be unduly expensive for them, were it not for the assistance they receive under the marginal production schemes. The selection of the holdings which should receive assistance under the scheme, requiring as it does an assessment of the degree of 'marginality' in each case, obviously calls for a good deal of local knowledge, and the schemes are administered by the agricultural executive committees under the central guidance of the Department. The committees, assisted by the Department's Inspectors, have all made careful surveys, as a result of which each has classified the holdings in its area.

Unlike most subsidies, the marginal agricultural production schemes, which are made periodically by the Secretary of State under powers conferred by the Agriculture (Scotland) Act, 1948, are selective in operation and a good deal of freedom is given to the committees in the administration of them. The procedure is that the Department agrees each year with the Treasury the amount of money that can be made available, and it then fixes the maximum rates of assistance that can be offered for various types of work. (The operations that at present receive aid include the regeneration of worn-out grassland, the reclamation of derelict land, the erection of temporary fencing and cattle shelters and the construction of pit silos, while payments are also made towards the cost of seeds.) The funds at the disposal of the Department are allocated among the committees, who make offers of assistance at the appropriate rates to the individual farmers for the work to be carried out. These farmers must be on what is called the 'classified list of marginal farms', which was first compiled after a comprehensive survey, and is kept up to date by the committees. Some £1¼ million annually is now devoted to these schemes by the Department.

Other Land Improvement Grants

A number of other important grants for land improvement are administered by the Department.[1] Comprehensive schemes for the improvement of the land and equipment of farms on the higher ground—amounting to half the cost of the work done—may receive assistance under the Hill Farming and Livestock Rearing Acts, 1946–1954. The hill farms, which are a characteristic feature of Scottish agriculture, present special problems and the Secretary of State is assisted in his duties under the Acts by an advisory committee. Applications for the hill-farming grants are examined in the Department itself but the agricultural executive committees, and the Department's Inspectors, report on all the proposals received. By July, 1956, work at a total estimated cost of nearly £12 million had been approved, or was under consideration, which shows the scope of the improvement promoted under the Acts.

As part of the Secretary of State's concern for the improvement of the land, some mention must be made of his functions in assisting farms that have too little water and farms that have too much water in the wrong places. Under the Agriculture (Miscellaneous Provisions) Acts of 1941 and 1944, the Department can pay grants towards the cost of installing water supplies primarily for fields and farm buildings. The main object is to increase agricultural production, but domestic supplies for farmhouses and cottages may be included in schemes, where they form an extension to an existing or proposed farm supply.

[1] For ploughing grants and fertiliser subsidies see Chapter VI.

As regards the other problem of securing adequate drainage, this is, of course, one of the basic requirements of sound agriculture, and schemes for the financial assistance of arterial, hill and field drainage have been in existence for many years. Arterial drainage, which involves work on rivers and other main water courses, presents special problems, because it calls for the co-operation of all owners along the river bank. Anyone who has lived in a block of Scottish flats will know the difficulties of getting even half a dozen people to agree on the most obviously essential work. At various times the Secretary of State has been given limited statutory powers to carry out drainage works without necessarily securing the agreement of all the proprietors affected, but the problem is still far from a satisfactory solution. The present English River Boards system originated in East Anglia, where flooding is widespread and affects the lives of town and country dwellers alike, and it is therefore easy to spread the cost of the drainage work carried out by the Boards. In Scotland, where river valleys generally are steeper and narrower, fewer people are directly affected and flooding in towns is not common. At present, work on arterial drainage schemes is being carried out, wherever possible, with the co-operation of willing proprietors. The Agriculture (Scotland) Act, 1948, enables the Secretary of State to carry out the work with State-owned machinery where agricultural owners and occupiers ask him to do so, and under the Agriculture Act of 1937 the Department of Agriculture can pay half the cost of approved drainage works, whether carried out in this way or by private contractors.

SPECIAL FUNCTIONS IN THE HIGHLANDS AND ISLANDS

In the remoter parts of Scotland, agricultural interest predominates and the Department of Agriculture has therefore become responsible for encouraging a number of improvements in the Highlands and Islands. It makes grants, normally of 75 per cent., towards the cost of building or improving minor roads, bridges, piers and harbour works there; it makes grants and loans to crofters to help them in building or improving their houses or other buildings; and it keeps stores at various points in Skye and the Hebrides, from which crofters can get their building materials with all the advantages of bulk buying. It also collaborates with the Scottish Peat Committee in investigating methods of winning, drying and transporting peat (in the Highlands or elsewhere) so that it can be used for industrial purposes. The Department's interest is less in the peat as such than in the improvement and use of the land that will follow its removal.

D

LAND TENURE

As the guardian of the basic national asset, the land, the Secretary of State has certain powers and duties relating to the tenure on which agricultural properties are held. It has already been said that about two-thirds of the farms in Scotland are worked by tenants, and in addition there are a very large number of small agricultural tenants who may be generally classified under the term 'smallholders'. The relationship between landlords and ordinary farm tenants is governed by the Agricultural Holdings (Scotland) Act, 1949, and the Secretary of State has several powers and duties under that Act, most of which are delegated to the agricultural executive committees to exercise on his behalf. One of the main duties is that of deciding whether notices to quit should be allowed to operate.

The other statutes affecting land tenure are the Small Landholders (Scotland) Acts, 1911–1931, and the Crofters (Scotland) Act, 1955. These Acts govern the occupation of land under a special form of tenure, the main features of which are that the occupier is responsible for providing his own equipment, including buildings, and, on vacating his holding, is entitled to compensation for the 'permanent improvements' to the extent that these are suitable to the holding. In general, these Acts apply only to holdings not exceeding 50 acres in extent (excluding any share in common grazings) or £50 in annual rent. Prior to 1st October, 1955, the Small Landholders Acts applied throughout Scotland, but since that date the Crofters (Scotland) Act, 1955, has governed the occupation of such holdings in the seven crofting counties, namely Argyll, Caithness, Inverness, Orkney, Ross and Cromarty, Sutherland and Zetland. This Act, which restored a statutory meaning to the word 'croft', provided for the setting up of a new Crofters Commission[1] with the functions of 'reorganising, developing and regulating crofting in the crofting counties of Scotland', and conferred specific powers on the Commission to control the re-letting of crofts, to terminate the tenancies of absentee crofters, to authorise the granting of feus[2] to aged and infirm crofters who wish to give up their land but to retain their houses, to frame and implement schemes of reorganisation of crofting townships which have fallen into a state of disorganisation and decay, and to supervise the standard of husbandry on crofts.[3] Certain administrative duties

---

[1] The Commission consists of six members appointed by the Secretary of State. They do not represent any particular area or interest, but include members with a knowledge of crofting conditions and at least one member who can speak Gaelic. The staff of the Commission is provided by the Department.

[2] The feu is a form of land tenure peculiar to Scotland. It originated in the feudal system, and the word is derived from the same root as 'feudal'.

[3] A crofter might be described as the tenant of a piece of land which is less than 50 acres in extent or has a rental of less than £50, who holds his land under the Crofters (Scotland) Act, 1955.

formerly carried out by the Scottish Land Court (e.g. supervision of Common Grazings Regulations) were transferred to the Commission, which also acts as the agent of the Secretary of State in the administration of schemes of assistance for aiding and developing agricultural production on crofts. The Commission itself administers a scheme of grants specially adapted to crofting conditions and providing aid over a wide range of works of land improvement of the kind already described in this chapter. The Commission's functions are exercised subject to such directions of a general character as may be given to it by the Secretary of State. It is required to make an annual report to the Secretary of State and a copy of this report has to be laid before each House of Parliament.

LAND MANAGEMENT

The Secretary of State is himself an agricultural landowner, with estates throughout Scotland larger than those of any private owner. These are managed by the Lands Officers of the Department on his behalf and have been acquired, generally speaking, in two different ways. First, the Secretary of State is the land settlement authority in Scotland[1] and as such, at the end of 1955, owned 178 land settlement estates extending in all to nearly 452,000 acres and comprising over 4,000 holdings. About half of these, but about 90 per cent. of the total acreage, are in the crofting counties. The policy of land settlement originated with the Crofters Holdings (Scotland) Act, 1886, which formed a Crofters Commission[2] to give security of tenure and fair conditions of occupation to crofters in the Highlands and Islands. To assist the Commission in this work, the Act gave it power to assign land for enlargement of crofters' holdings. Later the Board of Commissioners set up under the Congested Districts (Scotland) Act, 1897, was given power to purchase land by agreement in the crofting counties both for the creation of new holdings and for enlargements. The Board of Agriculture was set up by the Small Landholders (Scotland) Act, 1911; it took over the land settlement functions of the Crofters Commission and the Congested Districts Commissioners, and was also given special powers to create new smallholdings on private estates throughout Scotland. (The Act also set up the Scottish Land Court and transferred to it the judicial functions previously exercised by the Crofters Commission, which was then disbanded.) Later Acts of 1916, 1919, 1931 and 1934 supplemented the Board's (later the Department's) powers to purchase land compulsorily as well as by agreement and, in the years between the wars, the creation

[1] In England and Wales the local authorities are responsible for land settlement.

[2] Disbanded in 1911 and not to be confused with the body of the same name set up in 1955.

of holdings was undertaken on a considerable scale all over Scotland. Since the Second World War, few further holdings have been created, but the estate management responsibilities of the Department have nevertheless increased.

This brings us to the second way in which the Secretary of State has acquired land. The Forestry Act of 1945, which reconstituted the Forestry Commission,[1] vested in the Secretary of State all land in Scotland previously held by the Commission and made him the Minister responsible for future purchases of land for forestry purposes. It sometimes happens that the Forestry Commission acquires suitable land which has come on the market but which it is not ready to plant for a year or two; or the property it has acquired may include good land which the Commission has agreed with the Department to leave in agricultural use. In either case, the Department undertakes the management of the land. The greater part of the land managed in this way by the Department consists of hill farms, from which, generally, it has been possible to allocate part of the grazings for planting without seriously impairing the economy of the farms. For the most part, the land is occupied by tenants. Exceptionally, where, having regard to the forestry programme, it is not possible to let the land, the Department undertakes the farming itself, until the Forestry Commission is ready to start planting. Wherever possible, land which is to remain permanently in agricultural use is sold. The amount of land managed by the Department as a result of acquisitions under the Forestry Acts changes from year to year, as one area goes for planting and another is acquired, but at the end of 1955, the total area of such land was 286,817 acres.

Thus, as a result of his various duties, the Secretary of State has become the major landowner in Scotland. Financial matters and general questions of policy are dealt with centrally from St. Andrew's House, while the day-to-day management of the estates is in the hands of Lands Officers, who are all qualified in agriculture or estate management. The type of problem met differs, of course—as the character of the estates does—as between the land in the crofting counties and that elsewhere, and as between the land settlement estates and the land acquired under the Forestry Acts. Many of the crofting settlements were created at a time when it was accepted as normal that the only access should be by sea or by footpath; under modern conditions, the provision of roads and such other vital amenities as a piped water supply has become a major management problem. Outside the crofting counties, the land settlement estates include both dairy and arable holdings and, in the industrial belt, small 'specialist' units which were created in the 1930s to supply the urban market with such produce as fruit, flowers and vegetables.

[1] See Chapter XXI.

The development of this last group of holdings, where pigs and poultry were also kept, was, however, hindered by difficulties in the supply of animal feeding stuffs and other necessities during the war; since then, for various reasons, conditions have not favoured the intensive development of many of the holdings.

CHAPTER V

Agricultural Production

THE Department's part in achieving the Government's aim of increased agricultural production has been to fertilise the agricultural field (if one may revive a bureaucratic cliché) with applications of research and subsidies, and this work has meant that its contacts with the farming world have necessarily been very close. Before looking at what the Department does in this way, it may be of advantage to review briefly the nature and structure of Scottish agriculture.

The relative importance of crop and livestock production has varied from time to time—during the wars, crops assumed greater importance than usual—but the basic structure of Scottish farming has remained remarkably stable. The influence of soil and climate, combined in normal times with the pressure of economic circumstances, has favoured livestock production. If one looks at the output of the Scottish farms in 1954–55—the total value of which was £152 million—four-fifths of this was from livestock products, consisting of milk (26 per cent.), cattle (21 per cent.), sheep and wool (14 per cent.), eggs and poultry (11 per cent.) and pigs (10 per cent.). The remaining one-fifth consists of potatoes (8 per cent.), cereals (7 per cent.), other crops (4 per cent.) including fruit, vegetables and sugar beet. An examination of the farm structure shows that about a quarter of all the full-time farms in Scotland are engaged in dairying, one-fifth in the breeding of young stock, both cattle and sheep, and about the same number in the rearing and feeding of stock for slaughter. On the other hand, only one-fifth are concerned primarily in growing for sale crops such as barley, potatoes and sugar beet. Hill sheep farms also play a substantial part in the Scottish farm economy. Market gardens and fruit farms are important in certain districts but, except for raspberries, the climate does not favour large-scale development.

Of the 4·4 million acres of cultivated land in Scotland—that is, land that is or at least might be put under the plough—a larger proportion than in England and Wales is in fact ploughed, much of it for the production of winter keep for stock, and a smaller area (only about a quarter) is kept as permanent grass. The remaining three-quarters is put through a course of rotational cropping (often of six or seven years' duration), with about 850,000 acres devoted annually to oats, $1\frac{1}{2}$ million acres to temporary grass and other large acreages to turnips and swedes, barley and potatoes in that order. Although the obvious feature of land use in Scotland is the extent to which it is determined by the needs of livestock production, Scotland is also well known as a producer of high-quality oats and barley for human consumption (for the national specialities of porridge and whisky respectively) and of seed potatoes. The yields per acre of the various crops compare favourably with those of other countries and over the past 40 years have increased by as much as 17 per cent. for oats, 23 per cent. for barley and 15 per cent. for potatoes, which shows the benefits of more scientific and intensive farming.

This brief review emphasises the diversity of Scottish farming and, therefore, the range of Government interest—for at every stage and in every aspect of crop and stock husbandry the Secretary of State, through the Department of Agriculture, has functions to perform. Since livestock husbandry depends on the production of feed from grass and arable crops, it is appropriate to discuss first the Secretary of State's responsibilities in crop production.

CROP HUSBANDRY

Seeds

The official recognition of the importance of increasing agricultural production is shown by the fact that in the sale of seeds, the old principle of *caveat emptor* some time ago ceased to apply. The country simply cannot afford the loss of production that would result from farmers buying and sowing weed seed or seed of low vitality in the belief that it was of good quality. A control dating from the 1914–18 war was therefore made permanent by the Seeds Act of 1920, under which the seller of seed must disclose to the buyer its percentages of purity, germination and weed seed content, as established by official test. The accuracy of the statements made by the merchants may be checked in Scotland by official sampling and testing at the Department's Scientific Services Station at East Craigs, Corstorphine, Edinburgh.

The work done at this Station is a good example of the less spectacular but none the less valuable activities of the Department which go on all the time, undisturbed by changes of Government, because Secretaries of State, of whatever party, have agreed on their importance to agriculture. Apart from the statutory duties mentioned above, the Department subjects new varieties of crops and plants to a rigorous series of trials at the Station, with the general aim of improving the standards of particular seeds and plants. Different types of grasses are tested to assess their value in seed mixtures; potentially valuable new varieties of potato are tested over a period of three or more years before being put on an official register; and a scheme for the certification of seed oats is operated under which certified seed is officially sealed and labelled when put on sale. The improvement of potato stocks has received particular attention, as a matter of Government policy, because there is a valuable Scottish export trade in seed potatoes. The increased yields of recent years are largely the result of the Station's work in promoting the selection of healthy seed for planting and the roguing (i.e. the detection and removal) of undesirable plants from the growing crop. The Department runs an official scheme for the inspection of seed potato crops, under which they are graded and certified and the seed sold from the higher grades of crop is inspected and sealed before it leaves the farm.

The Department's interest in, and responsibility for, agricultural research are dealt with later in this chapter, but it is relevant to mention here the work of the Scottish Society for Research in Plant Breeding, an independently governed organisation which, however, depends almost entirely on public funds paid to it by the Department. In its work on plant and crop improvement the Society has concentrated on cereals (especially oats); beans; potatoes; such herbage plants as perennial rye grass, cocksfoot and timothy; swedes; kale; and sugar beet. The Society aims at breeding a strain of plants that are hardy, productive and, as far as possible, resistant to disease.

Diseases, Weeds and Pests

Even the purest and best seed grows up in a world full of enemies, and agricultural production is threatened by disease, destructive insects and the activities of various animals and birds. Since the Colorado Beetle visited us in the 1870s and a peculiarly virulent form of mildew arrived—also from America—in 1906, it has been recognised that protective action by the Government is necessary, and in Scotland the Secretary of State has statutory powers to prevent the introduction of destructive insects or disease organisms from abroad and, if they have been brought in, to control their spread. Various orders are in force dealing with all these matters. It is now usual for imported plants to be accompanied by a health certificate from the exporting country, but the Department's inspectors can and do examine imported plants and other produce at the ports, and they also visit shops, nurseries and market gardens to see that plant diseases and pests are eradicated or controlled. Many other countries to which we export plants and seed potatoes are now equally particular, and the Inspectors examine consignments for export and give certificates of freedom from disease or insect pests which are recognised by the receiving countries.

The major animal pest in Scotland was, until recently, the rabbit, and in an attempt to clear it from the countryside (particularly where its numbers have been fortuitously reduced by myxomatosis) the Department, from time to time, designates suitable districts as clearance areas within which there is a legal obligation on occupiers of land to destroy rabbits; these areas are progressively extended as the campaign goes on. The Department also gives financial inducements to encourage the destruction of rabbits and other pests: for example, a grant is paid towards the cost of scrub clearance, which may be a useful auxiliary work in the rabbit clearance campaign; the cost of ammunition used in organised shoots of injurious birds is subsidised; and, because the assistance the fox gives in rabbit clearance is more than counter-balanced by the damage it does otherwise, grants are given to fox destruction clubs. The control of rats and mice is the duty of the local authorities, who receive grants towards the cost of the work from the Department and have the advice of its technical officers. The Department's inspectors also examine stored food for insect pests—in ships, dock sheds, trains, lorries, silos, warehouses, mills or farms—at all stages, in fact, where it is likely to become contaminated. An incidental, but not unimportant, duty of the Department is the control of rats, mice and insects in Government property throughout Scotland.

LIVESTOCK HUSBANDRY

Breed Improvement

As livestock farming predominates in Scottish agriculture, and as Scottish breeds are well known and have a high export value, it is not surprising that the Department of Agriculture has an even more direct interest in maintaining or improving the quality of livestock than it has in plant breeding. There may be differences of opinion about the details of the control but that there should be a strict central control in the interests of the breeders themselves is generally accepted.

Broadly speaking, all stallions, bulls and boars have to be licensed before they can be used for breeding, and the Department's inspectors will only pass animals that come up to certain known standards: there is, however, an appeal to an independent referee against the refusal of a licence. With the development of artificial insemination, it became clear that control was necessary to prevent abuses, and Parliament enacted[1] that artificial insemination centres should be operated only under licence and in accordance with regulations made, in Scotland, by the Secretary of State. Licences are also required for sale of semen from privately owned cattle or horses, and the import or export of all semen is controlled by the Department.

Apart from these statutory functions, the Secretary of State encourages the improvement of stock in various ways. Breeding societies can get grants from the Department to help them to obtain the services of bulls, boars and goats of good quality and assistance is also given for the improvement of sheep breeding. Two progeny testing stations are being established, one for pigs near Stirling and

[1] Agriculture (Miscellaneous Provisions) Act, 1943.

one for poultry near Edinburgh. In order to promote stock improvement on small farms, the Department contributes towards the prize funds at local agricultural shows; and in the Highlands, bulls, rams and Highland pony stallions are lent from stud farms run by the Department itself, and grants are paid to encourage the breeding of a better quality of Shetland ponies and of sheep. Subsidised veterinary services are available to crofters in the Highlands and Islands.

Poultry farming is increasingly important in Scotland, accounting now for over 10 per cent. of the country's total agricultural output, and the Department, to improve poultry stocks, publishes an annual register of breeding stations and hatcheries which have been inspected and from which stock and eggs of high quality can be obtained.

Animal Health

Animal health has been regarded as a suitable subject for Government intervention for over 200 years. Epidemics among farm animals have probably been the greatest single cause of loss to farmers throughout the ages, and after the year 1745, in which Prince Charles Edward landed in Scotland, had also been marked by the less romantic invasion of cattle pest from Holland, an Act was passed by Parliament empowering the King to make Orders in Council for the suppression of the disease and authorising the payment of compensation from public funds to farmers whose animals had to be slaughtered. Successive outbreaks of a variety of diseases led to the acceptance of increasingly strict control of animal health in Scotland as well as in England. When the Board of Agriculture for Scotland was formed in 1912, some anxiety was expressed in Parliament lest the setting up of a separate Scottish authority should result in a relaxation of this control, and animal health in Scotland continued to be handled by the Ministry of Agriculture. As recently as 1955, the Government decided, on the recommendation of Lord Balfour's Royal Commission, that animal health should be entrusted, as other livestock matters already were, to the Secretary of State. The Minister of Agriculture, Fisheries and Food, however, remains responsible for the operational control of epidemic diseases throughout Great Britain. Local authorities in Scotland, as in England and Wales, have the important function of enforcing Diseases of Animals Orders.

Of the duties so recently taken over by the Department, one of the most important is the administration of the laws relating to bovine tuberculosis and, in particular, the operation of the Attested Herds Scheme. Under this scheme, the object of which is the eradication of the disease, a herd owner in Scotland can apply to the Department to have his herd admitted to the Register of Attested Herds. The veterinary surgeons carry out a series of tests and if the herd is admitted, it becomes subject to rules designed to prevent the reintroduction of tuberculosis. A substantial area of Scotland, mainly in the centre and south-west, is now free of the disease and over 80 per cent. of the total cattle population of Scotland is now attested. The Department pays bonuses, either per head of cattle or per gallon of milk, for attested animals, as an inducement to enter the scheme. The progress made by the scheme has had very good results in giving the country a safer milk supply, and the Department of Health is also for this reason keenly interested in its operation (see also Chapter XIII).

Among other duties, the Department of Agriculture has taken over responsibility for the administrative control of arrangements for the import and export of animals and now runs the Glasgow export quarantine station. The supervision of quarantine premises for dogs and cats arriving in Scotland from abroad has also been taken over by the Department.

AGRICULTURAL EXECUTIVE COMMITTEES

In the functions for increasing agricultural production which have so far been mentioned, the Secretary of State acts directly through the Department. A number of his duties in relation to the promotion of good husbandry and estate management, however, have been delegated to eleven agricultural executive committees, along with various other matters. These committees, which were first formed during the last war mainly on a county basis (as they still are in England and Wales), have been retained as a feature of the Department's regional organisation, with one committee for each of eleven areas, because they were found to be a convenient way of providing an organisation to tackle the problem of improving agricultural production in peacetime. Each committee organisation represents that blend of the voluntary committeeman and the paid official which is a characteristic feature of modern British administration, since each consists of 12 members appointed by the Secretary of State (after consultation with the organisations representative of the farmers, the farm-workers and the landowners) and their secretarial and clerical assistance is provided by the Department, which also exercises a general supervision over their activities and offers guidance as required on any questions of policy or administration that may arise.[1]

The main task of the committees, then, is to maintain efficient husbandry and estate management in their area. Provided the land is being farmed efficiently and the type of farming is neither obviously unsuited to the soil nor likely to reduce its fertility, the committees do not usually concern themselves with the quantity or type of produce. But they do go into action when, in the course of surveying their area, they find that land is being badly farmed or managed. In

[1] See also pages 39-40.

the first instance, everything possible is done to secure an improvement by advice and persuasion. The low standard of farming may simply be due to lack of knowledge, and a transformation may be achieved by putting the farmer in touch with the agricultural advisory service operated by the three Colleges of Agriculture in Scotland. If, after keeping the farm under observation for a time, the committee sees no improvement, it is then required to take action under the Secretary of State's statutory powers.

If the committee's complaint is against bad husbandry, those concerned are first informed of the action that can be taken, and given an opportunity to be heard by the committee. Formal action begins by the firing of a warning shot in the shape of a notice indicating, in general, in what way the farm is found unsatisfactory. After that, the Committee may find it necessary to serve formal directions setting out what must be done to put the farm to rights; these directions may deal with the maintenance and repair of fixed equipment, or with cultivation or stock management. If a farmer fails to comply with the directions, the committee instructs its officers to enter the land and do the work at his expense. In addition, or as an alternative, it can recommend that he should be prosecuted. As long as the warning notice is in force, the committee must review it at least once a year to decide whether or not it should be renewed, and on each occasion the owner of the farm (if the occupier is a tenant) has a right to ask the committee to initiate proceedings to dispossess the occupier. If it refuses, he can demand that the case should be referred to the Land Court. The last resort open to the committee is to seek the Secretary of State's approval to the dispossession of the occupier of the farm (whether he is a tenant or an owner-occupier). If approval is given, the occupier has a right of appeal to the Scottish Land Court, and the Secretary of State must accept the Court's findings.

If the committee's complaint is against the owner on grounds of bad estate management, the procedure is roughly the same. The directions issued by the committee may require the owner to provide or replace expensive items of fixed equipment, and in certain circumstances he can ask that the proposal to issue the directions should be referred to the Land Court. In the same way as with bad husbandry, warning notices in cases of bad estate management are reviewed annually, but here the occupier has the right to request the dispossession of his landlord. Where an owner has to be dispossessed, he is bought out by the Secretary of State, who takes over as landlord.

Whether it is bad husbandry or bad estate management that the committee is considering, it is worth emphasising that dispossession is the very last resort and is only adopted when it is quite clear that the person concerned either cannot or will not look after the land satisfactorily.

THE INSPECTORATE

At this stage something should perhaps be said about the Department's Inspectorate, which plays an important part in securing farming efficiency and in the administration of all the schemes of stock and crop improvement, as well as in those for land improvement described in Chapter IV. To thousands of Scottish farmers and agricultural workers, the inspectors *are* the Department. In all, there are some 200 inspectors and technical assistants, all specially qualified (and many of them graduates in agriculture) as well as being men of practical experience in farming. They are stationed at the Department's regional offices throughout Scotland and, when an application for assistance under one of the schemes administered by the Department is received, they go out to examine the proposals on the spot, talk them over with the farmer and give all the help they can.

The inspectors, some of whom specialise in livestock, poultry or horticultural work, carry out a wide range of additional duties. They inspect fields of oats or potatoes to certify the crop; they examine bulls for licensing or for use at artificial insemination centres; and they earmark hill cattle and calves to show that a subsidy on them has been paid. They also assist the agricultural executive committees in assessing the standards of husbandry and estate management on individual farms; they supervise the restoration of opencast coal sites to agricultural use; they assist in pest control; they inspect agricultural imports and exports; and, among many other duties, they advise on the allocation of seasonal farm labour.

AGRICULTURAL RESEARCH AND EDUCATION

In agriculture there is an unusually close relationship between administration, research, education and practice. The research is not carried on in a void but has a very real application to the business of practical farming. The link between the research workers and the farmers is provided by the three Agricultural Colleges, which—as will be seen shortly—also run an advisory service for their areas. The co-ordination of the arrangements is the responsibility of a body called the Scottish Agricultural Improvement Council. The Council is composed of the Directors of all the Research Institutes in Scotland, the Principals of the Agricultural Colleges and representative farmers, and from its composition it is able to act as a two-way system; not only does it ensure that the results of any promising piece of research do not stick in the laboratories of the research institutions but percolate as rapidly as possible into ordinary farming practice; it also sees that farming problems that may provide a fruitful subject for investigation, are brought to the notice of the research workers.

The Secretary of State is responsible for the general administration

of agricultural research in Scotland and under successive Secretaries of State the policy carried out by the Department has
been gradually to establish and develop eight separate research
institutes for the study of the various aspects of agriculture. The
Department seeks the advice of the Agricultural Research Council on
all scientific matters that arise in the administration of these institutes,
such as the programmes of work, the appointment of scientific staff
and the provision of scientific equipment. One of the Agricultural
Research Council's responsibilities is the co-ordination of agricultural
research over the whole of the United Kingdom. The Scottish research institutes receive public funds through the Department for
both capital and maintenance purposes. The following list of those so
far set up, with the dates when each was established, shows the steady
development and expansion of agricultural research in Scotland: the
Rowett Research Institute for Animal Nutrition at Bucksburn, Aberdeen (1913), the Scottish Society for Research in Plant Breeding at
Roslin, near Edinburgh (1920), the Animal Diseases Research Association at Gilmerton, near Edinburgh (1920), the Hannah Dairy
Research Institute at Kirkhill, Ayr (1927), the Macaulay Institute for
Soil Research at Craigiebuckler, Aberdeen (1930), the National
Institute of Agricultural Engineering Scottish Station at Howden,
near Edinburgh (1949), the Scottish Horticultural Research Institute at
Invergowrie, Dundee (1953), and the Hill Farming Research Organisa-
tion with its administrative office in Edinburgh (1954). On a smaller
scale, some research is carried out on crop plants at the Department's
Scientific Services Station,[1] and on agricultural economics in the Farm
Economics Branch of the Department. The latter work is done in
close co-operation with the agricultural economists of the Colleges of
Agriculture.

The three Agricultural Colleges, which teach scientific and practical
agriculture and also provide an advisory service for farmers, are all
older than the Department itself. The oldest, the West of Scotland
College, which has its headquarters in Glasgow and is responsible
for the south-west of Scotland, was incorporated in 1899. The south-
east is covered by the Edinburgh and East of Scotland College,
founded in 1901, and the extensive and difficult terrain of the north
and north-east by the North of Scotland College, which has its headquarters in Aberdeen and was established in 1904.

Each College has a Board of Governors responsible for the general
policy, administration and finance of the College. The Board consists
of about 25 people, all of whom give their services voluntarily, and
on it are represented local authorities, the Department, the Universities, various farming organisations such as the National Farmers'
Union of Scotland, the Scottish Farm Servants' Union and the Royal
Highland and Agricultural Society of Scotland, and such other bodies

[1] See also page 47.

as the Scottish Women's Rural Institutes. The Governors have a wide discretion but—necessarily, since they receive through the Department substantial financial assistance from the Exchequer—they do not have complete autonomy, and staff appointments and all important matters of policy that involve financial considerations must have the approval of the Department.

The teaching provided at the Colleges is rather outside the scope of this book. At each College, students can take courses for the Scottish diplomas in agriculture, dairy husbandry, dairy technology, horticulture and poultry husbandry, and the Colleges also provide part of the teaching for the university degree of B.Sc. in Agriculture. The Colleges own their own farms on which practical instruction can be given.

In addition to doing this work, each College provides a County Advisory Service, with local advisers dispersed throughout the College area, roughly one for each county. To simplify the organisation of the Service, some of the larger counties are subdivided into two or more areas and some of the smaller ones are grouped together but, even so, there is a considerable variation—from about 1,000 to over 3,000—in the number of farms in an adviser's area. At the county office the adviser will probably have an agricultural assistant to help him, as well as a poultry and dairying adviser (usually a woman) and a horticultural adviser. Bee-keeping and machinery advisers usually cover several counties and their services are available on demand. The greater part of the adviser's time is spent in visiting farms at the request of farmers, but they also arrange lectures, farm walks and demonstrations of methods and techniques. Some 80,000 visits are paid annually and the lectures and demonstrations are attended by about the same number of people, which gives an idea of the extent to which farmers make use of the Service.

The advisers in the field have behind them at each College a strong team of specialists—most of them the heads of their own particular departments—who do a good deal of research and investigation into practical agricultural and veterinary problems and may, if necessary, themselves visit farms at the advisers' request.

Not only is this Advisory Service a means by which the farmer in a small and remote farm can benefit from the most recent discoveries in the research laboratories, but in Scotland it comes to him free from any possible bureaucratic taint, since the advisory staff of the Colleges play no direct part in Government regulatory or control work. The Department of Agriculture would not like to think that its inspectors, who do this latter work, are on that account regarded with hostility by the farmers they visit, but there are perhaps advantages—since the size of Scotland makes it possible to organise things in this way—in having the visits for administrative and for advisory or educational purposes carried out by different people.

FARM LABOUR

Without a skilled and adequately remunerated labour force, the measures that have been described for improving agricultural production would be of little avail. The Department exercises some special responsibilities with regard to the adequacy of the labour force and the regulation of wages.

Wages

Agricultural workers, in Scotland as well as in England, enjoy the benefit of having a system for the fixing of minimum wage rates laid down by law. The rates for Scottish workers, the hours they are to work and their entitlement to holidays, are all fixed by a statutory body called the Scottish Agricultural Wages Board[1] which consists of six employers' representatives nominated by the National Farmers' Union of Scotland, six workers' representatives nominated by the Scottish Farm Servants' Section of the Transport and General Workers' Union and a Chairman and four independent members appointed by the Secretary of State. The Board can consult with 11 District Wages Committees, also set up by law, which are familiar with local conditions; these District Committees also have certain functions in connection with wage rates for partially incapacitated workers. Both the Board and the District Committees have secretaries provided by the Department, and its Wages Officers visit farms to investigate complaints and to see that the wages paid and the conditions of work are in accordance with those laid down in the orders of the Wages Board. The Department also has the duty of enforcing the Board's orders if necessary, and this may involve court action.

Harvest Labour

Since the need arose to increase cultivation at the beginning of the war, the Department has organised schemes to supplement the normal harvest labour force. The Department makes arrangements for children released from school under the Education (Exemptions) (Scotland) Act, 1947, to assist farmers to gather the potato crop. City children are billeted in hostels in the main potato-growing areas and local children are transported daily to the farms where their services are required. Some 26,000 children took part in potato lifting under the scheme organised by the Department in 1955 and in addition to that about 14,600 worked on potato lifting during their school holidays. It has not been found possible so far to dispense with the services of schoolchildren for this work.[2]

---

[1] Set up under the Agricultural Wages (Scotland) Act, 1949.
[2] See the *Report of the Committee on the Employment of Children in the Potato Harvest*, Cmd. 9738.

COLLABORATION WITH OTHER BODIES

Annual grants are made by the Department towards the administrative costs of the Scottish Agricultural Organisation Society, which is concerned with the encouragement of co-operation in agriculture and has aided in the establishment of marketing societies for fruit, vegetables and eggs, and of societies for the supply of fertilisers, feeding stuffs and seeds and for crop and grass drying. The Department also collaborates with the Development Commissioners, who provide financial assistance from the Development Fund for a number of other rural organisations such as the Scottish Country Industries Development Trust (which promotes rural crafts and industries), the Scottish Women's Rural Institutes and the Scottish Council of Social Service.

CHAPTER VI

The Agricultural Guarantee System

THE agricultural depression of the 1930s, the exigencies of war-time, and the economic difficulties of the post-war world—all these led to one conclusion. The country simply could not afford to neglect its agriculture; the Government had to encourage home food production but the farmers could not be expected to produce more without an assurance that they would not be producing at a loss and that their produce would find a market. Out of these conditions, which applied to Scottish and English farmers equally, there came the Agriculture Act, 1947—Part I of which provided guaranteed prices for a number of commodities. In the words of Section 1 of the Act, it should be the Government's general object to promote and maintain 'a stable and efficient agricultural industry capable of producing such part of the nation's food and other agricultural produce as in the national interest it is desirable to produce in the United Kingdom, and of producing it at minimum prices consistent with proper remuneration and living conditions for farmers and workers in agriculture and an adequate return on capital invested in the industry'. The determination of the policy by which this very desirable and comprehensive aim is to be achieved is the joint responsibility of the Secretary of State for Scotland, the Minister of Agriculture, Fisheries and Food, and the Home Secretary (as the Secretary of State concerned with agriculture in Northern Ireland).

THE EXPANSION PROGRAMMES AND PRICE POLICY

The great expansion of agricultural production during the war was not unnaturally followed by a relaxation of effort in the immediate post-war period, but difficulties over the external balance of payments made it necessary in August, 1947 (the month in which the Agriculture Act became law) to give a new impetus to production in the United Kingdom. This was called the Agricultural Expansion Programme. Price increases were designed to encourage expansion where it was most needed and to help farmers to finance the breeding and purchase of livestock and the purchase of machinery. The programme was aimed at increasing the net agricultural production of the United Kingdom to 50 per cent. over the pre-war figure, and 'production targets' were set for the main commodities, especially those which at the time had the highest value as dollar-savers, such as pigmeat, eggs, beef, mutton and cereals.

The immediate results of the expansion programme were satis-factory. There was a rapid increase in the output of milk, eggs and pigmeat and an appreciable but smaller increase in the production of beef and mutton. By 1949–50 the total agricultural output of Scot-land had increased to 39 per cent. above the pre-war level. In 1950–52, however, there were signs that the expansion programme was losing momentum, and in 1952 a new programme was announced. The broad objective was to raise farming output over a period of years to at least 60 per cent. above pre-war levels, though this was to be accompanied by a return to greater freedom in marketing. In the event, the return of a free market has ended the period of agricultural expansion-at-any-cost and ushered in a period where the nature and degree of further expansion must depend on such factors as the level of unit costs within the industry and the character of consumer demand. During 1952 and 1953 the Department was engaged, along with the other Agricultural Departments and in consultation with the National Farmers' Union, in working out new methods by which the price guarantees—which were valued highly as providing both stimulus and stability—could be preserved when a free market was restored. The result of these deliberations was a Government White Paper[1] issued in November, 1953, on the de-control of food and the marketing of agricultural produce. This indicated the Government's intentions for the commodities guaranteed under Part I of the Agri-culture Act, 1947, and made it clear that the production and market-ing of each commodity had to be considered separately—there was no single solution. The Government undertook to consider sympa-thetically proposals for agricultural marketing schemes and in ap-propriate cases to make use of producers' marketing boards in administering Part I of the Act.

THE FARM PRICE REVIEW

Effect is given to the policy of guaranteed prices through the annual review of the economic conditions and prospects of the agri-cultural industry which the three Ministers concerned with agriculture (see page 58) are required by the 1947 Act to undertake. This survey, known as the Annual Farm Price Review, is carried out in consulta-tion with representatives of the three National Farmers' Unions, and following it, the Government is required to provide guaranteed prices and assured markets—not for all agricultural produce but for 12 of the major products.

The system of annual reviews, although only given statutory authority in the Act of 1947, originated early in the Second World War. In December, 1939, the Government decided to fix prices for the main farm products in order to increase production and to enable

[1] Cmd. 8989.

farmers to pay their workers more. The prices were later raised more than once, because the farmers were able to show that their costs of production had increased, and from these war-time reviews there developed the idea of a comprehensive annual review. The Agricultural Ministers are empowered by the 1947 Act to hold a special review in addition to the annual review if a sudden and substantial change in costs or other conditions (coming in between annual reviews) seems to make one necessary. And because it is recognised that livestock producers, whose cycle of production must extend over several years, have a special need of stability, the 1947 Act requires the Government to fix minimum prices for livestock and livestock products for some years ahead.

The Annual Farm Price Review has become one of the major events of the agricultural year, and what is decided at it has a considerable effect on the financial position of most farmers. The interests of Scottish and English farmers are by no means identical, and the Secretary of State for Scotland and the representatives of the Department of Agriculture have to see that, in the Review as at all other times, the particular requirements of Scottish agriculture are met and that in the framing of United Kingdom policy due regard is paid to special Scottish conditions. (The representatives of the National Farmers' Union of Scotland, on the other side of the table, have the same task.) The Review takes up a good deal of the time and thought both of Scottish Ministers and of senior officers of the Department. The terms of Section 1 of the Act of 1947, quoted at the beginning of this chapter, give a general statement of the objective but they inevitably leave many difficult questions to be settled each year by discussion. How much food *is* it desirable to produce at home? What are the minimum prices possible? What is 'proper remuneration', or an 'adequate return' on capital?

The price guarantees for the different commodities are implemented either by the Agricultural Departments direct or through producers' marketing boards set up under the Agricultural Marketing Acts, 1931 to 1949. The guarantees take various forms, but by far the most common is some type of deficiency payment representing the difference between average market prices and standard prices determined at the Annual Review.

The 12 products—fat cattle, fat sheep, fat pigs, milk, wool, eggs, wheat, barley, oats, rye, potatoes and sugar beet—which enjoy guaranteed prices and assured markets under the 1947 Act account in fact for 90 per cent. (by value) of all Scottish farm produce. The most important omissions are fruit and vegetables, the production of which in Scotland on a commercial scale is localised, and store livestock. These are immature sheep and cattle sold by one farmer to another, and they are the main product of over 6,000 Scottish stock-rearing farms as well as of many crofts and part-time farms. Many of these farms are in the uplands, where the physical and climatic conditions make other forms of production difficult, and they are an important source of young stock for fattening on the lowland farms. But they benefit only indirectly from the system of guaranteed prices and it is one of the Secretary of State's special responsibilities to see that their production is maintained—and if possible increased—by other means, such as production grants.

Although the system of guaranteed prices determined as a result of annual reviews of the condition and prospects of the industry has become well established, there has been a growing tendency since food control finally ended in 1954 for farmers to criticise the system as an inadequate basis for a long-term policy for agriculture under the new conditions of free marketing. Farm costs have continued to rise while, despite the increasing efficiency of the industry, farm incomes have tended to decline somewhat since 1952–53. Moreover, the return of freer trading conditions, together with an improved world food situation, has exposed home agriculture to increasing competition from imported food, which in turn has its effect on the cost of agricultural support. Against this background, there has been a recent tendency for farmers to regard price reviews rather as an 'annual upheaval' than as a means of giving assurance for the future. Matters came to a head at the 1956 annual review, when for the first time the three Farmers' Unions felt unable to accept the Government's price determinations as a fair and reasonable settlement. The Government, in the *White Paper on the Annual Review*, 1956,[1] recognised that each annual review by its nature can afford assurance for only a comparatively short time ahead, and in November, 1956, the Government was able to announce new long-term assurances which had been worked out in consultation with the three Farmers' Unions, who welcomed them as a sound and satisfactory basis for future confidence and the necessary forward planning in the industry.

The new arrangements, which were set out in a White Paper,[2] involved no fundamental change in the Government's agricultural support policy based on the principles of the 1947 Act. They represented, however, an important development of the assurances under the Act and of the methods for giving them effect. The principle of annual reviews, as against reviews at longer intervals, was endorsed, since it was considered essential that account should be taken in good time of changes affecting the economic condition of the industry. But greater precision was imported into the guarantees beginning with the 1957 Review, by providing first that the total value of the guarantees (including production grants) should be maintained at not less than $97\frac{1}{2}$ per cent. of the total in the preceding year, plus or

[1] Cmd. 9721.
[2] Cmnd. 23.

minus any increases or decreases in the costs of production that have occurred on the commodities to which the review applies, since the last annual review; and secondly, that the guaranteed price for each commodity—crops, livestock and livestock products—should be maintained each year at not less than 96 per cent. of the guaranteed price for the previous year. For livestock and livestock products, and in recognition of the special needs of producers of these, it was further provided that, in any period of three years, reductions in the guaranteed price for a particular commodity should not together exceed 9 per cent. Special reviews may still be held, but only to meet exceptional changes in farming costs, and under certain specific conditions. Finally, to stimulate more rapid modernisation of farms, the White Paper referred to the Government's intention to introduce a new scheme of grants for assisting the provision of permanent field equipment and long-term improvements.

The Agriculture (Silo Subsidies) Act, 1956, authorised one new scheme of assistance which is now in operation, and legislative provision for the new arrangements generally is being made. The guarantees determined as a result of the 1957 Price Review are set out in a White Paper.[1]

PRODUCTION GRANTS

The other method which the Department employs to encourage agricultural production and to improve the health of the Scottish agricultural body is direct production grants, the grants being applied where they are most needed. Some mention of these direct grants— which are, of course, available in England and Wales also—has already been made in Chapters IV and V, but this account of the techniques employed by the Department would not be complete without some reference to them.

There are broadly two kinds of production grant. First, there is the general type of grant for which all farmers are eligible and which is designed to strengthen a weak spot in the farm economy by the application of a stimulant as near the source of trouble as possible. For example, in 1952, when there seemed to be a danger of a serious fall in the production of crops, grants per acre of grassland ploughed up were reintroduced to encourage farmers to grow crops on land that would otherwise be left permanently in grass. (There had already been ploughing grants during the war, when increased crop production was necessary both for direct human consumption and because we could not import fodder for livestock.) To improve the yield of crops per acre as well as increasing the acreage of land under the plough, a new fertiliser scheme was started. The rates of the fertiliser subsidies are reviewed each year at the time of the Annual Review;

[1] Cmnd. 109.

in 1955–56 they amounted to approximately 26 per cent. for nitrogenous and 36 per cent. for phosphatic fertilisers and 60 per cent. for lime. Also in 1952, because of the need to produce more beef, the Government gave farmers an incentive to breed and rear more calves for beef production by offering £5 per head for calves of not less than eight months old born within a given period. (The subsidy has since been increased to £7 10s. for heifer calves and £8 10s. for steer calves, and about £2 million is now paid annually under this scheme.)

Secondly, the Department may apply a selective type of grant to particular producers whose special circumstances and difficulties require it. The small hill and upland farmers who work difficult land in remote areas are in this category and, to assist them, the marginal agricultural production schemes described in Chapter IV were introduced. The hill cattle and hill sheep subsidies, although quite distinct in character, are other selective subsidies of this kind. Under the hill cattle subsidy scheme, as an inducement to hill farmers to increase the productivity of their land and the fertility of their grazings by keeping more cattle, the Department pays £10 a head for breeding cows and in-calf heifers which form part of a regular breeding herd kept all the year round on hill land. About £1¼ million a year is paid out under this scheme. The hill sheep subsidy is even more selective. It is in essence the result of a review of the economic position of hill farming which, apart from wool, does not produce any of the commodities covered by the price review system. The subsidy is designed as a stabiliser to counteract the effects of unfavourable economic conditions and the rate of payment depends on the state of hill sheep farming. Since the subsidy was introduced in 1941, as much as 16s. per ewe has been paid following a bad season; in the years 1953 to 1955, following good seasons, no payment was made, but 5s. per ewe was paid in 1956.

STATISTICAL INFORMATION

The Department could not operate this elaborate mechanism of price guarantees and production grants effectively if it did not have reasonably complete statistics about the level both of farm output and of farm incomes for Scotland as a whole and for different areas and types of farm. It therefore obtains twice a year from the farmers, in June and in December, a statistical return which shows areas of crops, numbers of livestock, the number of men employed, and other information. From the returns it is possible to see, county by county, the changes that take place in crop and livestock production and so, with the additional information that is obtained from marketing boards and other sources, to build up an assessment of the value and volume of Scottish agricultural output.

DEPARTMENT OF AGRICULTURE FOR SCOTLAND

Organisation, 1957

		* Professional, Scientific and Technical Staff, Inspectorates, etc.†	Other Establishments
	Division A— Price Policy and Marketing: Livestock Products Fatstock	Chief Inspector and staff (General Duties, Livestock, Poultry, Horticulture and Pest Control Inspectorate)	Crofters Commission Area and Agricultural Executive Committee Offices (11)
Deputy Secretary	Division AA—Price Policy and Marketing: Crops Horticulture, etc. Statistics	Chief Lands Officer and staff Technical Development Officer Chief Surveyor and staff Chief Engineer and staff	Scientific Services Station, East Craigs, Edinburgh Animal Quarantine
	Division F— Education Intelligence Research	Advisory Officer in Agricultural Economics and staff Director of Scientific Services and staff Chief Marketing Officer and staff	Station, Glasgow Divisional Veterinary Offices (19) Stud Farms, Inverness
	Division G— Labour Food Subsidies	Chief Fatstock Officer and staff Food Infestation and Rats and Mice Control Officers Chief Wages and Safety Inspector and staff	
	Division C— Agricultural Executive Committees: Landlord and Tenant Farming Efficiency Pests Control	Eggs and Milk Officers Peat Survey staff	
Under Secretary	Division D— Highlands: Land Use Crofters Estate Management		
	Division E— Hill Farming Livestock Improvement Animal Health		
	Division H— Land Drainage Estate Management Land Use		

Secretary

Division B— Establishment

Division I— Finance

Liaison Office (London)

* The professional, scientific and technical officers may undertake work for any Division. They report to the particular Division with which at any given moment they are operating, and are not linked to any particular division in the chart.

† The services of the Veterinary staff of the Ministry of Agriculture, Fisheries and Food in Scotland are at the disposal of the Secretary of State in carrying out his functions in respect of animal health.

PART THREE

The Scottish Education Department

CHAPTER VII

Education in Scotland

A RECENT annual report on education in Scotland, presented by the Secretary of State to Parliament, begins with some notes on 'Learning to Read' and ends by recording the gift to the Royal Scottish Museum of important collections 'one of *Hemiptera-Homoptera* and one of Scottish freshwater leeches (*Hirudinea*)'. It is a rough but useful indication of the range of his interest, and that of the Scottish Education Department, in the education of the Scottish people; his statutory responsibilities begin with children of under five and extend to a wide variety of institutions and bodies concerned with the further education of those who have left school.

The Education (Scotland) Acts make the local education authorities responsible for ensuring the provision of all forms of education, except University education, in their own areas, but also assign to the Secretary of State certain functions involving general supervision or specific approval. The Secretary of State is also responsible, through the Scottish Education Department, for controlling the distribution of parliamentary grants.[1] The amount of money provided by Parliament for education in Scotland is very large (in 1957–58 it was nearly £50,000,000), and it is natural that the Secretary of State should be required to see first that the education provided is on lines approved by the Government of the day, and secondly that the best possible value is obtained for the money spent. It is fair to add that over a substantial part of the field there is no significant difference of view between the political parties.

The Education (Scotland) Acts give the Secretary of State power to make formal Regulations laying down general requirements for schools and for such matters as the education of handicapped pupils, the provision of school meals and school milk, the award of bursaries, the training of teachers, their salaries and their superannuation; the payment of grant to education authorities is also controlled by regulation. These Regulations are not, however, an arbitrary method of direction. The Education Acts provide that new regulations should first be published in draft and not finally made until 40 days have elapsed. This gives an opportunity to anyone interested to consider them in advance, and amendments are often made as a result of the representations received. When the Regulations have been

[1] See Chapter XII and footnote on page 94.

made, they are laid before Parliament and may also be discussed there.

The Secretary of State's guidance of public education is also exercised less formally by departmental circulars and memoranda, by discussions at St. Andrew's House and locally through H.M. Inspectors. To ensure that he knows the views of those most closely concerned, there is regular consultation on questions of general policy with the Association of Counties of Cities, the Association of County Councils in Scotland, the Association of Directors of Education, the Educational Institute of Scotland, the Association of Headmasters of Secondary Schools and other bodies. And where advice on some aspect of general educational policy is required, the Secretary of State may appoint an Advisory Council on Education in Scotland, two-thirds of the members of which must represent the views of the various bodies interested in education. Towards the end of the war, for example, a Council was set up to undertake a comprehensive review of the Scottish educational system in relation to the special problems of the post-war period. As a result, 24 reports were produced on a variety of educational topics, and some of these—notably those on Primary and Secondary Education—aroused widespread interest. The Council was reconstituted in February, 1957 (see page 89).

In addition to the responsibilities already mentioned, the Secretary of State has general supervision over approved schools (which in England and Wales are the concern of the Home Secretary) and is the responsible Minister for questions relating to public libraries, local museums and art galleries in Scotland. He is also directly responsible for the management of the Royal Scottish Museum.

The Secretary of State discharges all these educational responsibilities through the Scottish Education Department. The Department was formed as long ago as 1872[1] and it is therefore by now a familiar part of the Scottish educational scene. At present its office staff numbers 271, the Inspectorate 98 and the staff of the Royal Scottish Museum 96; the headquarters of the Department is in St. Andrew's House, but more than half the office staff works at Government Buildings, Saughton, in the suburbs of Edinburgh. The organisation of the Department is shown in the chart on page 101.

Before going on to discuss in the succeeding chapters some of the more important parts of the Department's work, it may be useful to give a brief account of the Scottish educational system, which differs significantly from that of England and Wales. The principal statute on the subject is the Education (Scotland) Act, 1946, which consolidated the earlier legislation.

The main responsibility for the provision of education in Scotland —both at school and later—rests, as has already been said, with the local education authorities. (These are the town councils of the four

[1] See Appendix I.

cities—Edinburgh, Glasgow, Dundee and Aberdeen—the county councils of 29 counties and the joint county councils of Moray and Nairn and of Perth and Kinross.) Most of the schools in Scotland are run by them, but there are also grant-aided schools, conducted by voluntary managers who receive grant direct from the Department; and independent or private schools, which receive no direct grant of this kind, but which, like the others, are subject to inspection. In January, 1956, there were 3,198 public (i.e. education authority) schools, with 834,042 pupils, 31 grant-aided schools with 15,293 pupils and some 165 independent schools with about 21,500 pupils. Thus in Scotland only about 5 per cent. of schools are independent and they account for a little over 2 per cent. of the pupils; in England and Wales, about 15 per cent. of the schools are independent and 8 per cent. of all school children attend such schools.

Attendance at school becomes compulsory at the age of 5. Education authorities are required to provide nursery schools for children between the ages of 2 and 5, where the demand is great enough; but so long as there are still shortages of staff and accommodation for pupils of compulsory school age, the development of nursery schools is necessarily slow. Between the ages of 5 and 12, children attend the primary school. The broad lines of the curriculum are prescribed by the Secretary of State, but the school authorities draw up the detailed scheme of work for each school, which is subject to the approval of H.M. Inspector of Schools for the district in which the school is situated.

Between the ages of $11\frac{1}{2}$ and $12\frac{1}{2}$ pupils are promoted from the primary school to a secondary school. (In England and Wales, they leave the primary school a year earlier.) There are various types of secondary school course, and in order that pupils should be assigned to the course from which they are most likely to benefit, they take intelligence and other tests, the results of which are considered, along with the teachers' estimate of each child's attainments, by a promotion board. Before the pupils are finally allocated, the parents' wishes are considered, and if there is a dispute between the parents and the education authority as to the suitability of a particular course for a pupil, the parents can appeal to the Secretary of State.

Secondary school courses are of two main types—those normally lasting three years, which take the pupil up to the minimum school leaving age of 15 and are called junior secondary courses, and those lasting five or six years, called senior secondary courses, which should, if all goes well, lead to the Scottish Leaving Certificate awarded by the Department.[1] Both types of course continue the general education begun in the primary school but the emphasis

---

[1] The former correspond roughly to the courses provided in secondary modern schools in England, and the latter cater, broadly speaking, for pupils of the type admitted to grammar schools and secondary technical schools.

varies according to the needs and abilities of the pupils. There are, for example, literary, commercial, technical, domestic and rural courses as well as special modified courses for pupils of limited ability. Some schools offer only junior secondary and some only senior secondary courses; in others, which are known as 'comprehensive schools', both are provided. Again, most secondary schools take both boys and girls, but in the cities there are several, mostly founded last century, for boys or for girls only. The scheme of work for each secondary school must be approved by H.M. Inspector of Schools for the district.

As a general rule, the education provided by local authorities—both primary and secondary—is free, and pupils who receive free education also receive free books and stationery. A few local education authorities, however, have taken advantage of a provision in the Education (Scotland) Act of 1945 which enables them to maintain some fee-paying primary and secondary schools, provided that this can be done without prejudice to the free education in their areas.

There are only 15 grant-aided secondary schools not run by the education authorities but they are mostly large and of considerable standing. In order to qualify for grant, these schools must comply with the same requirements as those managed by the education authorities.

To complete the picture of school education in Scotland, mention must be made of children who need special treatment because of some physical or mental handicap. Where necessary, such children are educated in special schools or classes where they must remain until they are 16.

Education can, and ideally no doubt should, be continued from the cradle to the grave, but the law does not require it to be carried beyond the age of 15. Thereafter, strong personal interests or motives of self-advancement may encourage one to go on with the process, but the education is in fact voluntary. The Act of 1946 did indeed provide for the establishment of junior colleges to give compulsory part-time education to those who have left school but are still under 18, but this part of the Act has not yet been brought into operation.

Further education—that is, organised education after leaving school —is largely vocational, and its development has not been the same in Scotland as in England and Wales. In England, the system was broadly based on a larger number of technical colleges run by local education authorities, and the development of higher institutions has come more slowly. In Scotland, a number of 'Central Institutions', each serving the needs of a region, had come into existence by the first decade of the present century. Each was run by an independent governing body representing industrial, educational and other interests in the region, and from the outset they were designed to provide, in addition to less advanced courses, the highest forms of instruction, and facilities for

research and discovery. Most of the local outposts of further education—that is, the further education centres run by local education
authorities—were set up later, to give both full-time and part-time
courses on a more elementary level, and they have been profoundly
influenced by the Central Institutions. Since Scotland is a comparatively small country, with a population heavily concentrated in a
few industrial areas, the system by which advanced technical education is provided regionally and not locally, has worked well, and the
16 Central Institutions—of which seven are concerned with the
strictly 'technical' subjects—have grown steadily in importance and
expanded their buildings, their range of courses and the number of
their students. In 1955–56 there were in all 28,442 students at the
Scottish Central Institutions; at the further education centres, about
4,500 students took full-time courses, and a further 24,500 part-time
day courses, while the number taking evening classes was about
189,000, divided about equally between vocational and non-vocational
studies.

To complete this general account of education in Scotland, it
should be added that many people who never enter the doors of a
further education centre or a Central Institution are yet caught in
the net of what the Education (Scotland) Act of 1946 describes accurately, if not very invitingly, as 'voluntary leisure-time occupation
in organised cultural training and recreative activities . . . for persons
over school age'. There are many national organisations—the
National Associations of Boys and Girls Clubs, the Women's Rural
Institutes, the Churches, the Girl Guides and the Boys' Brigade, for
instance—which provide this for young people or for adults in their
local branches and clubs with the support of the local education
authorities. Some education authorities also organise their own youth
centres, clubs and camps and provide their own recreation grounds.
And there are a host of unofficial organisations, such as music
appreciation clubs, drama clubs, discussion groups and gardening
societies, to which education authorities can give financial assistance
because they provide an approved type of 'voluntary leisure-time
occupation'. Rather as M. Jourdain discovered with admiration that
he had been speaking prose for years, so someone may find that the
enjoyable society to which he belongs is a part, and an important
part, of further education.

CHAPTER VIII

Schools

THE organisation of school education in Scotland has been greatly simplified since the early years of the Scottish Education Department. Then, there were nearly 1,000 elected School Boards, to say nothing of the independent schools and the voluntary organisations with an interest in education. (It is not surprising that in their first year (1872–73) the newly established Board of Education in Edinburgh[1] found it necessary to write over 12,930 letters and to issue about 7,000 circulars.) Today, as will have been seen from the sketch in the previous chapter, the overwhelming majority of children attend schools run by the 35 education authorities and most of the dealings of the Department are with those authorities.

THE EDUCATION AUTHORITIES

Before describing some of the principal activities of the Secretary of State and his Department in relation to schools, it may be useful to describe how the education authorities organise themselves to carry out their functions. Each authority must appoint an education committee, constituted in accordance with a scheme approved by the Secretary of State, and thereafter delegate to it its educational powers and duties; certain financial matters are reserved for the authority itself. The education committee must always contain a majority of elected Council members, but added to these there are people with educational experience and a knowledge of the needs of the various kinds of school in the area. There must be women on the committee, and representatives of religious denominations, but beyond that each authority is free to form the type of committee best suited to its area. For the more detailed work of management of schools or groups of schools the authority must appoint—unless it can convince the Secretary of State that it should not do so—local sub-committees of the education committee, and further members are added to these sub-committees to represent the teachers, the parents and other interests. Each education authority has a Director of Education, who is their principal adviser in matters of education.

The Department's supervision of education in schools covers a wide variety of matters—the buildings, the equipment, school attendance, the conveyance of pupils to school, staffing, the curriculum,

[1] See Appendix I.

teaching methods, the allocation of primary school pupils to secondary courses, school meals, bursaries—there are too many for them all to be described but the following sections give an account of some of the most important.

To establish certain basic standards in public and grant-aided schools the Secretary of State has made Regulations known as the Schools (Scotland) Code,[1] compliance with which is a condition of the payment of grant. The Code is a comprehensive one: some of the principal matters dealt with are the admission of pupils to public schools; the numbers and qualifications of teachers; the number of days the school must meet during the year; the size of classes; the keeping of registers and pupils' progress records; the general scope of the education to be provided; and the submission and approval of schemes of work. To allow for flexibility, the Code provides that the District Inspector can authorise departure from certain of the regulations in exceptional circumstances.

Each authority must draw up a scheme for the provision of education in its area and have it approved by the Secretary of State. The scheme sets out what schools the authority manages, how many children they accommodate, what type of education is provided, what proposals there are for new schools, and so on. In short, it is a survey of what is already being done and what still needs to be done. Before approval is given, the schemes and any amendments to them are referred for examination to H.M. Inspector for the district, whose experience gives him a close knowledge of the authority's area, and he discusses with the officers of the education authority any points that give him concern. Has the authority taken account of impending housing developments in a particular district? Can the additional children that may be expected be accommodated in an existing school, or should a new school be built, or an existing school be extended and perhaps modernised at the same time? Should there not be courses in navigation in an area with a strong seafaring connection? When agreement on such points has been reached, perhaps after a meeting between representatives of the authority and of the Department, the scheme is approved.

SCHOOL BUILDING

The school is the most ubiquitous—if not always the most beautiful—of our public buildings and is certainly used by more people than any other. At present, schools in Scotland provide for over 1,100,000 children, teachers and further education students, or more than one in five of the population—and that is taking no account of all those who use them as branch libraries, polling stations, community centres, etc.

[1] S.I. 1956, No. 894 (S.40).

F

Beyond approval of the authority's general scheme of educational provision, the only functions formally laid on the Secretary of State by statute in relation to school building are the approval of the plans of all new buildings and major alterations and extensions, the recognition of the work as qualifying for grant, and the sanctioning of the necessary financial borrowing by the authority. In practice the Department, having experience of what schools are being built throughout Scotland as well as in England and elsewhere, periodically issues circulars to guide education authorities on the type of building they are expected to provide and on the kind of accommodation that should be included if plans are to be approved. It would be agreeable if the Department could always be free to use the accelerator; occasionally the economic state of the country makes it necessary to apply the brake and to warn education authorities that certain types of building cannot be approved for the time being.

The main problem at present is to provide schools in the new housing areas that are springing up on the periphery of all the larger towns. A building problem would in any case have resulted from the large post-war housing programme, but it has been made more acute because the high post-war birth-rates have increased the school rolls and made the existing accommodation insufficient. This 'post-war bulge' moves along the educational system like a heavy meal along the body of a snake; the rolls of the primary schools will be up by 15 per cent. between 1951 and 1961 and those of the secondary schools by a lesser amount between 1959 and 1964, and even after that the school population is likely to remain for some time at a level considerably higher than before the war.

The present practice, when a new school is to be planned, is that the authority first of all calculates, from the number of pupils who will be using the school, the total floor area of the rooms that will be required for actual teaching purposes. When this basic area required for teaching has been approved, a prescribed percentage can be added for ancillary rooms, corridors, halls, etc., and sketch plans are then prepared on the basis of the maximum area thus arrived at for the whole school. If the building is well planned, it is possible to use a substantial proportion of this percentage addition to make the classrooms bigger than the minimum, and even to provide additional rooms. Projects are approved where the cost of the work does not exceed a given amount per square foot. Thus within the limits of area and cost, the authorities and their architects have wide freedom in the planning of new schools—and a strong incentive to design them in a way that will ensure that as much space as possible is used for teaching, which, after all, is the real purpose of the building.

The Department's interest is not confined to a rigid imposition of certain limitations; once it has been agreed in principle what accommodation is necessary, and before the plans are submitted formally for approval, the Department's architects give any help they can to those employed by the education authority, so that the new school may be architecturally and educationally the best possible within the prescribed limits. A building development team, composed of administrative and technical staff and one of H.M. Inspectors, has been set up within the Department to publish general advice by means of handbooks on the planning and construction of schools. The team has also designed buildings for certain authorities in order to demonstrate new methods. In these and many other ways the Department tries to help education authorities to build, at a reasonable cost, schools that are efficiently planned for their purpose and at the same time are attractive in appearance.

There is no essential difference between England and Scotland in school building policy, and the Department and the Ministry of Education consult each other regularly to ensure that what is done in the two countries is reasonably consistent.

CLOSING A SCHOOL

For various social and economic reasons the population shifts from one part of the country to another, and just as the Secretary of State frequently has to approve the construction of a school in a new housing area, so he periodically has the less pleasant task of approving a proposal by an education authority to close a school. The small rural school makes a very important contribution to the life of the community and neither the Secretary of State nor the education authorities will close one if it is avoidable. But sometimes—usually in a sparsely populated rural area where the population has greatly decreased—there are so few children that the retention of a teacher at a time of general shortage and the continued upkeep of the school buildings are clearly unjustifiable. Before the closure is approved, the authority must always show that satisfactory alternative arrangements can be made for the education of the remaining children and for conveying them to their new school if necessary.

An allied case is that of the small secondary department attached to a rural primary school. There may not be enough pupils for the organisation of a satisfactory secondary course or there may not be facilities for the practical work that should be included in such a course. If country children are to have the same opportunities for education as town children, there may be no alternative but to transfer the pupils to the nearest secondary department of a size that can provide the facilities. Here again, the Secretary of State does not approve the proposed closure unless it is very clear that the new arrangement is the best one for the pupils.

PROMOTION SCHEMES

Enough has already been said about the variety of secondary courses available to show that it is most important that each primary school pupil should be allocated to the course most suitable for him. Each education authority operates a promotion scheme approved by the Secretary of State showing the methods it proposes to adopt. Each scheme provides for a promotion board generally consisting of the Director of Education, representatives of the head teachers and staffs of primary and secondary schools and members of the education committee. The board has in front of it the teachers' estimates of each pupil's attainment and, usually, the results of intelligence and attainment tests, and it also considers the wishes of the parents and any exceptional circumstances. The common belief that the whole thing is decided by the intelligence test is quite incorrect. The Department has advised authorities that the pupil should always get the benefit of any doubt and be allowed to embark on the more ambitious course unless he is manifestly quite unfitted for it. If there is an unresolved dispute between the parent and the education authority as to a child's ability to profit from a particular course, the parent has the right of appeal to the Secretary of State; the case will then be investigated, and a full report made, by H.M. Chief Inspector for the area. There are relatively few appeals, and in most of them the Inspector's investigations have supported the view that the authority's decision was the best one for the child concerned. Furthermore, the original allocations may be reconsidered and a pupil transferred from one course to another if this subsequently seems desirable.

SCHOOL MEALS AND MILK

If a mid-nineteenth century dominie could return today to look at the school where he taught, many things would surprise him, but nothing more perhaps than the arrangements for providing each pupil with an inexpensive midday meal and free milk. It is a prominent feature of modern education that the pupil's physical well-being is not left to chance, and in recognition of the importance of proper feeding, Parliament laid on the education authorities a statutory duty to provide a school meals service in the schools under their management. It is one of the Department's responsibilities to see that the service is conducted efficiently and economically, and specialist School Meals Inspectors check the day-to-day working of the arrangements. In the older schools the service is sometimes carried on under difficult conditions, but in new schools, specially designed kitchens and dining-rooms are of course provided. The design, equipment and cost are carefully scrutinised by the Department's technical officers and approved expenditure is reimbursed in full.

The school meals service is financed in the following way. About half-way through each financial year, education authorities let the Department have estimates of the number of meals they will provide during the year and of the expenditure, both on the actual meals and on overheads, that they are likely to incur. These estimates are examined and compared, and the Department works out for each authority the cost per meal, covering both food and overheads, that will be approved. The authority must then keep its gross expenditure down to a figure equal to the product of the number of meals served and the approved cost per meal. If it does, its net expenditure—i.e. after the receipts from payments for meals have been deducted—will be reimbursed as part of the grants paid to it. Something beyond the authority's control—a sudden decrease in the demand for meals, an increase in the price of food, a wage award—may of course make it impossible for the authority to keep its expenditure down, but that will be taken into account when the grant is paid.

The Secretary of State prescribes the charge per meal that the authorities are to make and has laid down in Regulations that each authority must have a scheme of charges approved by him, providing for the full or partial remission of the prescribed charge where the parents cannot pay the full amount without financial hardship. Education authorities may also make a reduced charge where there is more than one child from a family at school.

In addition to the midday meal, authorities can, if necessary, provide light meals, breakfasts and teas, fixing a reasonable charge for these and remitting it where there would be financial hardship. Three-fifths of the net cost of this additional service is met by the Department.

Under arrangements made by the education authorities, one-third of a pint of milk daily is provided free to children whether they are attending education authority schools or other schools in the authority's area. The cost is fully reimbursed by the Department provided it is not greater than the retail cost of pasteurised milk; if difficulties of supply lead to a higher cost, the Secretary of State's approval of the arrangements made is necessary.

SCHOOL HEALTH SERVICE

The State has recognised for nearly fifty years that growing children ought to have special medical care, provided through a School Health Service. Although this service remained as a separate entity after the introduction of the National Health Service, it is in no way a substitute for it and the two are indeed closely co-ordinated. The School Health Service, which is provided by the education authorities, includes routine medical and dental inspection and free medical and dental treatment at school clinics, and many authorities also have

child guidance centres or clinics for the treatment of children with
psychological difficulties. Since the Service is organised by the education authorities, the Scottish Education Department is financially
responsible for it,[1] but the Department of Health for Scotland is
responsible for its administration.[2]

EMPLOYMENT OF CHILDREN—
YOUTH EMPLOYMENT SERVICE

The responsibilities of the education authorities and the Department for children do not end when they pass from the school into the
outside world. They must see first that children under 13 are not
employed at all (with one trifling exception which may be made under
byelaws), secondly that older children are not employed unsuitably
or for such hours as will interfere with their education, and thirdly
that children leaving school are helped in the choice of a career and
in finding a job. The limitations on the employment of children are
contained in the Children and Young Persons (Scotland) Act, 1937,
which also empowers education authorities to make byelaws—with
the approval of the Secretary of State—regulating the employment
of children and the employment of 'young persons' (i.e. boys and
girls between the ages of 14 and 17) in street trading. The Youth
Employment Service was set up under the Employment and Training
Act, 1948, and is controlled jointly by the Ministry of Labour and
National Service, the Ministry of Education and the Department. It
collects, and makes available to children and their parents, information about careers and opportunities for employment; it gives advice
to those who need it, and it gives positive assistance both to pupils
leaving school in finding suitable employment, and to employers in
finding the kind of young workers they need. In some areas the
Service is operated direct by the Ministry of Labour, but 12 Scottish
education authorities, which between them are responsible for 64
per cent. of the school population, run the Service in their areas under
arrangements approved by the Ministry.

APPROVED SCHOOLS

One last type of school remains to be mentioned in this Chapter—
the approved school. The name—which to the uninitiated might imply
that all the other schools were *not* approved—is derived from the
Children and Young Persons (Scotland) Act, 1937 (and the corre-

---

[1] See footnote on page 94.
[2] In England, where a similar arrangement would have meant a division of
responsibility between two Ministers, the Ministry of Education is the responsible
department both financially and administratively. The Chief Medical Officer of
the Ministry of Health is also the Chief Medical Officer of the Ministry of
Education.

sponding English Act of 1933), under which 'children and young persons' who have been found guilty of an offence or who, in the opinion of the Courts, are in need of care or protection, are sent to certain specified residential schools 'approved for the purpose by the Secretary of State'. The Secretary of State's powers and duties in relation to approved schools are exercised for him by the Scottish Education Department. It is remarkable that although the overwhelming majority of ordinary schools are run by the education authorities, the important and rewarding but difficult work of running the approved schools is mainly done by voluntary boards of management—only one of the 21 approved schools in Scotland is conducted by an education authority (Glasgow) and although the other education authorities pay their share towards the cost of running the schools, they have no direct responsibility for them. There were about 1,350 pupils in the schools in 1956—1,150 boys and 200 girls.

The approved school is in essence a boarding school for difficult boys and girls where they will benefit from a good education and a better environment than they have had hitherto. Under the Act, children and young persons sent to an approved school under a Court Order may be retained there for three years—or until they are 15 years and 4 months old, if they have not yet reached that age when the three-year period has expired. The school managers can, at their discretion, allow the pupils to live outside the school 'on licence', but the Secretary of State's consent is required first if the pupil has not been in the school a year. It is the duty of the Secretary of State to see that the pupils are placed out on licence as soon as their conduct has improved sufficiently to justify it, and after 18 months' to two years' training many pupils can be allowed out. The school managers supervise the pupils while they are out on licence, and continue to do so at the end of their period of detention—either for a period of three years or until they reach the age of 21, whichever period is the less. Welfare officers help the managers in the work of supervision.

Because the pupils are in the approved school for a comparatively short time, it is obviously important that they should receive an intensive education. In three of the schools, all the pupils attend ordinary day schools run by the education authority (as pupils out on licence do in any case), and some of the other approved schools send selected pupils to outside day schools. Where instruction is given within the approved school itself, there is a qualified staff and particular attention is given to practical subjects—carpentry, shoemaking, tailoring, agriculture, gardening and dairying for the older boys, and cooking, laundry work, dressmaking, housewifery and commercial subjects for the older girls.

From the very nature of the work and because there is usually no intervening education authority, the Department's contacts with the approved schools are close and constant. Although the boards of management run the schools, the Department is responsible for supervision of every aspect of the administration. Indeed the work of the branch that deals with approved schools is a miniature replica of the work of the Department as a whole—dealing, as it does, with schoolroom work, technical training, staff salaries and conditions, building, legislation, meals and general welfare, accounts and finance. Through H.M. Inspectors, some of whom have special responsibility for approved schools, it sees that the premises, staffing and curricula are satisfactory and that everything possible is done for the health and physical well-being of the pupils. The arrangements for supervision of pupils at the end of their detention are checked; complaints and appeals from parents are investigated; negotiations are carried on with the boards of management about staff salaries and conditions; training courses for the staffs are organised. The financial side of the schools in particular brings a regular flow of work. The schools may have income of their own from the sale of their produce or from legacies, and there will be a small income from the contributions which the parents make, if they can, towards the maintenance of their children, and which are collected by the education authorities. The Department must scrutinise the estimates and accounts of receipts and expenditure and, on the basis that it shares the deficit equally with the education authorities, calculate what weekly contribution per pupil will have to be paid to the Managers by the education authorities.

CHAPTER IX

H.M. Inspectorate and the Scottish Leaving Certificate Examination

H.M. INSPECTORATE

FOR most Scots, one of H.M. Inspectors was the first representative of a Scottish Government department they met; the Inspector's life seemed perhaps, in the eyes of a child, an easy one, spent in passing from school to school, asking a few apparently artless questions in each. School visits are in fact a major part of the Inspector's work, but the real importance of the Inspectorate is that it prevents the central administration, the local administration and the schools themselves from working in isolation. It is easy in St. Andrew's House to forget what life is like in a small village school; it may not be easy in a small school to keep abreast of new developments or to understand why the administrators act as they do. The Inspectors can do a great deal to ensure better understanding and to help educational progress throughout the country.

The Inspectorate has always played an important part in the work of the Department and indeed there were Inspectors before a separate Scottish department was formed. The present Inspectorate consists of a Senior Chief Inspector, six Chief Inspectors, including one for Further Education, 72 Inspectors and 18 Assistant Inspectors. Recruits to the Inspectorate, except for a few with specialised duties —e.g. in connection with the school meals service—are all required to have had successful service as a teacher. The great extension in the range of school studies in the past 30 years or so is reflected in the wide variety of specialist qualifications required in the modern Inspectorate, which now includes experts in technical, commercial, nautical and domestic subjects, agriculture, art, music and physical education, as well as in the traditional school subjects.

For purposes of inspection, Scotland is divided into 19 districts, each in charge of an Inspector. A populous area such as Edinburgh, Glasgow or Lanarkshire forms a district on its own and so does an extensive area such as Inverness-shire; smaller or less populous areas are combined to form a single district. The Inspector in charge has other Inspectors to assist him according to the size of the district. The districts themselves are grouped in five divisions—South-Eastern, South-Western, Western, North-Eastern and Highland—

each under the general supervision of one of H.M. Chief Inspectors. H.M. Senior Chief Inspector, who is stationed at St. Andrew's House, supervises and co-ordinates the work of the whole Inspectorate and acts as the Department's chief adviser on strictly educational matters. He has also a special responsibility for the training of teachers and represents the Department on the National Committee for the Training of Teachers. The six Chief Inspectors meet periodically under his chairmanship to discuss, and advise the Department on, matters of general educational policy; they also act as consultants and advisers on any questions that arise on any of the aspects of education within their spheres, and are responsible for liaison with the Training Colleges for Teachers.

The Inspectors in charge of districts have very varied functions. They are directly responsible for the inspection of all kinds of schools and educational establishments, and for ensuring that accommodation is adequate and staffing satisfactory. Their relations with the Directors of Education are very close, since not only do they act as liaison officers between the Department and the Directors—which involves them in discussion of many aspects of the administration of education—but they discuss with the Directors (as well as with the teachers and the headmaster or headmistress) points that have emerged during their school visits, and thus help to keep each Director informed of the work of the schools administered by his education authority.

Visits to schools take up the greater part of the time of the Inspectors and in making them they are concerned not only with the actual education of the pupils but with accommodation, the general organisation and the staffing of the schools. So far as possible, schools are visited every year, but the amount of attention required naturally varies enormously—just as the schools themselves vary from the country school with one teacher and a handful of pupils to the big city school with, perhaps, over 1,000 pupils. In the secondary schools, where instruction is usually given by specialist teachers, the inspection is largely done by Inspectors who are specialists in their respective subjects. The Inspectors must satisfy themselves that the Code is being observed—which is a condition of the payment of grant—but their inspection is not an inquisition, an occasion for fear and the use of whitewash; it is rather aimed at helping the teachers to surmount their difficulties and to make their teaching as effective as possible. To quote the Advisory Council on Education in Scotland: 'Increasingly in recent years the Inspectorate have come to be looked on, and have come, we believe, to look on themselves, as above all consultants and collaborators, able to bring to the problems of any one school experience culled in many, and to contribute to the solution of difficulties a judgment at once disinterested and well-informed. To stimulate by discussion and suggestion, to spread ideas and be a link between school and school, to provoke the unreflective to thought and to awaken healthy doubts as to the sufficiency of familiar routines—in such service lies the most valuable function of the Inspectorate, and we would stress the very special value of its guidance and encouragement to the hundreds of small schools, where teachers, often inexperienced, are working under conditions of difficulty and isolation.'

Further education centres are inspected in much the same way as schools, but here a great deal of the work is done by specialist Inspectors of technical and related subjects. These Inspectors also serve on committees concerned with technological awards such as the National Certificates, and, along with District Inspectors, on various bodies concerned with technical education. Some Inspectors are employed almost entirely in the school meals service and a few are mainly concerned with informal further education. The former, in addition to visiting schools, give general advice on the planning and layout of school kitchens and dining rooms, and on dietary and menus. The latter take an interest both in what education authorities themselves are doing to provide social, cultural and recreational activities, and in what is being done, with assistance from the authorities, by the various voluntary organisations.

In order that the best possible use should be made of the expert knowledge and experience of the Inspectorate, a number of panels of Inspectors have been formed to deal with primary, secondary and further education and with the various subjects in the secondary curriculum. These panels not only advise the Department but prepare memoranda which are printed and issued for the guidance of teachers. The convener of a subject panel usually plays an important part in the Leaving Certificate Examination (which, as will be seen below, occupies a good deal of the time of the Inspectorate during part of the year) and he also undertakes the inspection of that subject in the colleges for the training of teachers.

In addition to their regular duties the Inspectors take part in local conferences of teachers to discuss memoranda issued by the Department, and they also, on occasion, take a share in courses for teachers, under the auspices of the National Committee for the Training of Teachers.[1] They also join in the work of bodies concerned with various aspects of education, such as visual aids, school broadcasting, school libraries and the Youth Employment Service. H.M. Inspectors sometimes represent the Department at educational conferences at home and abroad, and their services have been made available to Commonwealth and foreign Governments and to international organisations.

[1] See Chapter X.

THE SCOTTISH LEAVING CERTIFICATE EXAMINATION

Since the examination was started in 1888, a great many Scots have also formed an early acquaintance with the Scottish Education Department through the Scottish Leaving Certificate Examination. The Leaving Certificate corresponds broadly to the General Certificate of Education in England, but whereas the English examination is run by examining boards based on Universities or groups of Universities, the Department has the sole responsibility for running the Scottish examinations and for awarding the Certificate. There is, however, a close link with the Scottish Universities; a pupil who has secured the necessary passes in the Certificate is exempted from the entrance examinations of Scottish and other British universities, and the Scottish Universities Entrance Board in fact uses the Leaving Certificate papers for its own Spring Preliminary Examination. A large number of professional bodies also accept the Leaving Certificate for the purposes of exemption from their own entrance examinations.

The Regulations laid down by the Department for the award of the Certificate are issued annually by circular; they are varied from time to time, in accordance with changing conditions. Candidates must be in attendance at school and must have taken an approved course of secondary education extending normally to five years. The award of the Certificate by the Department is thus the culmination of a course of education the general lines of which have been laid down by it.

The Department has always been anxious to avoid over-pressure on the pupils and also to avoid any unfairness in the results of the examination. A pupil may not always do himself justice, but the examiners try to take account of his normal performance. This is done by obtaining for each candidate his teachers' estimates of the marks he should be capable of scoring in each subject. If the school estimates and the candidates' marks correspond well on the whole, a good deal of importance is attached to the estimate in deciding whether to pass a candidate who did less well in part of the written examination than his school thought he would. The Department has published memoranda on standards of marking so that the teachers and the examiners will as far as possible judge on the same basis.

A Chief Examiner is appointed by the Department for each subject. It is his duty to see that the question papers are satisfactory in scope and standard, and—by preliminary discussion and, if necessary, subsequent adjustment of their pass marks—that the various examiners adopt so far as is practicable the same standards of marking. The Chief Examiner pays particular attention to any case where there is a serious discrepancy between the school estimate and the mark scored in the examination. If he thinks it necessary, he can send for evidence of the candidate's work at school, and in exceptional cases he may ask one of H.M. Inspectors to visit the school to discuss the matter with the headmaster and the teachers concerned.

To run the examination successfully requires an elaborate and efficient organisation. The question papers are set and the preliminary arrangements made during the winter, the candidates are writing their answers in March, and within three months the Department has issued the results of the examination. The completion of the task within this period calls for concentrated effort, both by those members of the Inspectorate concerned and by a specially augmented office staff. Some idea of the scale of this annual task may be gathered from the figures for 1956: in all, over 100 question papers were set; over 400 invigilators and 300 examiners were employed; the number of candidates exceeded 12,000, and the number of books of answers corrected approached 100,000. A full account of the development of the Examination down to 1951 is included in the Secretary of State's Annual Report, *Education in Scotland in 1951*.[1]

[1] H.M.S.O. Cmd. 8515.

CHAPTER X

Teachers

SO FAR, in the chapters dealing with the work of the Scottish Education Department, the teachers have been mentioned only incidentally. But every stage of their career—their recruitment to the profession, their training, their salaries and conditions of employment and finally their superannuation—gives rise to administrative problems which, to a greater or lesser extent, are the concern of the Secretary of State and the Department.

TRAINING

In dealing with the training of teachers, the position of the Department might roughly be said to be that, having drawn up the rules of the game, it interferes with the play as little as possible. Regulations by the Secretary of State lay down the conditions of entry to the seven Training Colleges; they also prescribe in broad general terms the nature of the courses provided; they set out the conditions of award of the various teacher's certificates (which are awarded and issued by the Department on behalf of the Secretary of State); and they set out the financial arrangements under which the Training Colleges are conducted. Any questions of doubt that arise under the Regulations —for example, whether a person who has not passed the normal Scottish examinations is eligible for entry to a Training College, or whether a teacher educated and trained outside Scotland is eligible for a teacher's certificate—come before the Department. And lastly, after the deduction of the income from fees, 60 per cent. of the approved net expenditure on training (75 per cent. of capital expenditure) is met from the Education (Scotland) Fund,[1] the balance being met by the education authorities in proportion to the number of teachers they employ.

Within the general requirements laid down by the Secretary of State in Regulations (which can be amended to suit changing circumstances), the professional training of teachers in Scotland is the responsibility of the National Committee for the Training of Teachers. This body, set up in 1920, consists wholly of members elected by education authorities. It functions through what is called the Central Executive Committee, which is composed of members of the National Committee with added representatives of the teaching profession and of other educational interests such as the Universities. The Central

[1] See Chapter XII and footnote on page 94.

Executive Committee is responsible for the general administration—including the finance—of the Training Colleges, for the appointment and remuneration of staff, for the fixing of fees and for regulating the number of students to be admitted. Each of the seven Training Colleges is managed by a local body composed of education authority members, teachers and representatives of other educational interests, including the Churches and, where appropriate, the Universities. Each College has a good deal of liberty in drawing up its courses of training, and as a result each has a character of its own.

All men who attend the Colleges are required to have a University degree—unless they mean to teach physical education, art, music, educational handwork or other 'technical' subjects—but women need not be graduates. The length of the training is generally one year for a student with a degree (or a diploma from a Central Institution) and three years for other students. Students who successfully complete the Training College courses are awarded provisional teaching certificates, and on completion of two years' satisfactory service on probation at an inspected school receive the appropriate teacher's certificate from the Department. There are three main kinds of certificate:

(1) The Teacher's General Certificate, which qualifies for teaching in primary schools.
(2) The Teacher's Special Certificate, which qualifies for teaching one of the usual academic subjects at any stage in a secondary school, and is usually awarded only to a person with a first or second class Honours degree.
(3) The Teacher's Technical Certificate, which qualifies for teaching a 'technical subject' such as art or agriculture, and is normally awarded to holders of the diploma of one of the Central Institutions. The Training Colleges themselves provide the courses—normally lasting three years—which lead to the diplomas in physical education and in educational handwork.

Teachers with one of the three types of certificates are commonly known by the convenient though ugly term 'certificated teachers'.

Courses are provided at the Colleges for teachers who seek an additional qualification as a specialist teacher of very young or of handicapped children, and during the summer vacation and at convenient times during the session there are courses at which serving teachers can have further instruction.

RECRUITMENT

Since the war, the Department has had to concern itself increasingly with the recruitment of teachers. Before the war, Scotland had 29,000 teachers. The war itself depleted school staffs and since 1945 a variety of factors—notably the raising of the school leaving age to 15 in 1947, the high post-war birth-rates, the development of further education and the need to reduce the size of classes—have sharply increased the demand for more teachers. In 1955 there were 35,000, and whereas the average number of pupils per teacher was 27 before the war, it is about 25 today—with, however, wide variations in either direction. The percentage of University graduates in the profession is now 45 (it was 42·3 in 1939) and many of the non-graduates hold diplomas in the different 'technical' subjects. Thus, although all the rowing has been against the current, perceptible progress has been made. Nevertheless the education authorities would like to see a further 1,800 teachers employed.

To meet the difficult post-war situation, two special schemes were introduced under Regulations made by the Secretary of State: the Emergency Scheme and the Special Recruitment Scheme. Both schemes have been administered, under the general supervision of the Department, by the National Committee for the Training of Teachers and approved expenditure under them has been met in full from the Education (Scotland) Fund.[1]

The object of the Emergency Scheme, which was begun in England and Wales and in Scotland when the end of the war was in sight, was to bring into the profession people who, having served in the war and having developed a desire to teach, were prepared to reach a standard of education roughly equivalent to that normally demanded of prospective teachers. Nearly 6,000 people (four-fifths of them men) were accepted under the Scheme—the care taken by the Selection Board is shown by the fact that almost as many were rejected— and they received maintenance grants for themselves and for their dependants while they took the courses. The Scheme was to transfuse new blood but not diluted blood: many of the entrants were encouraged to take University degrees, their training courses were of about the normal length, and they have proved in no way inferior to the normal entrants. Indeed the Scheme—which, having dealt with all the ex-service students who wished to avail themselves of it, has now been closed—has produced a group of teachers whose varied experience makes them a stimulating element in the profession.

The Special Recruitment Scheme, which applied to Scotland only, was launched in 1951, to give people from other walks of life an opportunity to prepare themselves for teaching. Under this Scheme, also, maintenance grants are paid for the candidates and their dependants while they qualify to enter a University or Training College and while they study there. The educational requirements and the training are the same as for normal entrants to the profession. Out of some 2,600 candidates accepted, about 900 are now teaching in the schools.

[1] See footnote on page 94.

Leaving out of account these two special schemes, normal recruitment to the profession considerably exceeds the pre-war level. Teaching is therefore still proving attractive to young men and women who are at the stage of choosing a career. But the needs of the expanding educational service are such that there is no room for complacency about the supply of well-qualified teachers. There is still a shortage of teachers generally, and an acute shortage in particular categories. The Secretary of State has initiated investigations into these shortages —for example, in 1957 the Advisory Council on Education was asked to consider measures to meet the increasing demand for teachers for secondary education[1]—and their relief is one of his most difficult problems. The Department has also done all it can to make known to pupils, students and parents the advantages of higher education and the need for more teachers.

SALARIES AND CONDITIONS OF SERVICE

Education authorities themselves appoint the teachers they employ and in general they also determine the conditions of employment. The exceptions to this general statement are that teachers are protected by statute against arbitrary dismissal, that a woman teacher cannot be dismissed for the sole reason that she has married, and that the salaries paid must be in strict accordance with the national scales prescribed in Regulations made by the Secretary of State.

The Secretary of State normally prescribes what the salaries should be for a period of three years; the Regulations at present in force will remain in operation until 31st March, 1960, unless they are amended before that date. Before he makes salary regulations, the Secretary of State consults the National Joint Council, a body representative of the education authorities and of the teachers, which has been set up for the purpose of salary negotiations under a neutral chairman appointed by the Secretary of State. Having taken account of the Council's recommendations—which carry great weight—the Secretary of State must publish the Regulations in draft and consider the comments he receives from interested bodies and individuals before laying the Regulations before Parliament.

The Regulations prescribe a basic salary, the amount of which is dependent on the teacher's qualifications. They also lay down the amount of the special additions to salary for teachers in posts of special responsibility, such as head teachers and principal teachers of subjects in secondary schools. A woman has hitherto received about five-sixths of the salary of a similarly qualified man but as a result of Regulations made in 1955 the salaries of women are gradually being assimilated to those of men over a period of seven years.

The Regulations apply only to the salaries of teachers employed

[1] For its Interim Report, see Cmnd. 202.

G

by education authorities but there is a natural tendency for the salaries of other teachers to move correspondingly.

It will be seen, then, that the Department is brought very closely into salary questions: it must maintain close liaison with the National Joint Council, estimate the cost of salary changes, advise the Secretary of State on the drafting of the Regulations and, once the Regulations have been made, deal with any questions on them that may arise.

PENSIONS

The other major interest which the Department has in teachers is their superannuation, and this is considered separately in the chapter on the Financing of Public Education in Scotland (Chapter XII).

CHAPTER XI

Further Education

THE interest of the State and the local authorities in providing education for children has for long been well established; but it is a more recent development that the education authorities, with Government assistance, should have a duty to concern themselves with the education of people who have left school. Further education, because it is voluntary, presents special problems. Small children receive their education rather as they receive their food—the more palatable it is, the better, but it is chosen for them; at the secondary school stage an element of choice begins to appear. But the purveyors of further education no longer have, as it were, a monopoly. They have entered a world of fierce competition from other activities and have to consider not merely what is good for people but what people want. A class is useless if no one attends it, and so they must study the arts of publicity, and how to attract people into further education.

At the further education centres, which are nearly all run by education authorities, courses are given in a wide range of subjects. Many of the centres have to make use of day-school premises, which restricts their activities to the evenings, but there are about 60 with their own premises, and in these, day-time as well as evening classes are held. Many of the classes are vocational—in technical, commercial and other subjects. A recent development is the full-time 'pre-apprenticeship' course which enables boys and girls who have left school to continue their general education and at the same time to receive vocational training for careers in, for example, building, engineering or nursing. Another notable development affects those who have actually begun a career: employers in commerce and industry, as well as in the public service, are coming to recognise that their young employees will be more useful if they can supplement their practical experience by part-time courses, and many firms release them from work one day a week, so that they need not study entirely in the evening but can take the major part of their courses during the day.

There are also, in the further education centres, evening classes in literature, science, art, music, drama and other subjects which can broadly be summed up under the word 'cultural'. These classes usually meet once a week for one and a half to two hours. Part of the time is devoted to questions and discussion. The education authority for the area runs most of the classes, which are often arranged in co-operation with a University Extra-Mural Department.

The Department does not exercise a close and detailed control over the work of the education authorities in further education, but the general requirements to which they must conform in running further education centres have been laid down in the Further Education (Scotland) Code, 1952. The Code covers, in very general terms, such matters as qualifications of staff, size of classes, schemes and records of work, premises and equipment, and so on. The centres are visited periodically by H.M. Inspectors, who examine the schemes of work and the education provided, and report to the Department. Education authorities are required to obtain the Department's approval of the qualifications of any new teacher in further education; for full-time teachers the approval is required before appointment. The authorities supply the Department with particulars of the courses they provide, and with statistics of the number of students attending them.

As well as the further education centres conducted by the education authorities, there are Central Institutions, each of which provides more advanced education within its own specialised field, which may be art, music, commercial subjects, technology, domestic science or agriculture. Typical examples are the Royal College of Science and Technology, Glasgow, the Scottish College of Commerce, Glasgow, the Edinburgh College of Domestic Science, the Dundee Institute of Art and Technology, and Robert Gordon's Technical College, Aberdeen. There are three agricultural colleges, which are the concern of the Department of Agriculture.[1] The basic courses at the Central Institutions are of three or four years' duration and lead to a diploma or associateship of the College. These awards, which are granted with the approval of the Secretary of State, are widely recognised as being of high standing. As the Central Institutions have a special place in the Scottish educational system (they are all listed in Regulations made under the 1946 Act) and as their costs, so far as not covered by fees, endowments, etc., are defrayed by the Department through the Education (Scotland) Fund,[2] the Department takes a more detailed interest in their administration than it does in that of most other educational establishments. The Department's approval must be obtained for the courses provided, the number, qualifications and salaries of the teaching staff, the conditions on which the Institutions award their diplomas and certificates, and the amount of the fees they charge. The consideration of these matters and of the finances of the institutions constitutes a major part of the Department's work in further education. In 1954–55, the Department paid through the Education (Scotland) Fund £930,774 or 62 per cent. of the total cost of running the Central Institutions.

Various national voluntary organisations were mentioned in Chapter VII as providing informal further education, and as receiving

[1] See Chapter V.
[2] See footnote on page 94.

financial assistance locally from education authorities. The Department deals with the Scottish headquarters of these organisations, and, when it seems necessary, gives grants towards their administrative expenses and towards the cost of training leaders, wardens and other workers. It is also represented by assessors on various bodies concerned with educational or cultural activities, such as the Arts Council, the University Grants Committee, the Imperial Institute and the Council of Industrial Design.

THE ROYAL SCOTTISH MUSEUM

A chapter dealing with education outside the school is perhaps the appropriate place to mention that the Government finances, and administers through the Scottish Education Department, the Royal Scottish Museum in Chambers Street, Edinburgh, which houses a wide variety of important collections of scientific and artistic material. The Museum, which was established in 1854, is under the charge of a Director and has four departments—of Art, Archaeology and Ethnology, of Natural History, of Geology, and of Technology— each under a Keeper.

The Museum plays an important part at all levels of educational activity. The Edinburgh Education Authority arranges regular visits of school classes—including children from schools outside Edinburgh—in the summer months; students from the University and Central Institutions situated in Edinburgh pay more specialised visits; there are evening courses run for the Workers' Educational Association; and scientific and learned societies hold evening meetings in the Museum. The Natural History Department, with its attractively arranged models of birds and animals and its special Children's Gallery, and the Technology Department, with its examples of power producers from the early steam engines to the latest jet engine and with its many working models, are perhaps the most popular with the school children, but all four departments have valuable and well-displayed collections. The collections are continually being overhauled and the most modern methods of lighting and display are used to enhance the usefulness and attractiveness of the exhibits.

The Department is responsible for dealing with all establishment matters—appointments, salaries, conditions of service, superannuation, etc.—for the Museum staff, and the Director must seek its approval for the holding of special exhibitions, for purchases of over £100 in value and for the loan, exchange or disposal of objects in the collections. The Department also deals with other Government departments on behalf of the Museum—for example, with the Ministry of Works about accommodation and with the Treasury about special purchases.

CHAPTER XII

The Financing of Public Education in Scotland

IN the preceding chapters a short account has been given of the Scottish educational system and of the responsibilities of the Secretary of State and the Scottish Education Department for that system. It may already be apparent that even if the Government were indifferent to the quality of education provided in Scotland, it is financially involved to such an extent that it could not dissociate itself from educational administration.

Not only is the payment of Parliamentary grants in aid of expenditure one of the major functions of the Department, but the arrangements for the financing of public education in Scotland are sufficiently unusual to deserve some description.[1] It may be helpful to begin with a summary of the main Parliamentary Vote for which the Department is responsible:

PUBLIC EDUCATION, SCOTLAND (1957–58)

Subheads					£
A and B	Administration and Inspection	..	..	..	427,770
C.1	General Grant in Aid	..	..	..	47,537,842
C.2	Superannuation of Teachers ..	..	..	..	3,559,000
C.3	Milk in Schools	..	..	..	1,670,000
D	Royal Scottish Museum	..	..	..	74,551
E	Other Services ..	..	..	..	339,297
	Gross Total ..	..	..	..	53,608,460
Z	Deduct Appropriations-in-Aid	..	..	..	4,211,409
	Net Total ..	..	..	..	49,397,051

The amount of the General Grant in Aid (Subhead C), which is by far the largest part of the vote, is mainly determined in accordance with the Goschen or $\frac{11}{80}$ formula. This formula was originally applied to education in the Education (Scotland) Act, 1918, and with certain exceptions it secures for Scotland (a) the equivalent of monies formerly paid into the Education (Scotland) Fund from the Local Taxation (Scotland) Account; (b) a sum equal to that expended

---

[1] If proposals now under discussion are implemented, the arrangements described in this Chapter will be materially affected. The bulk of the education grant would be merged in a new general grant, and this would entail the disappearance of the Education (Scotland) Fund.

from the Parliamentary Vote for Education in Scotland in 1913/14; and (c) $\frac{11}{80}$ of the amount by which the grants for education in England and Wales (excluding the sum corresponding to (a)) exceed those paid in 1913/14.

The money received under the General Grant in Aid (Subhead C) is paid into a fund called the Education (Scotland) Fund, which is, as it were, the main irrigation channel through which the Parliamentary Grants flow into Scotland, and from which money passes by subsidiary channels to maintain and develop the national system of education. The Fund also receives (under Subhead D) $\frac{11}{80}$ of the amount voted for the superannuation of teachers in England and Wales, and the superannuation contributions from teachers and their employers in Scotland are paid into it. On the payments side of the ledger, the Fund bears the cost of the teachers' pensions and also pays to the Exchequer, in respect of teachers' and employers' superannuation contributions, not the sum actually received but $\frac{11}{80}$ of the sum of the contributions received in England and Wales. When these prior charges have been met and grants paid to various bodies other than education authorities, such as voluntary schools and Central Institutions, the remainder of the income is applied in grants to the education authorities. In 1955–56, £35,345,990 out of a total of £43,263,738 went to the authorities.

The Secretary of State has made grant regulations which govern the way this money is distributed to the education authorities. The formula that controls the amount of grant paid to each authority is that it receives £6 per pupil plus 60 per cent. of its net total expenditure on education *less* the amount which a given rate levied in the authority's area will produce. The last of these is really a balancing figure and the rate can be varied from year to year according to the size of the balance available in the Fund for distribution. In its main features, this method of distribution bears many of the distinguishing marks of what is called the 'block grant' system. Its most notable feature is that the total sum available for distribution is not dependent on what the authorities spend, but is pre-determined by the $\frac{11}{80}$ arrangement referred to above. This arrangement enables the total sum available for distribution in Scotland to be applied in the way that best suits Scottish needs and circumstances. The grants to other bodies are also governed by regulations made by the Secretary of State.

The financial work of the Department is done by the Finance and the Accountant's Branches. The Finance Branch prepares the annual estimates, makes all the payments from the moneys voted by Parliament, and keeps the accounts for this expenditure and for the Education (Scotland) Fund. It receives the annual estimates of the education authorities and makes enquiries about any item of expenditure or income that seems to call for explanation. From the authorities' estimates it calculates, by the use of the formula, the estimated amount of grant that each authority should receive; the grant is then paid in monthly instalments and any balance due is paid over when the annual accounts of the authority have been received and scrutinised.

The Department is also empowered to examine the accounts of the education authorities in order to ensure that their expenditure on education has all been properly incurred, that the conditions of grant have been fulfilled and that where the specific approval of the Secretary of State is necessary, it has been obtained. After this examination, which takes place at the offices of the authorities, the final balance of grant due to each authority is agreed between its chief financial officer and the Accountant's Branch and paid over.

The Accountant's Branch also scrutinises the estimates and accounts of the voluntary grant-aided schools and calculates the grant they should receive.

In accordance with the Act of 1946, the Accountant submits to Parliament every year an abstract of the receipts and expenditure of the education authorities and other bodies that receive grant, together with his annual report. The accounts of educational endowments are also audited within the Department to see that their expenditure has been in accordance with the requirements of their particular schemes, and a summary of the income and expenditure of the various classes of endowments is included in the Accountant's Report.

PENSIONS

Generally speaking, all whole-time teachers with approved qualifications, whether they work in grant-aided schools, in training centres, in colleges or in Central Institutions, are eligible for superannuation benefits under provisions administered by the Department, which also apply to some independent schools.

Under the provisions of the Education (Scotland) Act, 1956, Superannuation Regulations have been made which incorporate amendments required because of the provisions of the Teachers (Superannuation) Act, 1956. The main changes made by the Regulations are the increase in the maximum age of retirement from 65 to 70 years; the increase in the maximum period of pensionable service from 40 to 45 years, which will include the whole period of service and not, as previously, completed years only; the calculation of the pension by reference to the average salary of the last three years instead of the last five years of service; and an increase in the additional (lump sum) allowance from $\frac{1}{80}$ to $\frac{3}{80}$ of that average for each year of service after 30th December, 1956. The Regulations also provide for a disablement allowance calculated on a minimum period of 20 years' service (or such lesser period as the teacher would have completed when he reached 65 years of age) where the teacher's actual service is more than 10 years but less than 20 years. They also make provision for various minor improvements in benefits.

The contributions of teachers and employers, which were increased, from 1st October, 1956, from 5 per cent. to 6 per cent. of the teacher's salary, are not paid into a separate superannuation fund, but, as was mentioned above, into the Education (Scotland) Fund. A separate account is kept, however, of all revenue and expenditure. The Act of 1956 requires that an actuarial enquiry shall be held every five years from 31st March, 1956, and the resulting report subsequently presented to Parliament, to determine whether the account shows that the contributions are sufficient to support the benefits payable for service from 1st June, 1922. The Act provides that the deficiency as at 31st March, 1956, which is estimated to amount to about £36 million, is to be met by the Exchequer, and that any future deficiencies shall be met by a supplementary contribution from the employers.

The Regulations are administered by the Department through a Pensions Branch, and the various sections of this branch look after every detail of the arrangements, from the admission of teachers until the closing of the record when a pensioned teacher dies. Teachers who have received the Department's Certificate after a course at a training college must be included, but for certain others admission is optional and the Pensions Branch have to decide in each case whether the teacher is eligible. About 1,800 'certificated' teachers and about 70 others are included in the scope of the Regulations each year. For all those included, records are kept of their service and of the contributions paid by them and by their employers. As teachers retire, the amount of the benefits due to them is calculated, payment by the Paymaster General is authorised, and the payments are recorded. About 11,400 pensions are being paid at present, and every year about 800 new awards of pensions are made and 450 pensioners die.

The calculations for teachers who serve continuously until they reach retiring age are comparatively straightforward. But there are also teachers who leave the educational service altogether and must have their contributions repaid to them, and others who move between teaching and some other public service—such as the Civil Service, the National Health Service or local government—which has its own pension arrangements; each transfer means that the 'transfer value' to be paid or received by the Department has to be worked out. There are also adjustments to be made to the pensions of retired teachers who are re-employed in teaching—the number of whom has increased considerably in recent years—and contributions to be repaid where the teacher has died before any benefit became payable.

EDUCATIONAL ENDOWMENTS

As the names of many famous Scottish schools prove, endowments have long been a prominent feature of the Scottish educational tradition. Indeed, since it was as late as 1833 that Parliament first voted money to be used for education in Great Britain, the private benefactor was in the field long before the State. Some of those who set up trusts for educational purposes left reasonable latitude to their trustees in the use which they could make of the funds; others left very precise instructions as to the purposes for which their money was to be used. None of them could foresee what course education would follow long after they were dead. In some cases the State is now doing what the benefactor wanted to see done; in others the course of education has changed and left the endowment where it can no longer give any real benefit. The Court of Session has always had power at common law to alter the purposes of endowments, but this power was used only within narrow limits and in 1869 Parliament intervened by passing the first of a succession of measures which covered the next decade and provided opportunities to the governing bodies of endowments to apply their funds more usefully. But little was done under these measures, and it was only when an executive commission was appointed under an Act of 1882 that the great majority of the endowments in Scotland were overhauled and their usefulness extended to meet the changed situation brought about by the introduction of compulsory education in 1872.

With the passing of new Education Acts in 1908 and, particularly, in 1918, another overhaul of endowments became desirable, and a second executive commission was set up under an Act passed in 1928. When this commission went out of office in 1936, its powers of framing schemes for the future administration and application of endowments were inherited by the Secretary of State.

The Commission of 1882 worked on the general principle of amalgamating endowments on a school board area basis, and so made a radical reduction in their number. A further substantial reduction was achieved by the Commission of 1928, who followed the same practice on an education authority area basis with a view to achieving not only co-ordination between statutory authorities and governing bodies, but also more efficient and less expensive administration of endowments.

In 1948 the Secretary of State appointed a Committee to consider whether the administration of endowments was adequate to meet the demands of the modern educational world and, in particular, the changed situation created by the Education (Scotland) Act, 1945. This Committee, which reported in 1951, felt that the Secretary of State's existing powers were quite sufficient to enable him to do anything that might be required. They did, however, express some views about the purposes for which endowment funds should or should not be used. Thus they suggested that the provision of school meals, nursery schools and child guidance services, all of which are now undertaken by education authorities, should no longer be regarded as suitable for the expenditure of endowment funds. On the other hand, they recommended that endowments should continue to be used to provide bursaries, travel grants, special equipment for schools, cultural and recreational facilities, and educational experiments and research. As a result, the Secretary of State decided to initiate a general review of educational endowments in Scotland, with a view to bringing their purposes up to date where necessary.

In this review, all the endowments in the area of a particular education authority are considered together. (There is usually an area trust already in existence in each area, administered by the authority or by a special body set up by the Commissioners under the Endowment Acts.) When the review in any one area begins, it is explained to each governing body that the conditions of its endowment are to be examined, and each is asked to suggest in what way, if any, it thinks the administration of the endowment could be improved, bearing in mind the purposes of the endowment and the views of the Committee. A Commissioner appointed by the Secretary of State then holds a public enquiry in the district, at which the education authority is represented and at which the governing body can explain its views for or against any change. When he has received the Commissioner's report, and if he decides that the purposes or the administration of any of the endowments should be altered, the Secretary of State has a draft Scheme published together with a memorandum giving the reasons for any alterations that are proposed. If representations are received from the governing body or anyone else interested, there will be consultations and possibly even another public enquiry before the Scheme, amended as necessary, is finally made and published. Even at this stage, further representations may be made, or a dissatisfied person can submit a special case to the Court of Session or can petition the Secretary of State that the Scheme should be laid before Parliament. Finally, if all these hurdles are safely cleared, the Scheme is confirmed and is approved by the Queen by Order in Council. The system is an elaborate one, but it does ensure that no endowment is altered before all the arguments for and against a change have been heard.

The various reviews that have taken place have enabled endowments to supplement in a valuable way what is being done in Scotland from public funds. Despite the extent of the statutory provision for education today, endowments—if used with flexibility and imagination—still have scope to provide the stimulus to advance which has been their traditional contribution to Scottish education.

BURSARIES

It is now generally accepted that no promising boys or girls should be prevented by lack of money from carrying their education as far as possible. For this reason, education authorities may award bursaries. Some of these are to enable children to attend fee-paying schools, but the greater part are to make it possible for pupils of over compulsory school age to attend the fourth and later years of an approved secondary school course and to go on from school to a University, a teacher training college, a Central Institution or some establishment where they will receive further education. The authorities have complete discretion in deciding whether to award a bursary in any individual case, but the Secretary of State has made regulations to ensure that authorities throughout Scotland give bursaries which are adequate in amount, and that they calculate their awards on the same basis and make them on the same conditions. The regulations show how the expenditure on an applicant's education should be reckoned and what proportion should be met by the applicant himself—or by his parents—and the authority then awards a bursary to cover the balance.

There is no system of State Scholarships in Scotland similar to that operated by the Minister of Education in England and Wales. But a student of high attainment and promise, ordinarily resident in Scotland, who wins a competitive scholarship tenable at an English University, may have it supplemented by an allowance from the Education (Scotland) Fund to an amount which, together with any contribution the parents may be able to make, will meet the full cost of the course of study.

SCOTTISH EDUCATION DEPARTMENT
Organisation, 1957

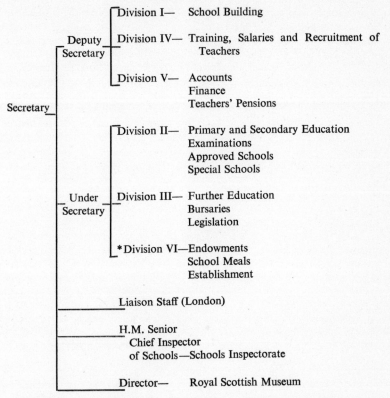

Secretary

Deputy Secretary
- Division I— School Building
- Division IV— Training, Salaries and Recruitment of Teachers
- Division V— Accounts
  Finance
  Teachers' Pensions

Under Secretary
- Division II— Primary and Secondary Education
  Examinations
  Approved Schools
  Special Schools
- Division III— Further Education
  Bursaries
  Legislation
- *Division VI—Endowments
  School Meals
  Establishment

Liaison Staff (London)

H.M. Senior Chief Inspector of Schools—Schools Inspectorate

Director— Royal Scottish Museum

* References from Division VI on Establishment matters are made direct to the Secretary; and on legislation and endowments direct to the Deputy Secretary.

PART FOUR

The Department of Health for Scotland

CHAPTER XIII

The National Health Service

SO far, the functions of the Secretary of State have been fairly clearly indicated by the titles of the departments through which he exercises them. The Department of Agriculture for Scotland does in fact deal with agriculture and the Scottish Education Department with education. Later chapters will try to show what lies behind the title of the Scottish Home Department. The Department of Health is somewhere between these two extremes; through it the Secretary of State exercises his general responsibility for the health of the Scottish people, and in particular for the working of the National Health Service in Scotland. But the Department also deals with a variety of other matters—such as housing, town and country planning, water supplies, sewerage and river pollution—which are in England the concern of the Ministry of Housing and Local Government.

The Secretary of the Department is assisted by three under secretaries responsible for the three main blocks of the Department's work: the health services, housing and general sanitation, and town and country planning. The organisation of the Department is given more fully on page 142. Its present staff numbers 974, of whom 165 are members of the professional and technical classes.

In view of the name of the Department, it is perhaps reasonable to begin the chapters on its work by looking at what is done by the divisions which deal with the National Health Service. There are other good reasons for doing so. Perhaps no part of the Secretary of State's duties directly affects so many of the people of Scotland; and because the Service is a new machine, built as recently as 1948, an examination of its working should help towards understanding modern administrative practice. Unfortunately the space that can be devoted to the subject in this book is limited and it therefore seems best to concentrate on the Department's rôle in helping to make the machine work, and on the particular features of the service which are different in Scotland and England.

It is fair to say that up to about 100 years ago the interest of the State and local government was confined to doing what seemed necessary to protect the healthy members of the public against contagion and infection; as the impulse to action was usually the first report of a new epidemic, progress was slow. Gradually, however, a public conscience in health matters developed and by 1947, when the National Health Service (Scotland) Act became law, the Department of Health had quite a variety of duties—in providing for the special needs of the Highlands and Islands under the Highlands and Islands (Medical Service) Grant Act of 1913, in guiding the local authorities in the running of the various medical services they provided, and so on. The creation of a comprehensive health service meant, however, in Scotland as in England, if not a complete break with the past, a tremendous increase in the Secretary of State's responsibility for the health of the country.

Even the most enthusiastic advocate of centralised control would hardly have suggested that the Secretary of State should administer and manage all the services for which he became responsible by the Act of 1947. Nor were they all services of a kind which it seemed reasonable or appropriate to ask local authorities to provide. The Act therefore divided the health service into three main parts: first, the provision of hospital accommodation and treatment and the services of specialists; secondly, a whole group of health services which may be described roughly as services for the promotion of health and the prevention of disease; and thirdly, the general practitioner services, which include the services of the family doctors, the dentists, the chemists, the ophthalmic medical practitioners and the opticians.

The job of the Secretary of State and the Department of Health is, broadly speaking, to keep a careful watch on the running of the machine, to see that it does its work, to improve it where improvement seems necessary and to provide the funds necessary for efficient and economical running. Within the Department, professional advice is given by the Chief Medical Officer and his staff, who specialise in the various branches of the National Health Service, while the Chief Medical Officer himself, in addition to keeping in close touch with day-to-day administration, watches the health of Scotland, with the medical statistics as a sort of control panel to tell him how things are going, and advises the Secretary of State on the medical aspects of policy. In accordance with modern administrative practice, the Act of 1947 also provided the Secretary of State with an advisory council of people outside the civil service altogether—the Scottish Health Services Council. The Council includes representatives of medical and dental practitioners, nurses and midwives, pharmacists, local authorities and hospital administrators, and it is assisted by Standing Advisory Committees with added members, which deal with the various aspects of the Health Service. There is a special Standing Committee to consider the problems of the Health Service in the Highlands and Islands.

The Hospital and Specialist Services

The Act put directly on the Secretary of State the duty of providing the hospital and specialist services and he does this through the agency of five Regional Hospital Boards, with headquarters in Edinburgh, Glasgow, Aberdeen, Dundee and Inverness. Actual control and management of the individual hospitals is carried out on behalf of the Regional Boards by 84 Boards of Management (corresponding to Hospital Management Committees in England and Wales). In July, 1948, when the National Health Service came into operation, the Secretary of State became the owner of over 400 hospitals with about 57,000 beds available for use; some of the hospitals were modern and in good condition, but many were neither. All these Health Service hospitals and the general planning of hospital and specialist services became the concern of one or other of the Regional Hospital Boards, and the Boards drew up for the Secretary of State's approval schemes for devolving to the Hospital Boards of Management the day-to-day running of the hospitals. In England, where the arrangements are otherwise similar, the teaching hospitals are run by Boards of Governors who are responsible not to the Regional Board but direct to the Minister; this distinction was not made in Scotland where the teaching hospitals provide a much larger proportion of the total number of hospital beds than they do in England. But the Board of Management of a Scottish teaching hospital must contain representatives of the University and of the teaching staff and, in order to safeguard the interest of the Universities in the provision of clinical teaching facilities, each Regional Board has a Medical Education Committee, on which the University is well represented, to advise it.

Another important difference between Scotland and England is that in England the local health authorities are responsible for providing the ambulance services; in Scotland, in order to avoid overburdening the smaller and poorer authorities and because the country is small enough to make a centralised organisation possible and efficient, the Secretary of State is himself responsible. He has entered into a contract with the Scottish Branch of the British Red Cross and the St. Andrew's Ambulance Association (who operate jointly for this purpose as the Scottish Ambulance Service) and the whole cost is met by the Exchequer. To ensure that this centralised service operates satisfactorily in each region, there are Regional Ambulance Committees on which the Regional Board, the Ambulance Service, general practitioners in the area and the W.V.S. are all represented. The Department has also made an arrangement with British European Airways by which they carry to hospitals on the mainland patients from Orkney, Shetland and the Western Isles who need urgent treatment that cannot be given locally.

Generally speaking, then, although the Regional Boards are the agents of the Secretary of State and carry out their functions subject to any directions he may issue, successive Secretaries of State have tried to give the Boards as much freedom as possible. Just as a wise landowner, having told his factor what he wanted, would leave the details of administration to him but would expect to be consulted about the buying or selling of land or the erection of buildings, so the Regional Boards require the formal approval of the Secretary of State before carrying out major building schemes and before entering into transactions for the acquisition or disposal of properties. But like many modern landowners, the Government has too many different calls on its money; this continuing financial stringency makes it necessary for the Department to keep fairly close control over current expenditure and capital investment and involves it in detailed examination of the Boards' annual estimates of expenditure, in regular analysis of costs and in a close scrutiny of building programmes and of individual projects costing more than £30,000.

Apart from the formal communications that pass between the Boards and the Department, there is a very useful informal relationship between the administrative and medical officers of the Department and those of the Boards through meetings and correspondence. In this way, as well as through more formal action when necessary, the Department can give advice and make suggestions.

Local Authority Services

To turn to the services for the promotion of health and prevention of disease, these were made by the Act the responsibility of the local health authorities—that is, the county councils and the town councils of large burghs. They include both powers and duties. Local health authorities are required to provide for the care, including the dental care, of mothers and young children; to provide midwives, health visitors and nurses, who will visit at home those who need their help; to make arrangements for vaccination against smallpox and immunisation against diphtheria and to carry out their duties under the Lunacy and Mental Deficiency Acts. In addition, local health authorities have been empowered to provide for immunisation against other diseases (against whooping cough for example, and recently—on a restricted scale—against poliomyelitis); and they are also empowered to provide care and after-care for the physically and mentally sick and to provide domestic help where it is required because of the presence of (as the Act comprehensively puts it) 'any person who is ill, lying-in, an expectant mother, mentally defective, aged or a child not over school age'.[1]

The relationship between the Secretary of State and the local authorities in health service matters is very like that which we have met—or shall meet—elsewhere in this book. The statutory responsibility is the authority's but it must submit for the Secretary of State's

---

[1] The School Health Service, provided by the county councils and the town councils of the four cities of Aberdeen, Dundee, Edinburgh and Glasgow in their capacity of education authorities, is referred to in Chapter VIII.

approval proposals for the carrying out of its duties. The authority then receives through the Department 50 per cent. of its approved expenditure.[1] The authorities mostly drew up their proposals in fairly wide terms, allowing themselves, for example, reasonable freedom to employ extra staff. The fact that the authority has itself to meet half the cost is regarded as likely to provide a sufficient brake on the expenditure. There is, however, a closer financial control over capital expenditure, since the authority needs the Secretary of State's sanction for any money it wishes to borrow, and may not spend more than £2,000 on a capital project without his approval.

The services provided by the local health authorities are not prevented from developing merely because they are cast in the mould of formal proposals. Sometimes at the Department's suggestion, sometimes at the authorities', the original proposals have been amended to provide for services that were only beginning to be developed when the Act came into operation. For example, all authorities have now made arrangements for providing B.C.G. vaccination against tuberculosis and, although they are not required to do so, all of them now run a domestic help service. Again, all local health authorities have undertaken the distribution of welfare foods, since July, 1954, as part of their arrangements for the care of mothers and young children.

General Practitioner Services

To organise the third group of services, the general practitioner services, the Act of 1947 set up new bodies called Executive Councils, which consist of a mixture of professional and lay members who serve voluntarily but are assisted by a salaried staff. There are 25 of these Executive Councils and five Joint Ophthalmic Service Committees. The doctors, dentists and chemists who give their services under the National Health Service do so under contracts with the Executive Councils, and the ophthalmic practitioners and opticians are similarly under contract with the Joint Ophthalmic Services Committees, which are drawn in each area from members of the Executive Council and of the professional organisations in the area. The actual services given by the various practitioners are perhaps well enough known to most people not to require description here. The methods of payment vary according to the service.

In each case, the practitioner is paid by the Executive Council, but the fee payable is laid down by the Secretary of State on the recommendation of the appropriate Whitley Council (or, for doctors and dentists, after negotiation with the profession's representatives). The doctor's remuneration varies according to the number of patients on his lists, with a special payment for doctors in remote areas in the

---

[1] If proposals now under discussion are implemented, these grants paid by the Department to local health authorities will be merged in a new general grant.

Highlands and Islands where the income reckoned in the normal way would necessarily be small. The chemist makes, and retains as part of his remuneration, the statutory charge of 1s. on each item on the prescription form and at the end of each month sends all his National Health Service prescription forms to the appropriate Executive Council, so that the balance due to him can be calculated and paid. (The calculations are made by Pricing Bureaux run by the Drug Accounts Committee,[1] who price all the more expensive forms in detail, and work out an average value for the rest by pricing a sample of them.) The dentist is paid for completed work on the authorisation of the Scottish Dental Estimates Board, a central body whose approval the dentist must seek before he provides dentures or certain other forms of expensive treatment; he also retains as part of his remuneration the statutory payments which the patient is required to make.

The general practitioner services are essentially local services and, in addition to fixing the fees payable, the Secretary of State's main function is to exercise through the Department a general supervision over them. The Department has to see that they are properly co-ordinated and that they work in smoothly with the hospital service and the local authority services. It also has to watch, since the general practitioner services are financed by the Exchequer, that they are run as economically as possible. The cost of these services is, however, largely dependent upon the public demand for them; if prescriptions are presented to a chemist, for example, he must prepare the medicines and will have to be paid for them. Where a public service of this kind does not even pretend to be self-supporting, it is not easy to decide—and in the last resort is a matter for decision by the Government of the day—how much it ought to cost. Obviously there must be some regard for economy all through the service and, for example, if a doctor's prescribing appears excessive or extravagant, he may find himself called before a committee of his colleagues to justify it.

The Department is responsible for various experiments made with a view to improving the service. For example, it has been directly concerned in the establishment and running of health centres—which in England it is the responsibility of the local health authorities to provide—and two centres, one at Sighthill on the outskirts of Edinburgh and one at Stranraer, have been built and are in use. Both are experimental, and while their operation will be carefully watched, it is not at present proposed to build any further centres of this type. It is hoped that some of the same advantages will be derived from a new scheme of a less ambitious and expensive kind, whereby interest-free loans can be advanced to groups of doctors to help them to provide joint consulting premises in which they can work in close association.

[1] This body covers Scotland and there is a similar body for England and Wales.

It should also be mentioned that the Secretary of State acts as a court for the consideration of appeals against decisions of the Executive Councils and other bodies, in various circumstances where there have been disputes or complaints.

It is convenient to refer to the Health Service as a machine, but the metaphor tends to obscure the fact that the service is run not by standardised cogs and pistons but by very individual human beings; in the general practitioner services in particular, the individual person is really more immediately important than the organisation, and the officers of the Department find that they can often more usefully guide the local development of the service by informal meetings, and by round-the-table discussion of problems as they arise, than by formal meetings and the issue of circulars and memoranda.

Whitley Council Work

These then are the three main branches of the National Health Service with which the Department has to deal. The activities of one other division of the Department cover the whole service. When the Act came into operation in 1948, it brought into employment under the National Health Service every variety and class of worker, from medical consultants to part-time cleaners, for all of whom conditions of service and salaries or wages had to be negotiated. Some of them were members of trade unions, some of small professional bodies, and some had no organisation responsible for looking after their interests. After a short reconnaissance into this jungle, two things were decided—first, that the negotiating machinery must work for Great Britain as a whole,[1] and secondly, that a series of the bodies commonly called Whitley Councils should be set up, each covering a fairly homogeneous group of staff. Each council has two sides—a staff side and a management side—and the decisions of the council are by agreement between the two sides. The Ministry of Health and the Department are represented on the management side and also provide the Secretariat for that side. Since 1948, although they have been heavily engaged in dealing with wage claims, the councils have substantially completed the very large task of prescribing salaries and conditions of service for nearly every type of health worker. The decisions of the councils, subject to the approval of the Secretary of State, are binding on the various employing authorities. In certain cases, local authority associations are parties to the decisions.

Medical Research

Research into the causes and treatment of disease is, of course, the life-blood of medicine in all branches of the service. While there are

[1] The Scottish and English contracting chemists, however, are represented by separate committees of the Pharmaceutical Council, each of which is autonomous.

full-time medical research workers in the Universities and elsewhere, most of the research in the National Health Service is carried out on a part-time basis by doctors working in hospitals, in general practice, or with local authorities.

To meet the cost of technical and statistical staff or of special equipment for clinical research of this kind, financial assistance is often required. This can be had both from the Exchequer and from the endowment funds that originally belonged to the voluntary hospitals. Part of these endowment funds have been merged in a central fund, and the income is used, under the control of the Scottish Hospital Endowments Research Trust, to finance major research projects. The principal source of Exchequer assistance is the Medical Research Council, which has a general responsibility for encouraging and assisting medical research throughout the United Kingdom. In addition, research may receive aid from Exchequer funds through the Department and through Hospital Boards. The Department, the Hospital Boards, and the Scottish Hospital Endowments Research Trust are advised on scientific questions by a special Advisory Committee on Medical Research in Scotland, appointed by the Secretary of State. Its members, who include two representatives of the Medical Research Council, are drawn from all the main sciences concerned, so that each research project that comes forward can be examined against a broad background of expert knowledge.

Conclusion

That, roughly sketched, is the organisation of the National Health Service in Scotland. It should be clear that the statutory responsibility for the running of the National Health Service in Scotland, which the Secretary of State exercises through the Department of Health, is no mere empty form. The parliamentary questions on the order paper and the contents of the morning's mail are sufficient to remind the Secretary of State of that. And some of the Department's most important work is in handling matters which do not fall wholly within the ambit of any one part of the Health Service or which the health statistics show to be a subject of more than local concern. A good example is the control of tuberculosis, a matter which is of national importance and one in which the Department, working through the existing local organisations, has the rôle of directing the forces and planning the campaign.

It will also be noticed, from what has been said, that the pattern of the National Health Service is one typical of modern British administration in that it relies for its working on an intricate balance between the paid and the voluntary worker, the expert and the layman. At the top in Scotland is the Secretary of State—salaried, admittedly, but a politician and not a health expert—assisted by the salaried administrative and professional staff of the Department of Health and by the unpaid advice of the Scottish Health Services Council. The three main branches of the Service are run respectively by the Regional Hospital Boards and Hospital Boards of Management, the local authorities, and the Executive Councils—all voluntary and mainly lay bodies, but assisted by permanent paid staffs who advise them and carry out their decisions. At its best, the system tempers lay inexperience with professional knowledge, and professional conservatism or over-enthusiasm with lay common-sense. And it does achieve progress, through all its network of Boards, committees and councils. One point may be noted—the 1947 Act does give the Secretary of State power to act in default of a local health authority, Hospital Board or Executive Council, if it fails to carry out its statutory duties. But this is very much a reserve weapon, and in general, provided the responsible bodies are moving in the right direction, the Department does not interfere to the extent of laying down the details of the route they take. The delegation of responsibility to voluntary boards necessitates acceptance of the fact that they will not welcome control in minor matters; the advantages that come from their knowledge of local conditions and personalities must be held to outweigh the danger that they may not all be equally quick in adopting the latest and most enlightened practices. To take one example, the Scottish Health Services Council has advised the Secretary of State that the old hospital practice of waking the patients at 5 A.M. is really unnecessary and the Secretary of State has commended this advice to the Regional Hospital Boards and Hospital Boards of Management. In time it will no doubt be adopted everywhere; in the meantime the reader who is unlucky enough to be roused from a sound sleep at 5 A.M. in a Scottish hospital will perhaps reflect that it is the price he pays for freedom from an excessively centralised control.

FOOD AND PUBLIC HEALTH

Closely connected with the public health, but quite separate from the Secretary of State's responsibilities for the National Health Service, are his functions in ensuring that the food supplied to people in Scotland is safe and pure to eat. In this work, as with much of the other public health work carried out by the Department of Health, the problem has gradually changed over the years; the fields closer at hand have been brought under cultivation and the labourers can turn their attention to those farther out.

The grocer family in the Happy Families pack were called Grit, which no doubt reflects the extent to which it was popularly accepted in the nineteenth century that the average grocer put grit or sand in the sugar. The result of the Food and Drugs (Adulteration) Acts, and of the efforts of the local authorities in obtaining samples of various kinds of food and in having them examined by the public analyst, has been that, as the figures in the Appendix to the Department of Health's Annual Report now show, the adulteration of food is no longer a serious problem in Scotland. The Department, which joins with the Ministries of Agriculture and Health in considering policy for Great Britain, is now able to lay more emphasis than before on the question of what foods should be subject to a legally prescribed standard of composition and to what extent the use of various substances in the preparation of food should be limited. The use of chemicals in the processing of food—for example, to provide artificial colouring or flavour or to improve the texture or the keeping quality of food—has greatly increased in recent years and needs close attention by the central departments.

Another matter which is receiving increasing attention and is a subject of public interest is food hygiene. The local authorities are responsible for this—as they are for keeping guard against adulteration—and the Department's function is to supervise what they do, and, if necessary, to encourage them to do more. Until the passing of the Food and Drugs (Scotland) Act, 1956, there was no comprehensive legislation about food hygiene, though since last century the sale of food unfit for human consumption has been illegal, and over the years a body of legislation has grown up to deal with particular aspects of food hygiene. Legislation to secure safe milk was among the first measures; then followed, in succession, regulations to set up a system of meat inspection at slaughterhouses, to control the quality of imported food, and to limit the use of unnecessary preservatives. Within recent years, regulations have also proved an effective means of improving hygiene in the ice-cream trade. The central administration for Scotland of all these statutes and regulations rests with the Department of Health.

The work of the Department in promoting a safe and hygienic milk supply throughout Scotland deserves mention. Since the Milk and Dairies Act of 1914 required dairymen to register with the local authority, and the local authority to make dairy bye-laws, there has been a steady improvement. A system of what are called 'special designations', administered in Scotland by the Department, has been in operation for some 30 years, as a result of which a dairyman who wants to sell milk described as 'Certified', 'Tuberculin Tested', 'Pasteurised', or 'Sterilised' must satisfy the local authority of the conditions in his dairy and obtain a licence. Progress has been so great that since the passing of the Milk (Special Designations) Act, 1949, it has proved possible to make orders requiring that in the four Scottish cities, and in most other towns, only milk with a special designation should be sold. The administration of the various Milk Acts is supervised by the Department through its milk inspectors, who make periodical visits to each local authority area and give practical advice to the officers of the local authorities on the technical problems that arise. Appeals made by dairymen to the Secretary of State against decisions of the local authorities are also considered in the Department.

No account of milk hygiene would be complete if it concentrated entirely on the dairy and neglected the cow. While the dairy is the responsibility of the Department of Health, the health of the cow comes under the Department of Agriculture. The two Departments work closely together and the safe milk scheme could not have been brought so near to completion without the aid of the bonus scheme for tuberculin-tested milk, administered by the Department of Agriculture through the Milk Marketing Boards, and the attested herds scheme, instituted by the Ministry of Agriculture and Fisheries and now—as a result of the changes recommended by the Royal Commission on Scottish Affairs in 1954—run by the Department of Agriculture.[1] Generally speaking, the division of responsibility is that the Department of Agriculture concerns itself with the economics and the Department of Health with the hygiene of milk production.

The Department of Health has for many years been concerned in supervising the standard of hygiene at slaughterhouses and the arrangements for the inspection of all carcases there. Now that many responsibilities for animal health have been transferred from the Minister of Agriculture to the Secretary of State, and the Ministry's veterinary staff are available to him, arrangements have been made to use these officers for supervising meat inspection throughout Scotland. The Department has also become interested in general policy for slaughterhouses. A by-product of Hitler's war was the closing of many small slaughterhouses, simply because meat rationing meant that the Government had to distribute meat only through the slaughterhouses which it operated. In consequence, there was a general improvement in the standard of hygiene and of humane treatment of animals. It was important not to lose these benefits when the time came for the Government to return slaughterhouses to their owners—who were, in Scotland, mostly local authorities. Now, under the Slaughterhouses Act of 1954, the opening of a slaughterhouse in Scotland requires the approval of the Secretary of State, and the Department in advising him must take account not only of considerations of hygiene, but of whether the new slaughterhouse is really necessary. At the same time, standards of construction and equipment are being laid down, and it will be the duty of the Department to see that these are attained in all the remaining slaughterhouses. In October, 1956, the Secretary of State announced that he intended to seek powers to close slaughterhouses if they did not comply with the standards after a reasonable time.

[1] See Chapter V, page 50.

CHAPTER XIV

The Care of the Aged and Infirm and the Welfare of the Handicapped

THE PASSING OF THE POOR LAW

IT has been mentioned more than once in this book that a Government department is an organism that develops and alters in response to social changes and the needs of the time. The history of the Department of Health illustrates this well. One of the Department's principal ancestors was the Board of Supervision for the Relief of the Poor. The modern approach to the work that used to be done by the Board and the Poor Law authorities is very different; and the work itself, so far as it concerns the payment of financial assistance, has left the Scottish Office and is handled by the Ministry of Pensions and National Insurance and the National Assistance Board. But social change also made it clear that the care of the aged and the infirm was quite a separate problem from that of unemployment or the relief of poverty. That work, because it bears a close relationship to the problems of housing and health which the Secretary of State deals with through the Department of Health, was added to his responsibilities in 1948 and allocated to this Department.

The Poor Law in Scotland—under which the care of the aged and infirm, as of others destitute, was controlled for so long—goes back to 1424, and Parliament was in the early days usually less concerned with the old and infirm, who gave comparatively little trouble, than with what a statute of 1535 described as 'maisterful and strang beggaris'. There were some privately endowed 'old people's homes' or almshouses such as the Trinity Hospital in Edinburgh so attractively described by Lord Cockburn,[1] but most of the poor relief was 'outdoor'—that is, it was administered to the recipients in their own homes in each parish under the arrangements of the kirk session and the heritors.[2] When it became evident in the first half of the nineteenth century that private charity was no longer able to meet the situation, a compulsory poor rate was introduced in 1845, parochial boards were set up and the Board of Supervision was established in Edinburgh to supervise and advise them. 'Outdoor' relief still predominated under the new system, but 'indoor' relief was provided in poorhouses for those who needed it. Care was taken that the poor-

[1] *Memorials of his Time*, chapter vii.
[2] The parish landholders.

houses should not be made so attractive as to tempt into them people who could possibly look after themselves outside. The aged, the infirm and the physically incapable were mingled with the 'fatuous poor', the husbands separated from the wives, and all submitted to strict discipline and provided with the minimum standard of subsistence in the most economical way possible. It is fair to remember that many of those who entered the poorhouses had been ill-nourished and deplorably housed outside them—nevertheless the entry of the State into this field of social welfare was not a very glorious one. The break-up of the old Poor Law began in 1908 with the Old Age Pensions Act and was stimulated by the Report of the Poor Law Commission in 1909. Later came the Health and Unemployment Insurance Schemes, unemployment assistance, the extension of the statutory hospital services and the new local authority health services. Finally, the National Health Service (Scotland) Act of 1947 provided a service under which the indigent and the feeble have the same rights as all others, and the National Assistance Act of 1948 achieved the complete repeal of the Poor Law.

THE NEW WELFARE SERVICES—GENERAL

It is a cardinal principle of all the welfare work done under the Act of 1948—and in this it is probably safe to say that there is no great difference of opinion between the political parties—that as far as possible old folk and the severely disabled, whether they are blind, deaf or crippled, should be encouraged and helped to take a normal part in the life of the community, and to live independent lives in their own homes if they can. The Department's rôle in this work is naturally enough an indirect one—to encourage the local authorities to use their various statutory powers and to try to ensure that the forces of the various voluntary organisations interested in old people are deployed as effectively as possible. As the department responsible for the National Health Service in Scotland, the Department of Health fosters the development of services, such as home nursing, home helps and so on, which assist old and handicapped people in their own homes. Sometimes the very people who need services of this kind do not know that they exist. The family doctor will often be the first person to learn of the social as well as of the medical problems of these people, and the Department has therefore asked all general practitioners to find out what particular services are available in their district and to see that they are used. Unsuitable housing may also contribute to the difficulties of old people who are trying to remain in their own homes—an old lady may be struggling to keep up a house that is far too large for her, while near by a large family are crammed uncomfortably into one they have outgrown. Because of the high proportion of old one- and two-roomed houses in Scotland, local authorities over the last 35 years have concentrated very largely on the provision of family houses of three, four and five rooms. The Department, exercising its responsibilities for housing, has, in recent years, suggested to local authorities that they should try to provide a proportion of small houses for old people and other small households. Local authorities often find that the building of small houses of this type releases larger under-occupied houses for those who need them.

Voluntary organisations do a great deal to help old people who are living alone in their own homes; they arrange for friendly visits to be paid, organise concerts and outings and do many other things of that kind. A central body called the Scottish Old People's Welfare Committee co-ordinates through local committees the activities of the various bodies in each district and the Department works in close co-operation with it and gives an annual Exchequer grant towards the cost of its headquarters expenses. Some of the bigger organisations (e.g. Women's Voluntary Services and the British Red Cross Society) have specialised in particular services such as the provision of meals and chiropody services for old people living at home.

RESIDENTIAL ACCOMMODATION

For old and infirm people who cannot carry on any longer in their own homes and have no one to look after them, the National Assistance Act requires the local authorities to provide residential accommodation. The idea of the old poorhouse has now been completely abandoned and the new homes are not restricted to the destitute, since it is recognised that the need for care and attention is not peculiar to the very poor. It has been necessary to continue to use many of the institutions built under the Poor Law, but they have mostly been modernised, improved and redecorated out of recognition. The new homes are mostly in smaller buildings, and the aim has been to make them as homelike as possible.

The Department necessarily takes a direct interest in the provision of old people's homes. Each local authority has made for the Secretary of State's approval a scheme outlining the needs of its area for accommodation of this kind and how it proposes to meet the situation. In addition the Secretary of State is prepared to pay a financial contribution towards the capital cost of each new home that is set up, provided it is approved by him and other statutory conditions are satisfied. The Department also gives advice—which is based on the experience of local authorities throughout Scotland—on the standards of accommodation and equipment. Local authorities can discharge their obligations by getting voluntary organisations to provide homes, and, if so, the Department gives the same help to them as it would to a local authority.

The Secretary of State has made regulations to deal with the registration and inspection of the homes and they are visited regularly —both the voluntary homes and those run by the local authorities— by the General Inspectors of the Department of Health on his behalf. Other regulations made by the Secretary of State lay down the minimum amount to be paid by the residents for their accommodation.

THE WELFARE OF HANDICAPPED PERSONS

The National Assistance Act of 1948 gave the county councils and the town councils of large burghs power to promote the welfare of the blind, the deaf or dumb, and other people with a severe physical handicap. The Act permits the local authorities to exercise their welfare functions through voluntary organisations, some of which have had a great deal more experience of this work than anyone else. The Act gives a pretty clear indication, however, of the sort of arrangements that Parliament hoped the authorities would operate, whether directly or indirectly, as soon as they could—there should be instruction to help people to overcome the effects of their particular disability; there should be special workshops where handicapped people could be employed or alternatively they should be helped in finding work which they could do at home; they should have opportunities for recreation and there should be an advisory service to let them know the facilities available in their district.

How do the Secretary of State and the Department of Health come into all this? The Act requires that a local authority which is going to help handicapped people should do so in accordance with a scheme —that is, it should set down on paper what it proposes to do—and that the scheme should be approved by the Secretary of State. It also enables the Secretary of State to convert the powers of the local authorities into duties so far as concerns any part of this welfare work. The Secretary of State thus has to watch the whole course of the campaign and to advise the local authorities in their work. Because the work was largely new to the Central Government as well as to the local authorities, he appointed an Advisory Council to guide him and its reports and suggestions have been passed on to the local authorities.

Progress has not been equally rapid all along the line. Welfare arrangements for the blind were already in existence in 1948, thanks to the Blind Persons Acts of 1920 and 1938, and as a result the Secretary of State felt justified in exercising the power given to him under the Act of 1948 to convert the powers of local authorities into duties as far as the blind were concerned. The Department produced a model scheme which was in the main adopted by the local authorities. Most of the local authorities make use of the voluntary organisations and give them financial help in their work but it is worth mentioning that the largest special workshop for the blind in Great Britain is run by Glasgow Corporation direct, on behalf of authorities in the West and South-West of Scotland. There is a voluntary co-ordinating body for the welfare of the blind in Scotland (of whom there are some 10,000 registered)—namely, the Scottish National Federation for the Welfare of the Blind, on which the various voluntary organisations, the workshops for the blind and the local authorities are all represented. The Department maintains regular contact with this body and makes an annual contribution towards its administrative expenses.

With the other classes of handicapped people, progress has been less rapid. Here the local authorities were largely breaking new ground and the Advisory Council found indeed that there were no reliable figures of the numbers of people requiring help. Although individual cases which come to the notice of the local authorities certainly receive help, some of the schemes which have been made by them are an earnest of future intentions rather than an indication that a welfare organisation has already been set up.

The Department, besides encouraging local authorities to develop their own welfare services, tries to help national voluntary organisations interested in the welfare of handicapped people. The Scottish Epilepsy Association, for example—one of the newer bodies—receives through the Department an Exchequer grant towards its administrative expenses.

FUTURE DEVELOPMENTS

Not everyone has an equal admiration for a 'Welfare State' but few can object to proposals for helping those who are too old and frail to look after themselves or to a policy aimed at enabling all handicapped people, whatever their disability, to play a full and useful part in the life of the community. The Secretary of State and the Department were given by the Act of 1948 the general direction of a welfare service with these among its principal objects. In some branches of the work, such as the care of the blind, the general framework has been set up and it now only needs time and capital to complete the job; in others, the foundations are still being laid. The task of the Department is to encourage the many workers and to co-ordinate their efforts. The means by which this is done— the administrative schemes, the advisory councils, the Exchequer grants—are not perhaps very interesting to read about, but many a novelist has had the same difficulty with a truly virtuous hero.

CHAPTER XV

Town and Country Planning

THERE are many areas of other people's land in the industrial areas of Britain which would convince anyone of the evils caused by lack of planning; and from this generally accepted proposition, people have come more reluctantly to accept that there should be some control over what they do with their own land. Thus the service of town and country planning, administered by the central government and the local authorities, has gradually come into being. The first timid appearance of planning as a statutory function was as a pendant to housing in an Act of 1909. It developed considerably between the wars, but town and country planning, in the form of a comprehensive system of control of land use, is almost entirely a post-war development, initiated by the New Towns Act of 1946 and the Town and Country Planning Acts—one for England and Wales and one for Scotland—of 1947.

The general object of town and country planning may be stated as the co-ordination and control of the development of land so as to secure the best use of all the available space, having due regard to both national and local interests and to the physical, social and economic welfare of the country. One might well feel that this was a task for an omnipotent and omnicompetent being, assisted by a small staff of archangels, but in practice responsibility for it in Scotland has been entrusted by Parliament to the Secretary of State, assisted by the Department of Health, and to the local planning authorities. Within the Department, the administrative divisions are assisted by professionally-trained technical planning officers, working under the supervision of the Chief Architect and Technical Planner (who also provides an architectural service for all the Secretary of State's departments). The work of the technical planners includes, besides study and research relating to basic planning principles, advice for authorities preparing their development plans, the technical examination of the plans when they are submitted, the hearing of advertisement appeals, and all the technical work on new towns up to the stage when the development corporation is ready to take over.

Officers of the local planning authorities deal direct with the Department in Edinburgh and are therefore personally known to their opposite numbers on the administrative or technical side in the Department; this makes for easier and smoother administration. The fact that the officers of the Department are stationed in Edinburgh (with the exception of two in Inverness) does not of course mean that they do not pay frequent visits to the district the planning problems of which they are discussing. Scotland is small enough to make it possible to have both central administration and local knowledge in the same system.

The local planning authorities are the county councils and the town councils of large burghs.[1] The development of new towns is the responsibility of development corporations appointed for the purpose by the Secretary of State, but the county council is the planning authority for any new town within its district. To give an example of the local organisation, the County Council of Fife is the planning authority for 22 small burghs and the new town of Glenrothes, but not for the large burghs of Dunfermline and Kirkcaldy or for St. Andrews, although all these are geographically within the county.

The Town and Country Planning (Scotland) Act, 1947, attempted to provide not only a comprehensive system for controlling the use of land but a solution of the problems of compensation and betterment—that is, of the difficulties that arise when extraneous circumstances cause an undue appreciation or depreciation in the value of land. The complicated financial provisions which were concerned with this matter were, however, abolished or amended by the Town and Country Planning (Scotland) Act, 1954, and need not be discussed here. The four main purposes of the 1947 Act, as amended, are: first, to enable the local planning authorities to think ahead by means of development plans so that the proposed pattern of land use throughout the country is generally known; secondly, to bring day-to-day development under their control by requiring express permission for it; thirdly, to arm them with power to acquire, develop or redevelop and dispose of land and to give Exchequer assistance for certain parts of this work; and fourthly, to deal with certain problems of what is called amenity, such as the preservation of trees and of buildings of architectural or historic interest, and the control of advertisements.

Even from this brief summary, it will be seen that the system set up by the Act is an all-embracing one; its introduction on 1st July, 1948, faced the local authorities, as well as the Department of Health, with a new and complex addition to the post-war problems they were already tackling. Generally speaking, the responsibility for operating the system rests with the local planning authority; it must take the initial action or make the initial decisions. As with many other social services, the Secretary of State's duty is to supervise and guide the authorities, to approve their actions or, if necessary, amend their decisions. Before considering the implications of this relationship on the administration of the various parts of the Act, it may be use-

---

[1] St. Andrews and Thurso, although not large burghs, are local planning authorities in their own right under the 1947 Act.

ful to look rather more closely at the Secretary of State's position as planning minister in Scotland.

Unlike the Minister of Housing and Local Government, who is the Planning Minister in England, the Secretary of State is also the Minister formally responsible for many of the most important services that make use of land—for agriculture, forestry, electricity supply, education, housing, the National Health Service, water supply and many others. He has recently become responsible for roads, which are sometimes described by planners with a taste for metaphor as the backbone of land use proposals, and in addition he has a general oversight of local authority structure and finance and as 'Scotland's Minister' an interest in the economic development of the country, and particularly of the Highlands and Islands. With some other ministers such as the Minister of Works (for the preservation of buildings) and the President of the Board of Trade (for development areas) he has joint responsibilities. All this puts him in a very good position for advising local planning authorities and for judging the planning problems that come to him from a national and not from a local or a sectional point of view.

More than almost any other service, planning calls for good liaison, and it would be idle to pretend that all this important work happens automatically. The process described by civil servants as 'keeping in constant touch' may in some Government departments mean nothing more than an exasperated telephone call once a month from A to B requesting information. But with practice—and this is undoubtedly facilitated by the fact that so many of the services are administered from St. Andrew's House and come under the same Minister—a procedure has been worked out by which the Department of Health sees that all those who ought to know about any proposed development are aware of it and have an opportunity to comment on it.

A good example of the Department's rôle is in the handling of the land requirements of the Services. The visitor to the Highlands will not travel far from Glasgow before he sees how the exigencies of war have left their mark on the countryside. These war-time scars were a reminder that some method must be devised to cover the activities of Government departments, which do not require to obtain permission from the local planning authorities. A procedure was worked out[1] to protect the public interest. Under this the Service departments regularly consult the Department of Health on all their varied requirements for land in Scotland—and for the use of sea areas also—and the Department in turn consults the local planning authorities and other bodies concerned (including various amenity and scientific societies). On occasion, the Secretary of State, acting as Scotland's Planning Minister, has had a public local enquiry held in order to

[1] Cmd. 7278 of 1947.

assist him in coming to a decision whether or not the proposals of the Service department should proceed and whether any modifications are called for.

Apart from these *ad hoc* consultations, the Department is represented on the Distribution of Industry Panel (a body convened by the Board of Trade) and, when the siting of a major project such as one of the larger electricity generating stations or an atomic energy station comes up for discussion, can itself convene the Scottish Physical Planning Committee. All the interested Government departments are represented on this Committee, which was set up for the discussion of such matters in relation to the fundamental planning problems of Scotland.

DEVELOPMENT PLANS

The basis of the system set out in the first part of the Act of 1947 is the preparation of development plans by the local planning authorities. The Act required the authorities to carry out a survey of their district and thereafter to prepare—and revise at intervals—a plan, which should define broadly the sites of proposed roads, public and other buildings, nature reserves and other open spaces, and indicate whether land should be used for agricultural, industrial, residential or other purposes. The plan is also required to indicate land subject to compulsory acquisition by either Government departments or local authorities and land which the planning authority itself intends to acquire because bad lay-out and obsolete buildings make 'comprehensive redevelopment' desirable. The planning authority has to take into account that areas which need comprehensive redevelopment are usually those where, over the years, a quart has been put into a pint pot. When the contents have been decanted into a new pint pot, the people and the factories which will not go in have to be found a home elsewhere. Lastly, the plan must show the stages by which it is envisaged that the proposals it contains will be achieved.

The Act left it to the Secretary of State to lay down in regulations and orders most of the details about what the plans should contain and how they should be set out. In the preparation of these instruments, the local authority associations were closely consulted through the medium of a working party composed of their representatives and officers of the Department.

When a development plan is formally submitted to the Secretary of State, it is accompanied by a report of the survey on which it is based. Experience has shown that a considerable time usually elapses before approval can be given, especially if the proposals are at all complex or controversial. No plan can be considered in isolation and proposals that involve shifts of population or major road changes have to be carefully studied and compared with the plans of neighbouring authorities. This consideration of one plan in relation to others is bound to slow things up, but it is essential if the Secretary of State is to carry out properly his central responsibilities for planning in Scotland.

The plans are dealt with in the now generally accepted way, by which the authority advertises that the plan has been submitted to the Secretary of State and displays it publicly in the localities where people interested are likely to see it. The authorities are encouraged by the Department to meet any objectors to the plan and it often proves possible to resolve their difficulties or to satisfy them by some minor modification. Where the objections are maintained, however, the Secretary of State normally arranges for a public local enquiry at which a person appointed by him—usually a senior member of the Scottish Bar—hears the objections and the local planning authority's answers to them. This person's report to the Secretary of State helps him in deciding what modifications, if any, he should make in the plan when he approves it.

It is not easy to summarise the points which the Department will look for in going over a plan on the Secretary of State's behalf. Each area has its own problems, and good planning consists less in the application of rigid rules than in dealing with each case on its own merits. In certain matters—the provision of schools, for example, or the construction of trunk roads—the interested Department has laid down standards, which are indeed known to the local planning authorities; in others, the Department of Health itself, dealing as it does with planning questions from all over Scotland, has built up a store of experience which is useful in assessing the merits of the particular proposals that come before the Secretary of State. The most difficult questions arise on the plans of the cities and of the other planning authorities in the central belt of Scotland—because it is in those areas that competition for the use of land is strongest.

One or two difficulties about development plans may be mentioned. First, it has taken longer for the local planning authorities to prepare them and the Secretary of State to approve them than the Act envisaged when it optimistically said that they should be submitted within three years and reviewed at five-yearly intervals. To start with, there were simply not enough planning staff to go round, and even when an authority had the necessary staff, the survey took a long time. The Secretary of State has therefore had to consent, as he has power to do, to extensions of time for many authorities. Nevertheless, progress has been made, and by 31st March, 1957, plans or part plans had been submitted by 38 out of the 57 authorities and 30 of them had been approved. Secondly, in their very nature, from the fact that they express intentions for the next 20 years, development plans have something in common with new year resolutions—no one quite believes in them. The ideal balance between elasticity and rigidity is hard to strike; if the plan cannot be adjusted to suit changing circumstances, it will clearly be more hindrance than help, but on the other hand, if it is to be continually altered and tinkered with, it will lose its value as an indication to the general public of what development is proposed, and all the laborious process of advertisement, objection, enquiry and approval will hardly have been worth while. The plans so far received have mostly, as was hoped, been realistic and constructive in their approach.

THE PLANNING CONTROL SYSTEM

The day-to-day control of development is of much more immediate, although of more limited, interest. After some initial misunderstandings, it is now generally appreciated that permission for any development must be obtained from the local planning authority before work can begin.

The Act of 1947 defined development very broadly as 'the carrying out of building, engineering, mining or other operations in, on, over or under land or the making of any material change in the use of buildings or land', but it left the Secretary of State to specify by order various types of development, many of them minor or underground, for which no specific application for permission need be made. Certain necessary but seldom used controls were given to the planning authorities by the Act itself—such as the power to modify or revoke permissions already given and to take action where someone has gone ahead without permission. But the chief administrative interest of the control system lies in the procedure laid down by the Secretary of State for obtaining decisions on applications for planning permission.

It was realised at once that the planning control system would bring not only large institutions but small firms and private individuals in contact with a difficult body of law, over matters which might be of the greatest importance to them. The Department has therefore done all it can to make the system operate as simply as possible. It has encouraged the planning authorities to give enquirers informal advice about the prospects of development being permitted and indeed the Secretary of State has explicitly provided by order that a general permission may be given, as a result of which the applicant knows that, subject to the settlement of the details later, he is safe in buying his land and sure of his right to build. When the actual application for planning permission comes in, the planning authority has the duty of considering the proposals in relation to its development plan (or what they mean to put in the plan) and of issuing its decision within a given time. It may grant permission either unconditionally or subject to conditions, or may refuse it altogether.

The applicant has the right of appeal to the Secretary of State against the decision (or if there has been undue delay, the absence of a decision). The applications received by the authorities vary enormously, from the proposal of a small developer to build himself a garage to the projects of the larger private or public corporations, which may be of national importance. The Secretary of State has power to require local planning authorities to submit to him proposals that are very controversial or of more than merely local significance, which in practice means that the decision is taken by him and not by the local authority. Controversial planning applications affecting trunk roads are now regularly dealt with in this way, since the Secretary of State has a direct interest as Roads Minister. Generally speaking, however, this course is rarely taken, and only at the request of the local planning authority or after consultation with it.

The Secretary of State almost invariably holds a hearing before deciding any planning appeal. If the case is one of great interest, a public enquiry may be conducted by a member of the Scots Bar. Normally, however, there is a hearing conducted by some other independent person, usually a retired senior civil servant or former local authority official. There are usually no points of law involved, and it is therefore possible to keep the proceedings informal and non-legalistic, which makes them both inexpensive and more comprehensible for the applicants or objectors. There is evidence that this feature of planning administration is appreciated by those concerned, and indeed the system, having passed its 'running-in' period, is now going smoothly. The number of appeals that reach the Secretary of State for his decision has tended to increase but is still relatively small; 237 only were received in the year 1956, this being the highest total since the 1947 Act came into operation.

It has been mentioned that the Scottish Planning Act of 1954 was mainly concerned with altering the financial provisions of the 1947 Act. It did, however, make one alteration in the planning control system. Where planning restrictions are imposed, compensation may now be paid in a closely defined range of cases. It falls to the Secretary of State to determine the amount of compensation payable and to make the payment. If it appears to him that the decision of the local planning authority which has given rise to the claim was a bad one, he can reverse the decision instead of paying compensation. The power is obviously not one that will be lightly used, and he is bound by law to consult the local planning authority concerned before using it.

PROTECTION OF AMENITY

The ultimate result of the powers which the 1947 Act gave to the Secretary of State and the local planning authorities should be—if those powers are wisely used—to make Scotland a more pleasant place to live in. An artist who was once bold enough to suggest to the Provost of a small burgh that some proposals of the town council's would not improve the amenity of the town was sharply answered: 'We ken oor ain amenities'. The 1947 Act was less confident of this and contained some important provisions with the specific purpose of protecting amenity, by the control of advertisements and the preservation of trees and of interesting buildings.

The worst horrors of bill-posting were perhaps already over by 1947, but if we are saved in Scotland from the excesses that make it so difficult to forget the names of the best-known *apéritifs* during a journey in France, it will be thanks to the Regulations made under the Act of 1947, which, for the first time, introduced a standard code of control, and made the display of advertisements subject to the consent of the local planning authority, with a right of appeal to the Secretary of State against the decision of the authority. This code has been a considerable success. 92 appeals were received in 1956, and this comparatively low figure was a major increase on previous years.

Scotland's heritage of woodlands and of notable buildings is small in comparison to that of some countries and to try to keep what there is, the Act gave the planning authorities power to make tree and building preservation orders, subject to confirmation by the Secretary of State. To guide the authorities in the preservation of buildings of architectural or historic interest, qualified investigators, on behalf of the Secretary of State, are compiling lists of buildings that are worthy of preservation. The Historic Buildings and Ancient Monuments Act of 1953 also set up an Historic Buildings Council for Scotland to advise the Secretary of State and the Minister of Works on this part of their functions. The listing of a building in itself secures that, at least while the local planning authority decides whether to make a preservation order, the building cannot be demolished or seriously altered.

No national parks have been set up in Scotland, but in five areas recommended by the Scottish National Parks Survey Committee as suitable, undesirable development can be checked by a requirement that the Secretary of State should be informed of all applications for permission to carry out development. The Nature Conservancy, which was established in 1949 and given special powers to acquire and manage land by the National Parks Act of that year, has established several reserves in Scotland, and the Department works closely with it.[1]

POSITIVE PLANNING POWERS

The planning control system which has just been described is the negative side of planning—the power to prevent something undesir-

[1] For National Forest Parks, see Chapter XXI.

able from happening—and that is the side which has so far been most in evidence in Scotland. But the Act of 1947 gave the local planning authorities positive powers to carry out the proposals for the use of land contained in their development plans, and in particular those for comprehensive redevelopment, by enabling them to acquire any necessary land, to clear away the results of bad building and mis-planning, and to lay out the land afresh. For work of this kind an Exchequer grant of 50 per cent. of the loss incurred is now payable, but, so far, these important powers have been comparatively little used.[1] The economic state of the country has made severe restrictions on capital development necessary; the need to provide new houses quickly made it necessary to concentrate on that task; and there was no extensive war damage in Scotland to make immediate redevelopment unavoidable. Schemes are, however, being undertaken in a number of towns, notably in Clydebank, Edinburgh, Greenock, Kirkcaldy and Paisley, and the first of several likely schemes in the City of Glasgow, that for Hutchesontown-Gorbals, was approved in February, 1957.

The Secretary of State is also concerned as Planning Minister with the allocation of suitable sites in suitable places for firms which want to open new factories. A firm cannot, in the last resort, be forced to open a new factory in any given place, but it will naturally prefer to go where there is labour available, and a measure of control was given by a provision in the 1947 Act that planning permission for any major industrial development should be granted only if the Board of Trade is satisfied that it will be in accordance with the best distribution of industry in the country. The Department has therefore worked closely with the Board of Trade in searching for, and keeping a register of, possible industrial sites that can be offered to enquiring firms, and they also try to see that the planning authorities of areas that need more industrial development make suitable provision for it in their development plans.

NEW TOWNS

The second of the major enactments on which the Secretary of State's town and country planning functions are founded is the New Towns Act of 1946. The origin of that Act lay in the recommendations of various committees and planning consultants that new communities should be established as a means of checking the tendency of population and industry to become concentrated in the big urban centres. The initiative in operating the Act in Scotland rests with the Secretary of State alone—in this it differs from the 1947 Planning Act —and it is his duty to select and designate the areas where it would

---

[1] If proposals now under discussion are implemented this grant will, save for major redevelopment, be merged in a new general grant.

be in the national interest to establish new towns, to appoint development corporations to plan and build the towns, and to supervise
them in this work. The procedure followed is the now customary one.
The Secretary of State publishes his proposals that a designated area
should be the site of a new town, those interested have an opportunity
to make objections, and if they sustain those objections a public
local enquiry is held.

Of the new towns so far established in Scotland, East Kilbride, the
oldest and farthest advanced, and Cumbernauld are designed to
relieve congestion in the City of Glasgow; and Glenrothes in Fife was
established in the expectation of a considerable transfer of miners
from the declining coalfield of Lanarkshire to the expanding one of
Fife. New towns are already the most spectacular visual achieve-
ments of modern planning.

Most towns have grown because they were needed or shrunk
because they were not. One cannot rely on such natural but uncertain
processes in the deliberate establishment of a new town, and the early
planning of each has involved the Department in a very wide range
of consultations. First, there must be talks with the Department of
Agriculture to ensure that the loss of agricultural land, which is inevitable, is kept to the minimum. There must be consultations with
the Ministry of Power and with the National Coal Board, who can
say whether there is any danger of subsidence on the site, and with
the Board of Trade about industrial prospects. The water supply
and drainage, and the road and rail communications, all have to be
thought about. Gradually, the development corporation takes over.
The task in the early stages is a formidable and complex one and,
although the Secretary of State's initial function is simply to designate
the site of the town, the Department usually makes rough layouts of
the whole area in order to be certain that it is adequate for the population and industry it is designed to take. It also helps the development
corporation in bringing into partnership the local authorities who will
have to provide the full range of services other than housing—water,
drainage, lighting, schools, classified roads and so on. The corporation's development proposals also have to be submitted to the local
planning authority.

TOWN DEVELOPMENT

It has emerged clearly in recent years that Scotland's main planning problem is how to achieve the decentralisation of population and
industry from the congested urban areas, and in particular from
Glasgow. It is generally accepted that houses and jobs will have to
be found outside that city for at least 300,000 people, as its densely
populated parts are cleared and redeveloped in accordance with
modern standards.

This is of course a long-term programme, but its magnitude is such that it will be necessary to employ all possible means of carrying it out. The new towns of East Kilbride and Cumbernauld can make a major contribution, but town development—i.e. the expansion of smaller existing communities—is also envisaged as playing an important part. Studies carried out by the Clyde Valley Planning Advisory Committee, a joint committee of the planning authorities concerned, have established that a considerable amount of town development is physically possible.

Administrative complications arise because the operations involve action by the authorities of the communities to be developed for the immediate relief of the people of Glasgow: the potential longer-term benefits to the communities themselves being less apparent. Following consultations with the local authority associations, legislative provisions to facilitate co-operation between Glasgow and these other authorities, including provisions for a special grant, were submitted to Parliament as Part II of a Bill introduced in January, 1957, which later became the Housing and Town Development (Scotland) Act, 1957.

CONCLUSION

Planning is essentially a long-term process. Many of the most intractable problems that beset local planning authorities today are the cumulative result of complex social forces at work 50 or more years ago when orderly land-use planning was not an objective; it may be many years yet before the full effect of the present planning system in redressing all this can be clearly seen. In the meantime, undesirable developments are being checked, and desirable projects encouraged, by the development plan system; there is positive good planning in the new towns and in the increasing attention paid to central re-development; and Government departments and local authorities are learning to work together to secure that land in Scotland is put to the best possible use in the interests of the community as a whole.

CHAPTER XVI

Housing, Water Supplies and General Sanitation

THE National Health Service and town and country planning are recent developments—so recent that it is not impossible to find people who regard the one as an undesirable innovation and the other as a lot of new-fangled nonsense. Both subjects took a great deal of parliamentary time and caused a great deal of political excitement in the period after the end of the war in 1945; if only for that reason it was perhaps appropriate to take them first among the functions which the Secretary of State exercises through the Department of Health for Scotland. The sector where the central government first became concerned with public health is now comparatively peaceful, and although they closely affect the environment of the individual citizen, such matters as statutory nuisances, drainage, scavenging and the control of offensive trades do not arouse strong political passions. All these matters—which may be grouped under the term 'general sanitation'—are primarily and very properly the concern of the local authorities, but the Secretary of State has important functions as a supervisor and co-ordinator. He has a measure of financial control, especially where he gives financial assistance to a local authority; he acts as a sort of court of appeal in a number of instances; and if a local authority fails to carry out the duties Parliament has entrusted to it, he has power to see that its job is effectively carried out.

It has already been mentioned in Chapter II that for the greater part of the nineteenth century Parliament felt grave doubts about state intervention and centralised control. But the great concentrations of population that resulted from the industrial revolution, and the threat of epidemics of such diseases as cholera and typhoid—what Professor Saunders has called 'the pressure of the brute facts of housing, health and hygiene'[1]—made it clear that some sort of supervision and control was necessary. The concept developed that it was a proper function of legislation to prevent the activities of certain individuals from interfering with or endangering other individuals or the community at large. Thus the Public Health (Scotland) Acts of 1867 and 1897 enumerated various objectionable things (badly constructed houses, blocked water-closets, polluted wells and so on) which might be declared to be statutory nuisances which the local authority must do something about—by taking the offending person to court if necessary. Apart, however, from his powers to take

[1] *Scottish Democracy 1815–1840*, by L. J. Saunders (Edinburgh, 1950).

action if the local authority fails to do what is required of it, the Secretary of State is not involved in the procedure for dealing with statutory nuisances. When Parliament turned to the control of what are described as offensive trades, the central authority was specifically brought in. Anyone who sets up one of these businesses—they are listed in the Public Health (Scotland) Act, 1897, and include such occupations as blood boiler, tallow melter and manure manufacturer—must obtain the licence of the local authority. The applicant can appeal to the Secretary of State if the local authority refuses, and, similarly, anyone who is injuriously affected can appeal to him if the licence is granted.

The Secretary of State has more positive functions under two other Acts: the Rag Flock Acts, under which he is responsible for laying down standards of cleanliness for the materials used in upholstery; and the Alkali, etc., Works Regulation (Scotland) Acts, which give him direct powers of control over the emission of noxious fumes from chemical works and provide him with an Inspector of Alkali Works to assist him. The chemical industry was singled out in this way for special treatment because its processes were so severely technical as to be beyond the competence of the ordinary sanitary inspector.

These and other powers are mainly concerned with prevention, but it also became recognised during the last century that if life was to be tolerable and disease kept under control, something more positive was required; an adequate, wholesome water supply would have to be provided, and should be publicly provided. More slowly came the realisation that in the long run it might be cheaper, as well as more agreeable, if the local authority provided proper sewerage and scavenging systems and prevented people from dumping piles of filth and rubbish in the street or in the nearest convenient stream. All this was eminently a matter for the local authorities but inevitably a certain amount of central supervision and financial assistance became necessary; the Secretary of State's concern with the environment of the individual accordingly includes functions relating to water supply and sewerage.

Like a house, a body of legislation on any given subject reaches an age when it needs a good deal of repair if it is to remain in use. The legislation which deals with the disposal of sewage has not yet been modernised, and the Secretary of State's functions are not defined in detail; but he exercises a financial control, because his consent to the necessary borrowing by the local authority is required, and because he gives financial help towards the cost of a number of sewerage schemes under the Rural Water Supplies and Sewerage Acts or under the Distribution of Industry Act, 1945. A modern legislative code for water supply, however, was provided in the Water (Scotland) Acts, 1946 and 1949, and these Acts, while they put on the local authorities the duty of providing a water supply in their own districts, give the Secretary of State a number of important duties which he carries out through the Department of Health.

He has, first of all, a general duty to see that local authorities throughout Scotland provide adequate water supplies.[1] In this he is assisted by a Scottish Water Advisory Committee. Rather as he requires education authorities to make an 'educational scheme' for their district, he can require a local authority to make a survey of its area with a view to finding out how much water is used in it, how much is likely to be needed in future, what sources are available and what is the best and most economical way of meeting the requirements of the area. Water supply is a matter which calls for co-operation between local authorities: a town will hardly ever be able to find all the water it needs within its own boundaries and a lowland county may have to prospect for water in the hills of an upland neighbour. A combination of two authorities for water supply purposes may be the best way of meeting the needs of both, and such a combination requires the approval of the Secretary of State, who can also bring it about compulsorily if it cannot be achieved by agreement.

When a local authority has found a new source of water, it must acquire the right to take the water; if it makes an agreement with all the proprietors concerned, it has to get the Secretary of State to make an order confirming the agreement; or it may ask him to make an order enabling it to acquire the water rights compulsorily. In either event, the statutes require the Secretary of State to make sure by advertisement and, if necessary, public enquiry, that the views of all those interested are heard. Orders of this kind may in the last resort be brought before Parliament, but it is usually possible to satisfy the various interests without even resorting to a public enquiry.

The Department is in a good position to observe the progress of water supply work in Scotland generally, since the Secretary of State's approval—given by order or otherwise—is required for the main items of capital expenditure on work of this kind and, in addition, much of the work done qualifies for financial assistance from the Exchequer under the Rural Water Supplies and Sewerage Acts. These Acts, which have made £105,000,000 available—the Scottish share is £30,000,000—for helping local authorities throughout Great Britain to provide water supplies and sewerage in rural areas, are an indication that the urgent need for work of this kind is no longer in the towns but in the countryside. The Department gets up-to-date information about the progress of the various works both through reports from the authorities and through its own engineering staff. Both on the administrative and on the technical side of water supply, the Department has become, over the years, the repository of a great deal of useful information and experience, and its advice is

[1] There are now no private water companies in Scotland.

often sought by local authorities when they come up against fresh problems.

As the land was tidied up, and a subterranean network of pipes marked the advances of sanitation, it became possible to think about cleaning up the rivers. The first Act of Parliament dealing with the prevention of river pollution was passed as long ago as 1876, but it proved ineffective, and a new Act passed in 1951 gives the Secretary of State a specific duty to promote the cleanliness of rivers in Scotland and to appoint, to assist him, an advisory committee representative of the local authorities, agriculture, fisheries and other interests. As the Act requires him to do, he has been setting up, since 1951, River Purification Boards for the areas drained by the principal rivers and their tributaries. These Boards, which are composed of representatives of the local authorities, agriculture, fisheries, industry and other interests, will each have powers to deal with and control pollution in its own area; by 31st March, 1957, eight out of the ten River Purification Boards contemplated had been set up.

The problems of sanitation alter as time goes on; new ones emerge, and what one generation accepted as inevitable, public opinion in the next regards as insufferable. Thus, atmospheric pollution is not a new phenomenon, but it is only recently that Parliament has passed legislation designed to reduce it. Under the Clean Air Act, 1956, when it is brought fully into operation, the emission of dark smoke from chimneys, railway engines and vessels will be prohibited, and the emission of grit and dust from furnaces must be minimised. Part of the Act came into force on 31st December, 1956, and town and county councils in Scotland can now declare all or part of their district to be a 'smoke-control area' in which it will be an offence to emit smoke from any chimney. The local authority is required to meet at least 70 per cent. of the approved cost of adapting a privately-owned house in a smoke-control area to enable smokeless fuel to be used, and in the case of its own houses meets the whole initial cost. The authority can recover from the Exchequer, through the Department of Health, an amount equivalent to a contribution of 40 per cent. of the cost of adaptation.

The advances of modern science may bring difficulties in the most unlikely places; to take an example from the past ten years, the general use of synthetic detergents for domestic purposes produced towering masses of foam and awkward chemical results at sewage purification works. Each problem, as it arises or as public attention is focused on it, must receive close attention, and the needs and interests of all those concerned must be carefully balanced. In all these matters, of course, the Department works in alliance with the Ministry of Housing and Local Government, and the experience of one country is available to the other.

HOUSING

A little has been said, earlier in this chapter, about the war on insanitary conditions that began about a century ago. It is from his concern with public health that the Secretary of State derives his present responsibility for housing. There were Acts before 1914 which permitted local authorities to build houses—such as the Housing of the Working Classes Act, 1890—but housing in Scotland was almost entirely a private activity. It gradually became realised, however, that deplorable housing conditions were really at the root of a great deal of disease and ill-health—to say nothing of unhappiness and frustration. The awakening consciousness of this, and, in particular, of the conditions in miners' rows, led to the appointment in 1912 of a Royal Commission on Housing in Scotland, which reported in 1917. The report is a long, thorough and remarkably human document and gives a vivid account of the insanitary, ill-planned and grossly overcrowded houses which the Commission found. The Commission made three main recommendations: that the housing of the working classes in Scotland should become the direct responsibility of the Central Government and of the local authorities; that the local authorities should have a definite obligation to build the necessary houses, or see that they were built; and that the State, for its part, should provide subsidies which would make it possible for the local authorities to let the houses they built at rents the tenants could afford—at levels, in fact, below the economic rent.

These principles were accepted by the Government after the First World War as the basis of their housing policy, and in 1919 the Housing, Town Planning, etc. (Scotland) Act put squarely on the local authorities the duty of seeing that enough houses were built to meet the needs of their districts. There are now 230 local housing authorities in Scotland—197 town councils (ranging from Glasgow with a population of over a million to New Galloway with one of only 300) and 33 county councils. They build for all classes of the community, since the restriction of their activities to houses for the 'working classes' was removed in 1949; the fact that one now finds it necessary to put the term in inverted commas gives an indication of the reason for the change.

Since 1919 the housing activity of the local authorities has, necessarily, increased steadily; since the Second World War, private enterprise has accounted for considerably less than 10 per cent. of the houses built in Scotland.[1] What has been the result of this revolutionary development? The census of 1911 showed that nearly half the population of Scotland lived in houses with only one or two rooms. The 1951 census—which provided a great deal more information about the size of houses in Scotland, the number of people living

[1] The percentage in England and Wales is much higher—about 30 per cent.

in them and the sort of household amenities each house contained—
showed that the proportion had dropped to under 30 per cent. but
that there was still a very disquieting amount of overcrowding.
Nevertheless very substantial progress has been made, especially since
1945, with a problem which must have seemed to those who first
read the Royal Commission's Report in 1918 to resemble the labours
of Hercules. Since 1919 almost 700,000 new houses have been built—
almost half the total stock of houses and sufficient to provide homes
for about half the families in Scotland.

Now, as a result of these Herculean labours, the nature of the
problem is beginning to change. Many of the smaller burghs and less
industrial counties are reaching the stage where every family has a
home of its own, and they are faced only with the modernisation of
semi-obsolete houses and the relief of what overcrowding remains.
In other areas, notably in Glasgow and in the industrial belt, the
need for new housing is still acute.

New Housing

From this short sketch of how the Government and the local
authorities came to go into partnership in the provision of houses,
the Government's constant difficulty will be obvious. It is no use
building inferior houses—there are enough of them in Scotland
already—but the amount any Government can afford to spend on
subsidies is limited and so the Secretary of State, acting through the
Department of Health, has to exercise financial control. The local
authorities, who know what actually needs to be done, formulate
their own programmes and are entirely responsible for letting,
managing and controlling their own houses. The Secretary of State
has issued a *Scottish Housing Handbook* for their general guidance,
which makes suggestions about siting, lay-out, design and equipment, and lays down the standards to which the houses built must
conform to qualify for Exchequer subsidy. At one time, the authorities had to obtain the approval of the Department at each stage of
their operations—for the choice of site, the lay-out plans, the house
plans and so on. Now, once planning approval has been obtained,
they need only certify—for houses of normal type—that their designs
are in accordance with the standards, and submit details of the
tenders they propose to accept. Provided the costs are reasonable,
the Department conveys the Secretary of State's approval and agrees
to pay a financial contribution on each house. The subsidy is fixed by
Parliament at an amount which, when taken together with a contribution which the authority makes from the rates, is intended to
meet the annual deficit arising on a new house—allowance being
made in the calculations for the cost of building, management and
maintenance, and for the income from rent.[1] There are additional

---

[1] See footnote on next page.

K

or alternative subsidies for houses in remote areas where the cost of building is particularly high, and for houses for agricultural workers.

The whole question of housing subsidies is very difficult. How much can the Exchequer afford, how much can the local authority afford, how much can the tenant afford, how great is the need for houses?—the political parties will not always agree on the answers but leaders of both the principal political parties have, over many years, expressed the view that housing subsidies should not be given to those who do not need them. At the same time, they have also recognised the principle that no one in genuine need of a house should be asked to pay more rent than he can reasonably afford. The Department's duty is to have as much relevant information as possible available, from past experience and up-to-date statistics, to help the Government of the day to formulate its housing policy.[1]

The Secretary of State has appointed to advise him on housing matters a statutory body called the Scottish Housing Advisory Committee, and the published reports of this body have given guidance to local authorities on such matters as *Planning Our New Homes*, *Choosing of Council Tenants* and *The Housing of Special Groups*.

Scottish Special Housing Association

Within their own areas, the New Town Corporations, which have already been referred to in Chapter XV, have responsibilities for housing similar to those of local authorities. Because of the greater Exchequer interest, however, the Department exercises a more direct control over the Corporations—as it does, for the same reason, over the Scottish Special Housing Association.

The Association is rather like a special force which the Secretary of State can use to supplement the efforts of local authorities in whose districts the need for houses is greatest, and to do special work which falls rather outside the responsibility of any one authority. It is incorporated under the Companies Acts, and has a Council of Management appointed by the Secretary of State. Since the war, besides building thousands of houses in districts where they are most needed, it has carried out the major part of a special programme of miners' houses. It also does a limited amount of experimental building on behalf of the Department, from which the local authorities all benefit. There is, for example, a housing scheme in Edinburgh devoted entirely to experimental and demonstration work; many of the houses in it are prototypes of new designs by the Department's architects and

---

[1] The Housing and Town Development (Scotland) Act, 1957, which became law on 17th July, 1957, revises the amounts of the existing housing subsidies payable in Scotland and introduces certain special subsidies. Subsidy is no longer to be related to the cost of the house, and the fixed contribution from local rates is abolished. The Act also makes changes in the scope of the operations of the Scottish Special Housing Association.

the scheme has been much visited by representatives of Scottish housing authorities.

The Association has no share capital and its working capital is normally advanced from the Consolidated Fund. (Where the Association acts as building contractors for Government departments such as the Forestry Commission or the Admiralty, or occasionally for local authorities, the commissioning body supplies the necessary capital.) The Department pays the same subsidy on the Association's houses as on those built by local authorities, and also makes a contribution equivalent to that made by the local authority from the rates.[1]

Existing Housing

It was mentioned above that many local authorities are now turning their attention to existing houses. This is an urgent problem, since some two-fifths of the population of Scotland are at present living in houses that are over 70 years old and about half in houses over 40 years old. A large number of these houses are structurally sound and it would be most uneconomic to demolish them and replace them merely because the interiors are obsolete. Many others, however, are hopelessly out of date and outworn and will have to be cleared away.

Local authorities were required by the Housing (Repairs and Rents) (Scotland) Act, 1954, to let the Secretary of State have for his approval their proposals for dealing with the unfit houses in their district—in the first instance to cover the three years 1956 to 1958. If the houses, although unfit, simply cannot be spared at present because there are not enough better houses in the district, the local authority can postpone their demolition, but must carry out work to make the houses at least tolerable to live in until such time as they are demolished. If the Secretary of State approves proposals of this kind, Exchequer subsidies are paid towards the cost of acquiring the houses and carrying out work on them.

Many authorities are faced with either individual houses or, more often, groups of houses which are so worn out through age and disrepair and so lacking in modern amenities that the only way to deal with them is to demolish them as soon as possible. If the general housing situation in the district permits, the local authority can either require the owners to close the houses and demolish them, or it can buy them and demolish them itself. It has power to acquire them compulsorily for this purpose, subject to the confirmation of the compulsory purchase order by the Secretary of State. If there are objections to the order, the Secretary of State will appoint someone —in important cases, usually a member of the Scottish Bar—to hold a public local enquiry.

Fortunately, as was said before, by no means all old houses are bad

[1] See also footnote on previous page.

houses. Those which are structurally sound may need only the installation of such modern improvements as a bathroom or a hot-water system. The local authorities can pay the owners of houses of this kind up to 50 per cent. of the cost of improvement, subject to a maximum grant of £400. The Department of Health, which pays a contribution towards the loan charges incurred by the authorities in this way, gives them general guidance on the type of work they should assist, and an authority must obtain the approval of the Secretary of State if it wants to pay a grant of more than 50 per cent. or more than £400. The authorities can also get Exchequer assistance amounting to 75 per cent. of the cost of modernising and improving houses they own themselves, and the same proportion of the cost of acquiring the houses, where they do not already own them. Each scheme of this kind is examined by the Department to ensure that the work will produce good houses at a reasonable cost. Some of the schemes that have already been carried out have resulted in the conversion of outmoded tenement blocks into modern flats and in the complete modernisation of groups of rural cottages, and others—some of them sponsored by housing associations like that formed by the National Trust for Scotland—have saved buildings of historical interest and architectural beauty and at the same time created comfortable modern homes.

Private Houses

The Secretary of State is, naturally enough, primarily concerned with public housing—there is no Government subsidy for privately built houses, except for houses erected by housing associations or for agricultural workers. But he has a general concern for the maintenance and improvement of what may be called the national stock of houses, and therefore for the standard of private building. The grants for the improvement of private houses have already been mentioned. The standards of construction for houses, as for all other new buildings, are controlled by building bye-laws made by the local authorities. These bye-laws all have to be submitted to the Secretary of State for confirmation and he could refuse to confirm them if it appeared that they did not set a suitable standard. In practice, most authorities follow closely the model bye-laws prepared by the Department. The bye-laws, of course, deal with the technical aspects of construction but the Department also does what it can to improve the design of private housing—for example, by its support of the Saltire Society's[1] annual award for the best-designed scheme of privately built houses.

The Secretary of State is also concerned to encourage house

[1] The Saltire Society is a body with headquarters in Edinburgh and branches in both Scotland and England, which 'exists to preserve the best in Scottish tradition and to encourage those who are contributing to the cultural life of Scotland today'.

ownership as a means of reducing the demand for the subsidised houses built by the local authorities. He encourages local authorities to lend money under certain approved conditions to people who need capital for the building, repair or improvement of houses, and since 1954 he has been prepared to join with a local authority in guaranteeing advances made by a building society in order that the society should make larger advances than they would without a guarantee.

One form of private house-building that may receive help from the State is that done by an approved non-profit-making housing association. A number of the employees of a firm, for example, may join forces to build themselves houses, or a body may be formed to provide houses for disabled ex-servicemen. The assistance is given through the local authority, which can also contribute. The Department of Health supervises the formation of the associations and indeed draws up the conditions which must be fulfilled if they are to qualify for assistance.

Private owners who wish to build houses for agricultural workers may receive assistance in the shape of a capital grant of £240 or £300 per house according to size. The scheme is administered by local authorities, who meet part of the cost, the remainder being met by the Exchequer.

STAFFING

From the description which has been given of the various duties of the Department in relation to general sanitation and housing, it will be obvious that they require a varied technical staff. The Department's architects, engineers and surveyors—who incidentally give technical advice to other departments in St. Andrew's House as well—examine the various schemes that are submitted for approval and they also carry out research into new types of house design and new methods of construction. The local authorities often seek their advice informally before submitting their formal proposals. The Department also has Housing Inspectors, each of whom pays regular visits to the local authority housing schemes in his area where building work is in progress, and examines in particular the standards of workmanship.

In the Department's work, much depends on good relations with the local authorities. It is not unknown for an official correspondence to take a wrong turning and end in a *cul-de-sac* from which it is almost impossible to extricate it by further letters. The Department has four General Inspectors—whose office dates from the days of the Board of Supervision for the Relief of the Poor—who have established personal and friendly relations with the authorities as well as with various voluntary bodies in their areas, and as a result can smooth over difficulties of this kind and report to the Department the strength of local feeling on any subject.

DEPARTMENT OF HEALTH FOR SCOTLAND
Organisation, 1957

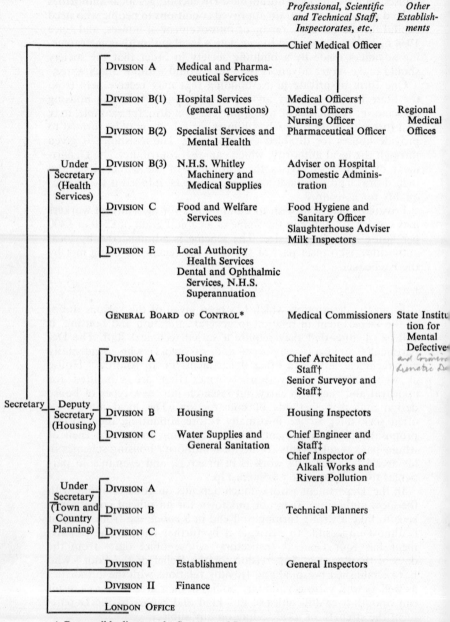

			Professional, Scientific and Technical Staff, Inspectorates, etc.	*Other Establishments*
			Chief Medical Officer	
Secretary	Under Secretary (Health Services)	DIVISION A — Medical and Pharmaceutical Services		
		DIVISION B(1) — Hospital Services (general questions)	Medical Officers† Dental Officers Nursing Officer Pharmaceutical Officer	Regional Medical Offices
		DIVISION B(2) — Specialist Services and Mental Health		
		DIVISION B(3) — N.H.S. Whitley Machinery and Medical Supplies	Adviser on Hospital Domestic Administration	
		DIVISION C — Food and Welfare Services	Food Hygiene and Sanitary Officer Slaughterhouse Adviser Milk Inspectors	
		DIVISION E — Local Authority Health Services Dental and Ophthalmic Services, N.H.S. Superannuation		
	GENERAL BOARD OF CONTROL*		Medical Commissioners	State Institution for Mental Defectives *and Criminal Lunatic De...*
	Deputy Secretary (Housing)	DIVISION A — Housing	Chief Architect and Staff† Senior Surveyor and Staff‡	
		DIVISION B — Housing	Housing Inspectors	
		DIVISION C — Water Supplies and General Sanitation	Chief Engineer and Staff‡ Chief Inspector of Alkali Works and Rivers Pollution	
	Under Secretary (Town and Country Planning)	DIVISION A		
		DIVISION B	Technical Planners	
		DIVISION C		
		DIVISION I — Establishment	General Inspectors	
		DIVISION II — Finance		
		LONDON OFFICE		

* Responsible direct to the Secretary of State.
† Serve all four Departments.
‡ Serve Scottish Home Department and Scottish Education Department.

PART FIVE

The Scottish Home Department

CHAPTER XVII

Public Order, the Care of Children and Miscellaneous Services

WHEN the Secretary for Scotland Bill was being considered by Parliament in 1885, Sir Lyon Playfair, it may be remembered, went so far as to refer to the new Minister as 'a haggis salted with education'. Education is a separate matter, but most of the original haggis, with some additional ingredients added, is now on the plate of the Scottish Home Department. The Department's functions, in fact, are such an elaborate and mysterious composition that an orderly, let alone a complete, analysis of them presents some difficulty.

It may be of interest to record first how the Department was formed. When the Secretary of State was apportioning among departments the various functions which the Reorganisation of Offices (Scotland) Act of 1939 gave him, he created the Scottish Home Department and gave to it the duties of the old Fisheries Board (whose origins went back to 1726) and of the Prisons Department (which was the successor of the Prison Commissioners appointed in 1877), as well as most of those which had been discharged by the Scottish Office since its formation in 1885. What had previously been the staff of the Scottish Office became in the main the staff of the Scottish Home Department, and the name Scottish Office, as we have seen, was thenceforth used to denote the Secretary of State's headquarters and the Scottish departments generally.

This new Scottish department came into being on 3rd September, 1939, simultaneously with the outbreak of the Second World War and thus is not yet 21 years old, but it embodies a much older tradition of administration. Not only was it created by a fusion of three administrative units formed in 1726, 1877 and 1885, but its functions, in so far as they derive from the duties of a Secretary of State at common law and under the Royal prerogative, go back far into history. So, while the Department may appear to be young in years, and while one may hope that it still shows youthful vigour, it is in a sense a kind of elderly changeling, already hardened in administrative sin, but rejuvenated by the legislative elixir of 1939.

In its organisation the Department conforms to the orthodox civil service pattern. The Secretary is assisted by four under secretaries and below them the Department is divided into 13 administrative divisions and one finance division in Edinburgh and one liaison division in London, each in charge of an assistant secretary. The detailed organisation of the Department is shown on page 178.

Apart from its Edinburgh headquarters, the Department has a number of establishments in other parts of Scotland. It staffs the sheriff clerk's office in each county; it maintains 12 prisons and borstal institutions in various parts of the country from Newton Stewart in the south-west to Peterhead in the north-east; it has fishery research stations at Aberdeen and Pitlochry as well as four fishery research vessels; it has Fishery Officers at 21 ports and maintains eight fishery cruisers and two dredgers; it administers training centres for the police, the fire service and the children service; and it runs—as if all this were not a sufficient variety—33 hotels and public houses in the Cromarty Firth and Gretna state management districts. Its present staff amounts to over 2,450,[1] of whom about 800 are at headquarters.

When an attempt has to be made to analyse and describe what these people do, there are various ways of setting about it. Perhaps the easiest, as well as the most easily understood, is to group the Department's functions according to the Whitehall Departments by which the corresponding functions are carried out in England. The table in Chapter I, which is by no means exhaustive, shows that the main tasks carried out by the Department in Scotland are in England spread over the Home Office, the Ministry of Housing and Local Government, the Ministry of Agriculture, Fisheries and Food, the Ministry of Power, the Ministry of Transport and Civil Aviation and the Lord Chancellor's Department. In addition, the Department has functions which in England are carried out by the Charity Commissioners and, in some matters relating to the development areas, it is required to act jointly with the Board of Trade. It also has certain responsibilities for the National Galleries, the Record Office and the Department of the Registers—roughly equivalent work in England being done by the Treasury—and for the Royal Observatory, which in England is the concern of the Admiralty. It provides its own fleet of fishery protection vessels, a service which in England is undertaken by the Royal Navy. To complete the story, it has had in recent years to concern itself increasingly with the general question of Scottish development and with the special problems of the Highlands and Islands and it is the Department through which the Secretary of State deals with many of the miscellaneous questions with which he is expected to concern himself as 'Scotland's Minister'.

POLICE

Amongst this heterogeneous collection of functions, it can perhaps fairly be said that the most important are those connected with the maintenance of public order in the broadest sense of the term. It is

[1] Not including staff at Sheriff Clerks' offices amounting to over 230.

the duty of the Secretary of State in Scotland, as it is of the Home Secretary in England and Wales, to see that the Queen's Peace is kept. Sir Frank Newsam, in his book on *The Home Office*,[1] has dealt fully with the conception of the Queen's Peace and it is perhaps enough to say here that it is the maintenance of those conditions of law and order which should be the normal state of civilised society. (It is more frequently mentioned in the breach than the observance—in the phrase 'a breach of the peace'.) The principal instruments in preserving the Queen's Peace are, of course, the police forces, and although the Secretary of State is not himself a police authority for any part of Scotland (as the Home Secretary is for the Metropolis), he must be concerned to see—and is indeed responsible for seeing—that the Scottish police are adequate and efficient. Her Majesty's Inspector of Constabulary for Scotland, who is appointed on the Secretary of State's recommendation, inspects all the police forces in Scotland each year and reports to him on their efficiency, and only if the report is favourable can the Secretary of State, through the Scottish Home Department, pay the grant which has been authorised by Parliament of 50 per cent. of the cost of maintaining the forces.

This, however, is only a small part of the work of the Department in connection with the police. That work is indeed worth considering fairly fully, not only because it is important in itself, but because, in spite of certain unique features, it is fairly typical of what the Department has to do in relation to other services and illustrates particularly well the need to establish friendly working relations between English and Scottish Departments concerned with the same subject. The Scottish police forces are maintained by the police authorities—that is, by the councils of counties and of most large burghs—but the policemen are not local authority officials. They are technically officers of the Crown,[2] with a special status which ensures their independence and gives them security in the tenure of their office. They are appointed by the Chief Constable, who is himself appointed by the police authority subject to the approval of the Secretary of State. Before recruiting to his force, the Chief Constable must be satisfied that each man complies with the qualifications as to education and physique which the Secretary of State has laid down in regulations. The training of all ranks of the police is carried on centrally in various branches of the Scottish Police College, the headquarters of which is at Tulliallan Castle, Kincardine-on-Forth, and which is maintained by the Scottish Home Department on behalf of the police authorities. Half the cost of running the College is met by Government grant. The number of policemen in each force

[1] Chapter III.
[2] But the Scottish constable does not take an oath to serve the monarch as his English colleague does. Instead he swears faithfully to discharge his duty as a constable.

requires the approval, through the Department, of the Secretary of State, and, if two or more police authorities wish to combine and run a joint force for the enlarged area, the arrangement must be approved by him. Subject to parliamentary approval, the Secretary of State may combine authorities compulsorily, but he has not so far exercised this power.

It was laid down in 1919, and is a sign of his special status, that a policeman should not be a member of a trade union. The conditions of service and the pension rights of the police are laid down in regulations by the Secretary of State, who, before making them, is required by statute to consult the Scottish Police Council, on which both the police authorities and all branches of the service are represented. There is, however, no obligation on him to do what the Council advises, and, because this aspect of the organisation was open to criticism, a new Great Britain Police Council was set up. This body has an Official Side and a Staff Side, with an independent chairman, and independent arbitrators to whom any dispute between the two sides can be referred. Until such time as the new body has statutory authority, the Scottish and English Police Councils remain in being, but their functions have become largely formal.

The policeman's tenure of his office is governed by the Police Appeals Acts and by regulations made by the Secretary of State. Once his period of probation is over, a policeman can only be dismissed, or required to resign, after his Chief Constable has held a hearing into a charge against him. If he is asked to leave the service—which, happily, is a rare occurrence—he has a right of appeal to the Secretary of State. These appeals may involve a judicial hearing by the Sheriff, and the Sheriff's report is then the main factor taken into account by the Secretary of State in determining the appeal. The Secretary of State's functions are discharged through the Home Department. The rarity of the duty does not diminish its importance, and indeed this part of the Department's work may be used to emphasise how essential it is that the Department should command the confidence of the police service. The morale of the service will very quickly suffer if policemen do not feel that their individual appeals are being considered and their wider interests looked after by a central department which is efficient, sympathetic and just.

Crime, like disease, is not confined by local government or national boundaries, and the individual police forces in Scotland must frequently co-operate not only with each other but with the English forces. It would, in the long run, be to no one's advantage if one authority could build up a particularly strong force by outbidding the others in the terms of service it offered. It has therefore been the settled policy for some years that police conditions of service should be uniform throughout Great Britain, and this has meant that the Department and the Home Office have had to work very closely together. The formation of the Great Britain Police Council has intensified these contacts as well as made uniform conditions easier to achieve. The two Departments discuss together the line their representatives should take at the Council meetings, so as to avoid adopting divergent policies. There may be special circumstances which justify divergences in minor matters, but, in general, the two Departments have to get together at the earliest possible stage in the consideration of any problem, to hammer out a common method of dealing with it. This same need exists in most of the other branches of the Department's administration and is met either by correspondence and direct discussion between the officers concerned, or by using the Department's small liaison staff as a channel of communication with the Whitehall departments.

COURTS OF LAW

The problem of maintaining the Queen's Peace does not, of course, end with the maintenance of efficient police forces. Malefactors, when they have been discovered by the police, have to be brought to justice. In Scotland, the police are not themselves responsible for prosecuting in the courts. They report the case to the appropriate public prosecutor—in serious cases the Procurator Fiscal—so that, if he thinks the evidence sufficient, he can bring the accused before the proper court of law. Even for these courts the Secretary of State has certain responsibilities. It is on his recommendation, though with the advice of the Lord Advocate, that the High Court Judges (other than the Lord President of the Court of Session and the Lord Justice Clerk) and the sheriffs and sheriffs-substitute are appointed by the Queen; and it is his duty to see that the courts are adequately staffed. The Department now runs a Scottish Court Service from which the administrative staff required by the High Court, the Court of Session and the sheriff courts is provided.

THE PROBATION SERVICE

The preservation of law and order requires that there should be some machinery for enforcing the decisions of the courts. If the criminal courts feel that an accused person, although undoubtedly guilty, is more likely to be recalled to the paths of rectitude by guidance than by punishment, they may put him on probation. The probation service, although extremely valuable, does not present any very unusual administrative features, and indeed the pattern is one that by now has become very familiar to the reader. The service is run by the local authorities through local probation committees and the Secretary of State, through the Home Department, defrays 50 per cent. of the cost and is responsible for the efficient working of the service. The way in which the service should be administered, and the status and remuneration of the probation officers, are laid down by him in regulations and the appointment of probation officers requires his approval. The Department runs training courses for probation officers, and guides and keeps in touch with the local operation of the service through special inspectors. An advisory body called the Scottish Central Probation Council has been appointed by the Secretary of State to guide him (and incidentally the local probation committees) on policy and administration.

PRISONS AND BORSTALS

The courts may also, of course, impose a fine, which will be collected by the appropriate clerk of court. But they may feel that a period of isolation from the normal community is necessary for the offender, in which case they will send him to prison if he is an adult, or, if he is a young offender, to a remand home for a short period of detention or to an approved school or borstal institution for training. In Scotland, where approved schools have long been regarded as educational rather than penal establishments, they are the responsibility of the Education Department (see Chapter VIII). But remand homes and borstals, as well as prisons, are the concern of the Home Department.

There is not much that need be said about remand homes. As their name indicates, they are institutions to which young offenders can be sent on remand while awaiting trial, or after trial while a psychiatrist or psychologist is making an examination on behalf of the court; or the courts may sentence a child or young person to be detained for up to a month in a remand home as a punishment. The homes are run by local authorities (county councils and town councils of large burghs) to whom the Home Department pays on behalf of the Secretary of State 50 per cent. of their approved expenses. The administration of the homes is governed by rules made by the Secretary of State, and Home Department inspectors visit them regularly.

For the running of prisons and borstals, on the other hand, the Secretary of State is directly responsible. This has been a central responsibility since 1877—and there is no evidence that local authorities want it back—and Scotland differs from England and Wales in that there are no Prison Commissioners to share this onerous duty with the Secretary of State.

There are now prisons at Aberdeen, Dumfries, Edinburgh, Glasgow, Greenock, Inverness, Perth, Peterhead, and (an open one) at Penninghame, near Newton Stewart; and there are borstal institutions at Castle Huntly, Cornton Vale, Dumfries Prison, Polmont, and —for girls—at Edinburgh and Greenock Prisons. Over 750 prison officers and specialists are employed in these establishments and there is, of course, a great deal of detailed work to be done in the construction and maintenance of buildings, in contracting for and purchasing supplies and in organising the routine of the prison itself, in providing suitable employment and industrial training, in supervising and looking after the well-being of the inmates.

In its prisons work the Department has to deal not merely with paper problems but with the problems of individual prisoners; in addition it has valuable and constructive work to do in advising the Secretary of State on questions of policy. It has to do its best to keep abreast of current doctrines in penology, to assess, from what it knows of the subsequent records of ex-prisoners and ex-borstal boys and girls, the value of the various kinds of treatment provided in prison and in borstal, and, so far as seems desirable, to introduce reforms. The organisation of corrective training and preventive detention, in order to carry out the requirements of the Criminal Justice (Scotland) Act, 1949, and the introduction of an open prison and two open borstals, are examples of recent reforms which have required much thought and planning, and have involved the Department in some unusual tasks. (Officers of the Department, for example, addressed a public meeting at Newton Stewart on behalf of the Secretary of State, in order to explain the proposals for the open prison at Penninghame.) The path of the reformer is not easy and, in the popular imagination, the civil servant has to be goaded along it by Members of Parliament with sharp instruments. But in its prison work, it can be said that the Department has advanced a very considerable distance since the days of the treadmill, when the effect of the prison sentence was to produce not so much a reformed character as a determination not to be found out next time.

Prison and borstal must necessarily be to some extent preventive and punitive in character; but more and more, in recent years, the emphasis has been on the need to make a constructive effort to rehabilitate those who are consigned to custody, and to make them into useful citizens. It would be too much to hope that the majority of the prisoners themselves should show much interest in this process (although they may be grateful for it afterwards) and the general public do not, on the whole, concern themselves with what goes on inside prison walls, unless unfortunate circumstances compel them to do so. Nevertheless the work goes on. It requires a personal understanding by the officers of the prison and borstal service of the individual people committed to their care—at least in those cases where the period of committal is long enough for reformative influences to be brought to bear. The Department's Director of Prison and Borstal Services and his staff therefore have to concern themselves constantly not only with questions of general policy and with the running of the various establishments, but with the selection, training and guidance of the officers who man them. In supervising the working of the system and in creating a proper understanding and sympathy between the service and the communities outside the walls, the Department is assisted by visiting committees, whose members are appointed by the neighbouring local authorities or, for borstal institutions, by the Secretary of State.

The rehabilitation of prisoners and borstal inmates is not, of course, regarded as complete when their sentence comes to an end. They have still, however well they may have responded to the training they have received, to make the difficult transition from the controlled life of an institution to the free life of the world outside. They have to resume what so many find difficult to support—the burden of personal decision. Under modern conditions the transition may be eased, since the latter stages of training may include work under conditions of freedom and trust—sometimes even outside the prison or borstal. But even in these cases a helping hand is needed in the early stages of freedom. A statutory body known as the Scottish After Care Council, the members of which serve voluntarily and which is assisted by officers of the Home Department, has the task of giving this help to all ex-borstal boys and girls and to ex-prisoners who have served sentences of three years or more. (Those who have served shorter sentences are assisted on release by the Discharged Prisoners' Aid Society.) The officers of the Department engaged on this work first make contact with those they are to assist while they are still undergoing training in the institution; and from material supplied by the prison and borstal governors they familiarise themselves with the personality, history and personal difficulties of each inmate. For the borstal boys and girls, they also have the benefit of information about their backgrounds collected by the psychiatric social workers now attached to the borstal service, and of reports from a psychiatrist who has studied each case. The officers find the inmates employment when they are discharged (with the assistance of the Ministry of Labour and National Service); for certain categories they select guardians who are willing to take an interest in them; and they generally help them to settle down to normal life. The success of this work is not easy to measure and there are many failures and disappointments in it; but there are also considerable successes to record in the carrying out of a piece of social service which only in Scotland is entrusted directly to officers of a Government Department.

THE ROYAL PREROGATIVE

Offences against law and order are, as we have seen, breaches of the Queen's Peace and it is therefore very proper that the right to pardon should be vested in the Sovereign. The exercise of the prerogative of mercy—which is generally used where humanity seems to require some interference with the strict course of the law, but can also be invoked to put right a wrongful conviction—is perhaps the most important surviving example of the royal prerogative. In Scotland the prerogative is exercised on the advice of the Secretary of State, who in turn relies on the advice of the Home Department. His task in deciding whether to recommend a free pardon[1] or a remission of sentence is a difficult and delicate one. It is never a light matter to interfere with the sentence of a court of law; in capital cases, a man's life rests in the balance as well.

Capital cases are invariably reviewed by the Secretary of State, whether or not a petition for reprieve is submitted. It is the task of the Department to present each case to the Secretary of State in the most complete and helpful way, taking account of every factor and of every piece of information that is available, whether or not it was before the court, and setting out the relevant considerations succinctly and impartially. The Secretary of State also has before him a report by the judge who took the case, and (in accordance with the advice of Queen Victoria!) it is also the custom to discuss each case with the Home Office, whose experience is much wider and whose consideration of any similar English case may disclose relevant points. But the decision whether or not to make a recommendation to the Queen is entirely that of the Secretary of State.

Capital cases are naturally in a class by themselves. But the Secretary of State may be—and indeed constantly is—petitioned by prisoners and others who have been convicted of crimes and offences, to recommend their pardon or a remission of their punishment. Every case that comes up in this way is fully considered and, if necessary, the help of the judge who heard the case may be invoked. But it is, naturally enough, seldom possible to recommend clemency. The Secretary of State's duty to advise the Queen on the use of the royal prerogative does not enable him to act as a court of appeal. What he has to do is to take into account any compassionate considerations, and any other facts that for some reason were not before the court, and to decide whether or not they would justify clemency. Within such narrow limits it is only occasionally that remission of sentence can be recommended, and justification for a free pardon is, for obvious reasons, even rarer. But periodically it does become evident that there has been an inadvertent miscarriage of justice which cannot be corrected through the normal processes of the law. For example, a legal decision about the speed limit for a particular class of vehicle recently made it necessary to recommend that free pardons should be given to a very considerable number of people who had previously been convicted of exceeding the speed limit. Every case investigated by the Department is submitted to the Secretary of State for his

---

[1] 'Pardon' is here used in a special sense, implying not merely forgiveness for an offence committed, but, where there has been an error of justice, the annulment of both conviction and sentence.

L

instructions, unless he has already given some general direction which covers it, and a free pardon or remission requires the issue of a formal warrant signed by the Queen and countersigned by the Secretary of State.

LEGAL AID

This discussion of the functions of the Home Department in relation to law and order would not be complete without some mention of the duties which the Secretary of State has comparatively recently acquired, and which he exercises through the Department, in the provision of legal aid in the courts for people who cannot afford to pay for it themselves. (In England this work is the responsibility of the Lord Chancellor's Department on the civil side and of the Home Office on the criminal side.) The legal aid scheme is actually operated by the Law Society of Scotland, who act for this purpose through a central committee on which the Faculty of Advocates are represented and to which the Secretary of State appoints two independent members. But the lines on which it is run are subject to the Secretary of State's approval and the entire cost—so far as it is not recovered from the litigants—is met from the Home Department's vote.

Legal aid is now almost fully available in the civil courts. Applications for aid are dealt with by local committees, or, if the case is to be taken in the Court of Session, by a special body called the Supreme Court Committee; and applicants not only have to submit to an assessment of their means by the National Assistance Board, but have to convince the committee that they have what the lawyers call a *probabilis causa litigandi*.

The provisions of the Legal Aid Act dealing with criminal proceedings have not yet been brought into operation. In the meantime members of the legal profession are continuing the centuries-old practice of acting gratuitously for any person on the Poor's Roll charged with a criminal offence in the High Court or in a sheriff court, if such person is unable to pay for his defence. Since 1953 an annual sum has been provided from the Law Charges (Scotland) Vote out of which honoraria are paid to some solicitors who defend poor persons.

FIRE SERVICE

So far, by the expedient of following the career of an imaginary wrongdoer from his arrest by a policeman trained in the Home Department's Police College into the law courts staffed by the Department's Court Service and thence either into one of the Department's prisons or into the care of the probation service, it would be possible to run a continuous, if a rather tenuous, thread through the Department's various activities. But that becomes increasingly difficult. There are, first of all, certain functions which, although not exactly concerned with law and order, are related to the protection of life and property. The Secretary of State is responsible in Scotland, for example, as the Home Secretary is in England, for the fire service and the civil defence service. The former is concerned with the protection of life and property both in peace and in war; the latter with the building up of an organisation to protect the civil population, or at least reduce the loss it would otherwise suffer, in any future war.

The history of the fire service in Scotland goes back quite a long way, and indeed Edinburgh could put forward a convincing claim to have had one of the earliest professional local brigades in Britain, founded in 1824. Edinburgh might also claim to have been the scene of one of the earliest instances of Government interference in fire-fighting, for when one of the largest fires in the history of the city took place in 1824, in the High Street, the Lord Advocate and the Solicitor-General were quickly on the scene, fiercely disputing with the Lord Justice Clerk, the Lord Provost and the Dean of the Faculty of Advocates as to who should take command of operations.[1] In spite of this promising start, progress was slow. It was most rapid in the cities (which of course were also the first to be provided with a piped water supply), but by 1938, when the Act was passed which made the provision of fire services an obligation on all local authorities, only Aberdeen, Edinburgh and Glasgow had taken a statutory obligation on themselves by means of local acts. After the Second World War, during most of which the service was nationalised, it was completely reorganised; and there are now only eleven brigades for the whole of Scotland—one for the City of Glasgow, administered by the Town Council, and ten for the rest of the country, administered by joint committees composed of representatives of the county councils and of the town councils of large burghs.

The Secretary of State stands in relation to the fire services in much the same position as he does in relation to the police. But there are important differences. One, which the local authorities do not allow the Government to forget, is that the Exchequer meets only 25 per cent. of fire service expenditure.[2] The Home Department, which pays the grant, also advises the Secretary of State on the conditions of service of firemen, which are laid down by him in regulations. Firemen, like policemen, have their conditions of service negotiated for Great Britain by a joint council, but there are no departmental representatives on the joint council and the central departments therefore cannot influence its recommendations in any way. If the Secretary of State and the Home Secretary dislike its recommendations or

---

[1] *Memorials of his Time* by Henry Cockburn, chapter vii. *Fires in Edinburgh* by Robert Chambers (Edinburgh, 1824).

[2] If proposals now under discussion are implemented, this and other *ad hoc* grants paid by the Department to local authorities (e.g., for child care and physical training and recreation) will be merged in a new general grant—see page 163.

those of the arbiters to whom disputed points may go, they can refer them back; and in the last resort the decision about regulations is, of course, their own. But the recommendations of the joint council are obviously not to be lightly disregarded.

The police organisation has been followed to the extent that there is an Inspector of Fire Services for Scotland, appointed by the Crown on the Secretary of State's recommendation, who reports on all brigades annually and whose assurance that each brigade is efficient is a condition of its receiving the Government grant. The Department is assisted in keeping in touch with the service throughout the country not only by the Inspector, but by a statutory body called the Fire Brigades Advisory Council for Scotland, which contains representatives of the authorities and of all branches of the service and sits under the chairmanship of an officer of the Department.

An important difference between the Department's responsibilities for the fire service and those for the police is in the arrangements for training. The Scottish Police College trains all ranks of the police force, but the fire service is much smaller—there are only 1,800 whole-time and 2,000 part-time regular firemen in Scotland as compared with over 7,000 regular policemen—and as a result it would not be economic to run officers' courses, which are highly specialised, for Scotland alone. There is therefore one college for Great Britain, and the two Departments and fire authority and fire service representatives from both countries are associated in its management. There is, however, a Scottish training school for recruits and junior ranks at Gullane, which is run by the Department on behalf of all the authorities.

CIVIL DEFENCE

The civil defence service, in Scotland as in England, is rather like a balloon—shrunken at present but sufficiently elastic to be capable of expansion to its proper size for use in an emergency. In its fullest state of expansion, civil defence would include the war-time duties of the police and the fire service as well as the organisation of services such as the Civil Defence Corps, which are required only in an emergency. Some aspects of civil defence, such as evacuation, the treatment of casualties and the care of the homeless, are the responsibility of the Department of Health, but it is the Home Department which is responsible for advising the Secretary of State on civil defence organisation generally and for planning the operational control which would become necessary in time of war.

During the war of 1939–45, the Minister of Home Security had specific responsibility for many of the individual civil defence services, and, over and above that, a co-ordinating responsibility for the operation of civil defence in Scotland. The Secretary of State, on the other hand, continued to exercise jurisdiction over the police, fire and casualty services, which were his peace-time responsibilities. This divided responsibility for a service whose efficiency depends very much on rapid, well co-ordinated action did not seem a very happy arrangement, and the Secretary of State—working through the Home Department—is now responsible for the central control and co-ordination of all civil defence in Scotland. Locally, civil defence is yet another function of the county councils and of the town councils of the cities and large burghs.

Civil defence in peace-time does not appeal to our national temperament (and in this the civil defence recruitment figures do not show any significant difference between the Englishman and the Scot). We like to be sure that there is going to be an emergency before we start to train for it. Once the first bomb falls, the Scot will put aside his golf clubs and, murmuring that someone should have done something about it, will join the nearest civil defence organisation. In the meantime, the civil defence administrator builds largely on shifting sands. He must rely mainly on his information officers to devise means of keeping up recruitment to the civil defence services; and, from what the experts can tell him of the destructive effects of the atom bomb, the hydrogen bomb and whatever worse horrors may lie hidden in the womb of time, he must try to ensure that an adequate organisation of well-trained people exists, at least in skeleton form, to meet the emergency if it should come. This work does not, in its essentials, differ greatly between Scotland and England and it involves the Home Department in very close contacts with the Home Office and other Whitehall departments, as well as in consultation with the local authorities and in the payment of grant towards civil defence expenditure. So far, it has been thought that research and the maintenance of central training establishments are matters most economically and efficiently handled by one department for the whole of Britain and they have therefore been left to the Home Office.

LICENSING AND STATE MANAGEMENT

One other part of the Home Department's work has some bearing on public order and safety—its responsibilities for the administration of the law about liquor licensing and for the running of the scheme for the state management of licensed premises. A nation's drinking habits are a part of the national character, and it is therefore not surprising to find that the Scottish licensing laws differ in many ways from the English. Drinking, in the country that produces Scotch whisky, is a serious business, and, by a natural reaction, what is usually called temperance takes a more severe form. The local licensing courts are differently constituted in Scotland; Sunday drinking in Scotland is reserved for the *bona fide* traveller; and the control of clubs in Scotland is much stricter than in England. Under the Scottish Temperance Act, which has no English counterpart, a community can, if it is so minded, determine by poll to terminate or restrict the sale of liquor in its area.[1] The Scottish legislation on this subject gives the Department a good deal of work—for example, in making regulations and confirming bye-laws—but the difference in the law for the two countries means that there is less need for continuous consultation with the Home Office on this than on some other subjects.

This is not true of state management of licensed premises. This scheme—operated in two enclaves, around Carlisle and Gretna on the border and in the Cromarty Firth district—originated in the 1914–18 war. The concentration of munition workers at Gretna and the creation of a major naval base in the Cromarty Firth resulted in an alarming amount of drunkenness, and the quickest and most effective remedy was for the Government to assume responsibility for the sale of liquor. The state took over practically all the licensed premises in the three districts, closed some, improved the rest, and has been running them ever since. The circumstances that brought the experiment into being no longer exist, but the system has been allowed to continue. In consequence the Home Department now runs 33 hotels and public houses. An Advisory Council, appointed by the Secretary of State and the Home Secretary jointly, and including prominent members of the brewing industry, advises both Ministers on the management of the licensed premises in the three districts and there is a local committee in each district. There is a general manager for the Scottish state management districts with an office in Glasgow and each district is in charge of a superintendent. Questions of policy and major matters of finance are dealt with by administrative and financial officers of the Department.

MISCELLANEOUS ACTIVITIES

With many of the other functions which the Department exercises in Scotland and which are the concern of the Home Office in England, there is no space to deal. There is the central administration of the Acts relating to shops, theatres and cinemas, to charitable collections and to the protection of birds and animals. And there is a series of Acts about the representation of the people which impose duties on the Secretary of State and, through him, on the Department. The Department's constitutional functions also include a great deal of formal and ceremonial business—the issue of warrants appointing the Lord High Commissioner to the General Assembly of the Church of Scotland, Lords-Lieutenant, various officers of state and regius professors; the constitution of royal commissions; the organisation of state visits by the Sovereign; and a whole range of duties

[1] Such determinations are at present in force in 39 areas.

of a similar kind. It is perhaps the only part of the duties of the Secretary of State which one of the pre-1745 Secretaries would recognise if he could return to the office today.

CARE OF CHILDREN

Perhaps the most constructive part of the Department's work is in the care and protection of children. The legislation is contained partly in separate Scottish Acts and partly in Acts that apply to the whole of Great Britain, and, although the traditions of the two countries differ, the accepted principles are now much the same in both. The Children Act of 1948 is the principal statute; it applies to both countries and was largely based on the reports of two separate committees, the Curtis Committee in England and the Clyde Committee in Scotland. In conformity with J. S. Mill's sound principle in *Representative Government* that 'there should not be several departments independent of one another, to superintend different parts of the same natural whole', the Children Act of 1948 concentrates on the Home Secretary and Secretary of State ministerial responsibility for children deprived of a normal home life. This responsibility had previously been divided between several central departments.

Sir Frank Newsam in his book on *The Home Office*[1] relates the work of child care and protection to the general aim, which runs through so much of that Department's labour, of promoting the Queen's Peace. Only too often an investigation into the early life of a criminal discloses a neglected childhood, and the Children Act provides that a child who, for some reason, has been deprived of parental care and guidance should be given a home and should have the same opportunities of becoming a useful citizen as a child living with his own parents in his own home. The Queen's Peace is thereby safeguarded and strengthened; but the work is also an end in itself.

Its scale is shown by the fact that there are some 10,000 children formally in the care of local authorities[2] in Scotland: 1,200 of them are looked after in homes run by the Churches and by voluntary bodies; 1,700 of them are accommodated in homes provided by the local authorities themselves; and 6,100 are boarded out with foster parents, in the way which has been customary in Scotland for over 100 years, but are subject to the careful and discreet supervision of the children's officers of the local authority. The cost of these arrangements is, of course, considerable, and a grant of 50 per cent. of the approved expenditure is paid by the Home Department. Over and above these children, there are about 2,600 who have been placed privately in voluntary homes; about 500 whose parents, for one

[1] Chapter VII.
[2] The county councils and the town councils of large burghs.

reason or another, pay someone else to look after them; and about 1,400 who are in process of being adopted.

The Department makes its influence felt in various ways. It has the usual formal duty of advising the Secretary of State on the making of rules and regulations about the conduct of the service and it also has to consider whether the expenditure of the local authorities is such as can properly rank for grant.[1] The Secretary of State and the Department have the advice of the Scottish Advisory Council on Child Care, a body of people experienced in this kind of welfare work as well as in local government, who give guidance on the running of the various branches of the service and help to keep the Department in touch with the most recent experience and thought. But the Department's real influence on the character of the service is exercised largely through the contacts made by its inspectorate. This expert body of workers is continually on the move up and down the country, meeting and talking to those in the local authorities and voluntary bodies who are actually doing the work of child care, and helping them informally with advice and guidance. In this work, the inspectorate helps to spread the ideas of the most enlightened workers over the country as a whole and to raise the good to the level of the best. The Department also runs training courses for those who want to take up work on the staff of children's homes, and specialist and refresher courses for those who already have experience. In these ways the best standards of child care are sympathetically and intensively inculcated. Little Buttercup in *H.M.S. Pinafore*, who practised baby farming many years ago, has now disappeared unregretted; but it would not have been a great improvement to have replaced her with cold and unsympathetic institutions. The task of acting *in loco parentis* is not one of the easiest of the many that Parliament has put upon the local authorities in recent years, but it is one of the most rewarding, and the authorities have taken great care in recruiting staff who are not only efficient and well trained but devoted to their work. And it is perhaps not a bad thing for its immortal soul that a Department whose normal functions tend to be of a regulative or negative character should have an opportunity for constructive social work.

[1] See footnote 2 on page 155.

CHAPTER XVIII

Local Government

AS we have seen, the Secretary of State's departments are closely concerned with various aspects of the work of the Scottish local authorities. But there must also be a department to advise him in the exercise
of his general responsibility for the structure and finance of local
government in Scotland. In England and Wales, these general local
government matters are associated administratively with housing and
town and country planning and dealt with by the Ministry of Housing
and Local Government. In Scotland, this work is done by the Home
Department. There are arguments for and against the Scottish practice, but the Royal Commission, which recently reviewed it, did not
recommend any change. Put broadly, the case for it is that general
local government is best dealt with by a department which works
with the local authorities but does not have a predominant interest in
any one subject. The Home Department satisfies this criterion better
than any of the other three Scottish departments.

The Department's local government work is varied, but can be
divided roughly between administrative and financial questions.
There are a great many points of purely local significance which, in
accordance with the Local Government Act, have to be submitted
to the Secretary of State by the local authorities for his consideration or approval. In addition, the Department has the difficult and
troublesome, but rewarding, task of watching the working of the
local government machine for the whole of Scotland. New legislation
may bring fresh responsibilities to the local authorities; the Department, from its own observation and from its regular contacts with
the three main associations of local authorities, should be able to
ensure that the course recommended to Parliament is agreed, by those
who will have to assume the burden, to be the one best adapted to
Scottish conditions. From time to time, still more radical questions
have to be considered. In 1929, for example, when the whole structure
of local government in Scotland was modified, it was the Scottish
Office (which was then in the position of the Home Department)
which advised the Secretary of State on the preparation of the
necessary Bill. There has recently been an examination of the local
government structure in England and Wales, in consultation with the
local authority associations in those countries. The circumstances
which made this review desirable in England and Wales did not exist

in Scotland, but the Home Department has watched closely what has been going on south of the Border, in order to be able to advise the Secretary of State on any possible Scottish implications.

The Department's local government work, however, goes far beyond questions of local government structure, for it includes all the general aspects of local government finance. The earlier chapters of this book should have shown clearly that the revenues of local authorities are only partly derived from the rates levied by them. In recognition of the financial burdens of the authorities and of the fact that they run services which are in the national as well as in the local interest, the State pays grants towards the cost of particular services such as education, housing and police; in each case, the central department responsible for the particular service pays the grant. But, apart from these individual grants, there is a general grant—known as the Exchequer Equalisation Grant. The way in which this is calculated is, as a glance at the Valuation and Rating (Scotland) Act, 1956, will show, only slightly easier to understand than the Schleswig-Holstein question (which only three people ever mastered, and one of them went mad) but the general object is simple enough—to bring up to the national average the rating resources of local authorities which are below that average. Without some assistance of this kind, a local authority such as a Highland county with a large surface area and a small population would be at a very serious disadvantage compared with, say, a compact and prosperous seaside town. The grant does help to even out the inequalities. A Christmas tree on which there is not a present for everybody is unlikely to be very popular, and when the gifts are unwrapped and compared there are not infrequently cries of rage and disappointment. It is the Department's duty to keep the method of distribution under close examination and to carry out formal reviews from time to time to make sure that the grant is working as fairly as possible; two such reviews have been carried out in the past four years.

It is also through the Home Department that the Secretary of State sanctions borrowing by local authorities to meet capital expenditure. Even before the war, English local authorities needed the sanction of a central department before they could borrow money; in Scotland before 1939, however, such sanction was needed only when the local authority's decision to borrow was reached by a majority of less than two-thirds of those present at the meeting. During and since the war, the need to ensure that the capital resources of the country are used to the best advantage has made it necessary that Scottish borrowing should be brought under closer control.

The Department not only has to work the existing financial machine; it has to examine it from time to time and see whether it needs overhauling or even rebuilding. A comprehensive examination of this kind was carried out recently by a departmental committee presided over by Lord Sorn and the report of that committee[1] recommended the complete recasting of the Scottish valuation and rating system. Its main proposals were that Scottish property should in future be valued on the same basis as English, and that the long-standing practice[2] of dividing the burden of rates between the owner and the occupier should cease. The necessary legislation to put the committee's recommendations into effect, now enacted in the Valuation and Rating (Scotland) Act, 1956, necessitated very specialised preliminary discussions with other Departments, with the local authority associations and with various experts in local government finance.

The Department has also been co-ordinating a review of the financial relations between central and local government in Scotland. As indicated in the footnote on page 155, that review may result in the replacement of a number of separate grants by a new general grant.

Although local authorities have recently lost some of the managerial functions they assumed during the last century—in hospital administration and in gas and electricity supply, for example—they have become primarily responsible, as a result of successive pieces of legislation, for many of the major social services, the local maintenance of law and order, the protection of property and the planning service. The importance of the Department's work in local government is correspondingly increased, since it alone is in a position to keep both structure and finance under general observation, and to advise, when creaks and groans suggest that the engine is labouring, what changes and adjustments seem necessary. Generally speaking, it is perhaps not unfair to say that the inclination of the local authorities is to seek larger Government grants and less Government interference, while the Department's aim is—not the exact opposite, but that ideal balance between local management and central supervision and support which will produce an efficiently working system.

This is perhaps the appropriate place to mention one peculiarity of the Scottish administrative system. Any local authority or other public body in Scotland which wants new powers of a kind that would be obtained by private Bill in England must, since 1899, seek them by drafting and presenting to the Secretary of State what is called a provisional order. The procedure followed in dealing with such applications is that codified in the Private Legislation Procedure (Scotland) Act, 1936. If there are objections to the provisional order which the promoters cannot or will not meet, a public enquiry is held in Scotland before commissioners selected usually from Scottish Peers and M.P.s. If the Secretary of State decides, on the recommendation of the commissioners or otherwise, to approve the order, he then

---

[1] Cmd. 9244.
[2] Greatly admired by one Chancellor of the Exchequer (Mr. Goschen), who would have liked to introduce it in England and Wales.

presents it to Parliament as a schedule to a Bill, and the Bill (which simply confirms the order) passes through Parliament under an expedited procedure. These arrangements take time, as such matters will, but they have been periodically modified and improved in accordance with the suggestions of the local authorities and others, and it can be said that they have been found in practice to be economical and convenient for the various bodies in Scotland who wish to obtain special powers from Parliament. The advantage of having the disputed points considered in Scotland itself rather than at Westminster is shown by the fact that, in the period of just under 60 years during which the procedure has been in operation, there have been only seven cases in which the order, as settled in Scotland and presented to Parliament for confirmation, has been seriously opposed.

PHYSICAL TRAINING AND RECREATION

The Physical Training and Recreation Act, 1937, enables the Minister of Education in England and Wales and the Secretary of State in Scotland to give grants to local authorities[1] and voluntary bodies to help them to provide such facilities for physical training and recreation as playing fields, village halls and community centres. The Department which pays the grants in Scotland is the Scottish Home Department—not the Scottish Education Department. Such schemes, however, often receive assistance from education authorities as well, and the two Departments work closely together to avoid any conflict or overlap.

[1] See footnote 2 on page 155.

CHAPTER XIX

Industry and Transport

THE general public always find it difficult to understand why the administrative civil servant is necessary at all. It is an old argument, and one which there is no space to reopen here, that the doctor should run the health service, the teacher our educational system, the engineer our water supply and drainage and so on. This book may perhaps have helped to show, first, that most disparate services do in fact present a number of problems that are essentially similar because they are administrative problems, and secondly, that to hammer out a comprehensive policy from the advice of a variety of technical experts and advisory bodies is an administrative task. Each service has, of course, its own special problems, which only the expert can solve, but the administrator must reach at least an elementary understanding of them.

Since its formation in 1939, when the Home Department took over the work of the Fisheries Board, its officers have had their versatility tested in this way by the addition to the Department's responsibilities, first, of electricity and then, very recently, of roads. The first of these in particular has demanded a mastery of at least such basic facts as what a megawatt is and what 'load factor' means, but, once the essential minimum of knowledge has been acquired, it will be seen that there is a great deal in the work that is not radically different from the Department's more traditional duties.

FISHERIES

There is a long tradition in Scotland of separate legislation and separate administration for fishery matters. The origins of the Fishery Board for Scotland, whose functions the Department took over when they were transferred to the Secretary of State in 1939, go back to 1726; and Scottish fisheries legislation goes back farther still, to Acts of the Scots Parliament. To look at these old Acts, incidentally, will correct the ideas of those who think that for Parliament to concern itself with the minor details of the operation of an industry is a degenerate modern development; long before we had a police force, long before the State showed any interest in housing or public health, Parliament legislated at great length on the subject of fish.

It may seem odd, now that responsibility for fisheries is vested in the Secretary of State, that the subject should be administered in Scotland through the Scottish Home Department when in England it is associated, through the Ministry of Agriculture, Fisheries and Food, with the other principal food-producing industry, agriculture. There is, however, no necessary connection between agriculture and fisheries, except that we eat the produce of both, and no logical reason why the two should be dealt with by the same Department of State. The case for leaving fisheries with the Home Department was recently reconsidered by the Royal Commission for Scottish Affairs, and it did not recommend any change.

The fisheries work of the Department occupies two administrative divisions and a great part of the time of an under secretary, and its ramifications are very wide. There are nowadays two statutory bodies, the Herring Industry Board and the White Fish Authority, concerned with the organisation and assistance of the two main branches of the sea fishing industry in Great Britain, and a good deal of the Department's work is with those two bodies, for whose appointment and supervision the Secretary of State is responsible jointly with the Minister of Agriculture, Fisheries and Food and the Home Secretary. (The White Fish Authority, incidentally, has a Committee for Scotland and Northern Ireland, whose Chairman acts as the Deputy-Chairman of the Authority.) Within the spheres of interest of the two authorities, the central departments have much administrative work to do. They provide, by means of a subsidy to catchers, the direct assistance which is at present available to both branches of the fishing industry; they advance to both bodies the money they require for making grants and loans for the provision of new fishing boats; and they also give assistance to the Herring Industry Board and the White Fish Authority for other purposes. Various actions of the authorities require the formal approval of the Secretary of State, and this adds to the need for close and regular contact between them and the fisheries departments.

Herring fishing is a more important part of the Scottish economy than of the English, whereas more white fishing is done from English ports than from Scottish. A working arrangement has been made corresponding to the balance of interest in the two countries, whereby the Home Department works particularly closely with the Herring Industry Board (whose headquarters are in Edinburgh) and the Ministry of Agriculture, Fisheries and Food with the White Fish Authority (whose main offices are in London). Government advances to the Herring Industry Board are made from the vote of the Home Department, and those to the White Fish Authority from that of the Ministry. But each of the fishery departments must, of course, keep itself informed of the state of the industry as a whole—for which their ministers are jointly responsible—and the departments work together in any major matters that involve discussion either with the statutory authorities or with various branches of the industry. The fact that there is a Scottish Committee of the White Fish Authority means that any particularly Scottish difficulties in that industry come to notice quickly.

Fishing in Scotland is carried on partly from one or two major ports (such as Aberdeen and Granton) and partly from scores of smaller harbours strung around the whole coastline of the mainland and the islands. The port that has an adequate harbour in a good state of repair is fortunate, for nowadays the cost of building, improving and maintaining these harbours is very great. They belong for the most part to local authorities and harbour trusts, whose resources are slender and who are constantly finding, as a result of storms or simply from the wear and tear caused by the ceaseless onslaught of the sea, that they are called upon to face heavy expenditure on repairs. To help them, the Department makes money available by means of grants and loans; each scheme has first to be carefully examined to ensure that it is necessary and well conceived and that the local body responsible cannot reasonably be expected to bear the full cost itself. In considering the technical aspects of these projects, the Department can call on the advice of harbour engineers from the engineering staff of the Department of Health. The Home Department also maintains two dredgers for work on Scottish fishery harbours; and, if the harbour authorities are unable to pay the ordinary charges, dredging may be carried out at a reduced charge—or even free.

The Scottish fishing fleet consists at present of about 3,300 boats manned by some 11,700 fishermen. Twenty-five fishery officers at the main ports (grouped in seven areas, each under an inspector) keep in touch with these men to give them whatever help is possible and to supply the Department with the statistical and other information needed for scientific and for administrative purposes. The coast is shared between them, so that every fisherman and every fishery harbour is in the district of one of them. These officers have quite a long history; they were originally appointed to inspect herrings and to apply the Crown Brand to barrels of cured herring, but they have survived to fulfil a much wider function and, as the link between the central government and the men who catch or who market the fish, they are now an integral and essential part of the Department's organisation.

The Department maintains a small fleet of fishery cruisers. In general, trawling and seining are not permitted within the three-mile coastal area, and the duty of the cruisers is to enforce this law for the protection of Scottish inshore fisheries and of the breeding grounds around the Scottish coast. In English and Welsh waters, this work of fisheries protection is done by the Royal Navy. The Navy's fishery protection fleet does usually have one ship in Scottish waters, but in the main the enforcement of the law against poaching there is undertaken by the Department's own vessels.

Both the Department and the Ministry have substantial scientific staffs who work partly in laboratories and partly in research vessels; the Department has a laboratory at Aberdeen and four research ships, and there is also important research on freshwater fisheries conducted in laboratories at Pitlochry and in various rivers and lochs throughout the country. The research was formerly financed in part from the Development Fund, and the Advisory Committee on Fisheries Research appointed by the Development Commission advises the Department on the programme of work and ensures that it is properly co-ordinated with research carried on by other organisations financed from public funds. The connection between fisheries research and the fishing industry is necessarily less direct than that between agricultural research and the farmers, because the raw material moves uncontrolled beneath the waves and arranges its own production. But the accumulation of knowledge about the habits and movements of fish will, in the long run, benefit the fishermen of the world. The need to avoid over-fishing is among the lessons that research teaches, and like many lessons, it is neither very popular nor very quickly apprehended.

It is, in fact, being increasingly recognised that the need to conserve the stocks of fish in the various fishing grounds of the world is a matter calling for international co-operation and there is a permanent international commission on the subject of over-fishing. There is also an international organisation for the proper co-ordination of fisheries research,[1] and whaling and such matters as the delineation of coastal limits also give rise periodically to discussion between the nations. Fisheries administration thus brings the Home Department into the world of international conferences, since these international problems are dealt with jointly by the English and Scottish fisheries departments, and some of their officers, indeed, spend a substantial proportion of their time abroad.

Freshwater fisheries are also an important part of the Scottish economy. The commercial salmon catch alone is worth probably £1 million a year, and both salmon and trout angling have a considerable indirect value, as a means of recreation and as an attraction to tourists. The Secretary of State has various responsibilities for freshwater fisheries—for example, for the control of disease and for the regulation of close seasons—and the Department advises him on these matters and, of course, on any legislation that may be necessary. To help it in carrying out these duties, the Department is advised by an inspector who keeps himself informed of the condition of the various fisheries throughout the country.

[1] The International Council for the Exploration of the Sea.

ELECTRICITY

The Secretary of State and the Home Department have been concerned with the electricity industry in Scotland since 1943, when the North of Scotland Hydro-Electric Board was established to develop the water-power resources of the Highlands and Islands and to give a supply of electricity outside the areas of other authorised suppliers. In 1948 the Board was made responsible for the whole work of generating and distributing electricity in the North of Scotland, and the Electricity Reorganisation (Scotland) Act, 1954, created the South of Scotland Electricity Board to take over the same functions in the South from the former British Electricity Authority. The responsibilities for Scottish electricity transferred by the 1954 Act from the Minister of Fuel and Power to the Secretary of State fell, naturally, to the Home Department.

As a result of these changes, the administrative structure for electricity has been somewhat simplified. There are now two all-purpose electricity boards in Scotland, each appointed by the Secretary of State and each responsible to him in the same way as the electricity authorities—both central and in the areas—in England and Wales are responsible to the Minister of Power. The Home Department is concerned with the general programme of development of the two Scottish boards and with the sanctioning of their borrowing, and it has a number of other duties in relation to them. Various matters are governed by regulations made by the Secretary of State, and there are others, such as new hydro-electric schemes and steam generating stations, which require his formal approval or confirmation; he requires advice on the appointment of members to the consultative councils, and to the special amenity and fisheries committees which advise on those aspects of electricity schemes; and there is a good deal of other work. Over and above these formal duties, the Department must keep in close and informal touch with the boards and their officers, because it is only in this way that a relationship of mutual trust can be established and that the Department can equip itself to advise ministers competently on electricity matters when they have to deal with them in Parliament or elsewhere.

The Department works in close co-operation with the Ministry of Power, because, though Scotland has its own problems—particularly in large-scale hydro-electric development, to which there is no close English parallel—there are many other matters in which the Government must maintain a common policy throughout Great Britain.

The separate administration of electricity supply in Scotland is of interest not only because it adds to the Secretary of State's responsibilities a further one of a quite novel kind, but because the structure of the industry is now different from that in England and Wales.

M

Each of the Scottish Boards is responsible in its own area for both the generation and the supply of electricity, whereas in England generation remains the responsibility of a central body and supply is the responsibility of separate area boards. The new Scottish arrangements are of interest also because there are in Scotland special opportunities of exploiting methods of generation other than the traditional one by use of coal. The use of water power has already been carried a long way; and research into the use of peat has reached the stage at which a pilot generating plant, burning peat instead of coal, is being erected. Scotland may also provide special opportunities of operating nuclear generating stations in conjunction with hydro-electric stations. Work on two nuclear stations belonging to the Atomic Energy Authority is already under way and another is planned by the South of Scotland Electricity Board. These stations will generate throughout the 24 hours. The real problem of electricity supply is, of course, the peak load; and already hydro-electric power —which can be turned off and on at will—is helping notably to solve it. If, however, it becomes possible, as it should, to use the electricity produced at nuclear generating stations when ordinary demand is low —for example, during the night—to pump water into storage reservoirs, the amount of hydro-electric power available at times of peak loads could be greatly increased.

ROADS

The principal administrative change recommended by the Royal Commission on Scottish Affairs was that the ministerial responsibility for highways, bridges and ferries in Scotland should be transferred from the Minister of Transport and Civil Aviation to the Secretary of State. This recommendation was accepted by the Government, and the Department took over this work from the Ministry on 1st April, 1956.

The main new responsibilities which the Secretary of State has acquired are the planning of the programme for the maintenance and improvement of trunk roads and classified roads—which involves problems of selection beside which the judgment of Paris was a simple matter—and the payment of grants to the highway authorities. A new division of the Department has been created to handle this administrative work and the Department has also taken over the Ministry's financial staff in Scotland. In order to provide the Secretary of State and the Department with the necessary technical advice, the Ministry's road engineers in Scotland have been seconded to the Department, under a Scottish chief road engineer.

The old Scottish Office did have certain limited responsibilities for roads before 1919, and in more recent years, while the responsibility still lay with the Ministry of Transport and Civil Aviation, the Home

Department was forced into a premature familiarity with the livelier aspects of highway administration, such as the controversy about the Forth Road Bridge, the progress of the scheme for the improvement of roads in the Crofter Counties, and the discussions about the expanded highways programme which was announced in 1955. There is, however, a great deal which is completely new to the Department in the work which has now fallen to it. It has, for example, to examine in detail the schemes which the highway authorities (that is, the county councils and the town councils of large burghs) prepare for major improvements or new work on classified roads, and it prepares similar schemes for trunk roads in co-operation with the highway authorities who act as agents for carrying out the work on such roads. It has to deal with the acquisition of land for the road programme, and it examines the development proposals under the town and country planning legislation which the Department of Health refers to it, to see how they affect the highway system. There is a good deal of new work in the negotiation of agreements, and the Department also has to examine the local authorities' proposals for the regulation of traffic and for the closure of roads.

The Royal Commission's recommendation was based primarily on the view that there would be advantages in having highways administration and the problems of highway authorities dealt with in Scotland by a department which was familiar with the Scottish scene rather than by the Ministry of Transport and Civil Aviation in London. It will be the Home Department's job to justify this view.

MACBRAYNE'S SERVICES

Another activity on the transport side is the Home Department's interest in the steamer services given to the Western Highlands and Islands by Messrs. David MacBrayne, Ltd. Many of the Western Isles would in all probability lack any regular steamer service if Government assistance (which amounts under the present ten-year agreement with MacBrayne's to an annual subsidy, subject to adjustment, of £360,000) were not given. It will be seen from this that, in the development programme for the Hebrides and Western Highlands, MacBrayne's services have a very considerable part to play.

The way governmental concern in MacBrayne's affairs is shared between the Ministry of Transport and the Scottish Home Department is an example of devolution to a Scottish department of affairs which can best be handled in Scotland and retention of other matters in the hands of the United Kingdom department. The formal agreement between the Government and MacBrayne's is in the name of the Minister of Transport and the reviews each year, under the agreement, to adjust the subsidy upwards or downwards are carried out in the first place by Ministry of Transport accountants. But the main stages of the review are the joint concern of the Ministry of Transport and the Home Department and the annual subsidy itself is carried on the Home Department's vote, which means that it falls to the Secretary of State to defend in Parliament the extent of the subsidy. Similarly, in everyday working, the Home Department and the Ministry of Transport have an equal concern in such matters as the approval of freight rates and passenger fares; and while the Ministry of Transport takes the lead in marine matters, it is the Home Department which takes a special interest in the part that MacBrayne's services play in the Highlands and Islands development programme. In this task they are, of course, assisted by the Advisory Panel on the Highlands and Islands.

The Home Department is also concerned with Government assistance to a number of local sea transport services elsewhere in the Highlands and Islands.

CHAPTER XX

Scotland's Minister

IT has been mentioned at intervals in this book—rather, perhaps, with the effect on the reader that repeated references to a treat in store have on a child—that the Secretary of State has certain non-statutory and to some extent unforeseeable functions as 'Scotland's Minister'. The time has now come to say something about these mysterious duties, which were described by the Gilmour Committee as 'penumbral', perhaps because they are carried out in that twilight world where more than one Government department operates and the responsibilities of each are difficult to distinguish.

The subjects that come up vary from day to day, from flint arrows to guided missiles, and from the harvesting of seaweed to the encouragement of electronics, and, when they do come up, they are troublesome. It could hardly be otherwise. People seldom write to the Secretary of State to say how well things are going. When they are not going well, he is immediately called upon to act. If he fails in his efforts, the ensuing misfortune is naturally attributed to him. If he succeeds, he comforts himself with the knowledge that he has done something for his fellow-countrymen, and marvels at the reticence of their appreciation. The departments endeavour to share these feelings.

The 'penumbra' is not easily described, since it may involve any matter in which Scottish interests in the widest sense are affected, but, in recent years, the major part of the work has come to be concerned with the economic condition of Scotland as a whole, and of the Highlands in particular. The custom has grown up that an annual debate on the state of the Scottish economy takes place in the House of Commons during the estimates season, and this has helped to give these rather shadowy responsibilities a more discernible and precise form. In order to be able to brief the Secretary of State for debates and for discussions with his Cabinet colleagues and with other people about Scottish economic questions, the Scottish Home Department has to co-operate very closely with the Board of Trade, the Ministry of Supply, the Ministry of Labour and National Service, the Admiralty and other departments concerned with industry and employment. Its interest in Scottish economic affairs as a whole also makes it the natural channel of communication between the Secretary of State and the Scottish Council (Development and Industry), the Scottish Tourist Board and the Scottish Board for Industry, and it is regularly represented at the meetings of all these.

The relationship of the Department with the Scottish Council is a very special one, and one of the most interesting examples of that partnership of official and voluntary effort which is common in modern administration. The Council is not a Government creature making noises acceptable to the Government through an apparently independent mouth. It is an independent body maintaining itself by public subscription and representing all the interests concerned in Scottish economic affairs—the chambers of commerce, the Scottish T.U.C., the banks, the local authorities and many influential private individuals. The Council has been most active since 1945 in stimulating developments to increase the general prosperity of the country, and, in particular, in promoting a better balance in the Scottish industrial structure, which has traditionally been rather underdeveloped on the side of light industry. The Council has been particularly successful in attracting American industry; something like 80 per cent. of the American firms which have settled in Great Britain since the war have come to Scotland.

The aims of the Scottish Council and the Secretary of State are largely similar, and, as the Council has normally used the Home Department as its channel of communication with the Secretary of State and indeed with the Government as a whole, it has been most necessary that relations between the Council and the Department should be close and friendly. The Department is represented at the meetings of the Council and of its committees, which are in fact often held in St. Andrew's House, and, when the Council wishes to meet a Minister other than a Scottish one, the Department arranges the meeting and the Secretary of State or one of the other Scottish Ministers is usually present.

This special relationship with the Scottish Council has involved the Home Department in discussing with other Government departments many matters for which the Secretary of State has no ministerial responsibility. For example, the vigorous interest taken by the Council in the reorganisation of the Scottish transport system under the 1953 Transport Act—an interest reflected in many other quarters and in both Houses of Parliament—meant that the Department had to discuss the Council's ideas in detail with the Ministry of Transport and Civil Aviation, while the Secretary of State had to be prepared to discuss transport matters both in the Cabinet and in the House of Commons. In the same way, the Council's untiring efforts to bring new industry to Scotland have involved the Department in frequent talks and a great deal of correspondence with the Board of Trade and other departments. Yet the only statutory recognition of the Secretary of State's concern with commerce and industry in Scotland is his association with the President of the Board of Trade in any revision of the boundaries of the Scottish Development Areas.

The relationship of the Scottish Tourist Board with the Department is very similar, except that, as the Board's interests are more specialised, the range of contacts required is narrower and the work involved is much less. When the Board has any submission to make to the Government, it usually does so through the Secretary of State, and amicable working relations have been established between the Board's officers and the Department.

The Scottish Council and the Scottish Tourist Board give the Secretary of State the benefit of their advice on matters which are not formally his responsibility, but in which he must take an interest because they concern the welfare of Scotland as a whole. The position in the Highlands is rather different. A great deal that goes on there—agriculture, road-making, hydro-electric development, housing, fishing, water supply, forestry and much else—*is* his formal responsibility. Each of these activities—including the work of two bodies of special importance to the Highlands, the North of Scotland Hydro-Electric Board and the Crofters Commission—has already been dealt with in its proper place, and to deal with them all over again in a separate chapter on the Highlands would be to admit that one was bewitched by those often-repeated words, 'the Highland Problem'. But there are certain general difficulties which arise because the Highlands, like the rest of Scotland, are making the transition from an old-fashioned to a modern economy. The difficulties are more acute in the Highlands because distances are greater, the population smaller, natural resources often less abundant. Many parts of the Highlands are in fact adapting themselves with remarkable success; other remote communities that have not the natural resources to support their present level of population show the distressing symptoms of a gradually declining and ageing rural population. To ease the process of adaptation and development, and as far as possible to arrest the process of decline, are matters that must be of concern to 'Scotland's Minister'. In addition to the various consultative bodies whose advice to the Secretary of State covers the whole country, he has as his official adviser on Highland affairs a special body known as the Advisory Panel on the Highlands and Islands, whose duty is to watch every aspect of Government activity in the Highlands.

The Highlands Panel has been in existence since 1947. Its members, who are appointed by the Secretary of State, include representatives of the Highlands and Islands county councils (that is, of the seven crofter counties, for Perthshire, though it may appear as part of the Highlands to tourists, is not so for administrative purposes), Members of Parliament, representatives of the Scottish Council and other persons chosen by the Secretary of State for their knowledge of the Highlands. From month to month throughout the year, groups of members work as separate committees on subjects of special importance and travel throughout the Highlands and Islands to get first-hand information on the subjects they are discussing. The full Panel meets four or five times a year, usually in Inverness. These meetings, like meetings of the groups, are attended by assessors from the principal Government departments concerned. The secretariat is provided by the Scottish Home Department.

The Highland Panel, with its all-embracing concern for the welfare of one part of the country, has for the first time enabled the Highlands and Islands to speak with something like a common voice. The rail, air and steamer services to the Highlands, freight charges, the road construction programme, forestry, industrial development, the difficulties of the fishing industry, whatever is a live issue in the Highlands, or may become one, engages the Panel's attention or may be referred to the Panel by the Secretary of State for its views. The Panel of course works in close collaboration with the Crofters Commission in its task of reviving the crofting areas of the Highlands and Islands.

With the help of the Panel, a programme of Highland development was prepared and published by the Government in 1950. This programme was not merely a general declaration of policy; it included details of a variety of work—on roads, piers, fishery harbours, water supply schemes and other projects—completion of which was regarded as likely to benefit the Highlands. The actual details of the programme have naturally altered with the years, as work has been completed, and as circumstances have changed the relative urgency of the various schemes. But the programme remains, and an important part of the work of the Panel has been to watch over its execution. To assist the Panel in this task, to keep under review the work of the various agencies concerned with Highland development and to keep Ministers in touch with the current problems, a committee of departmental representatives meets from month to month in St. Andrew's House. In addition to dealing with problems as they arise, this Highlands Committee provides progress reports for Ministers and for the Panel. In this way the inter-departmental committee can bring to the notice of Ministers or of the Panel any point where the advance seems to be held up or any matters which require special consideration.

The general position, then, is that Highland development is furthered by the local authorities, by Government departments and by a number of agencies appointed or assisted by the Government[1]— to which has recently been added the Crofters Commission. General oversight of what is being done, and of all the multifarious problems that arise, is effected by the Highland Panel, by the St. Andrew's House Highlands Committee and, especially for the crofting areas of the Highlands, by the Crofters Commission itself.

This brief account of the Secretary of State's functions as 'Scotland's Minister' cannot possibly deal with them all or do more than

[1] See the Report of the Royal Commission on Scottish Affairs. Cmd. 9212, page 82.

indicate the machinery by means of which he acts. But it may have been enough to show that this part of his duties is something quite different from the usual work of a departmental Minister. The Royal Commission went so far as to say that 'he is in a unique position in that, advised by such representative organisations as the Scottish Council (Development and Industry), the Scottish Board for Industry, and the Advisory Panel on the Highlands and Islands, he can claim to represent an agreed Scottish viewpoint over a very wide field'. One can agree with this, while adding respectfully that any Secretary of State who hoped on that account to escape criticism in that very wide field would be sadly disappointed.

SCOTTISH HOME DEPARTMENT
Organisation, 1957

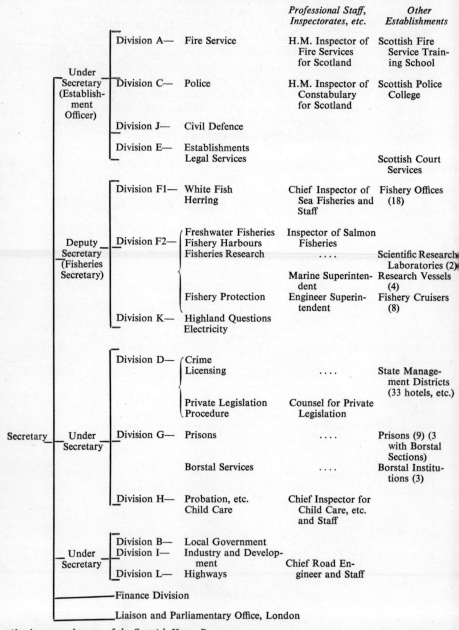

			Professional Staff, Inspectorates, etc.	Other Establishments
Under Secretary (Establishment Officer)	Division A—	Fire Service	H.M. Inspector of Fire Services for Scotland	Scottish Fire Service Training School
	Division C—	Police	H.M. Inspector of Constabulary for Scotland	Scottish Police College
	Division J—	Civil Defence		
	Division E—	Establishments Legal Services		Scottish Court Services
Deputy Secretary (Fisheries Secretary)	Division F1—	White Fish Herring	Chief Inspector of Sea Fisheries and Staff	Fishery Offices (18)
	Division F2—	Freshwater Fisheries Fishery Harbours	Inspector of Salmon Fisheries	
		Fisheries Research	....	Scientific Research Laboratories (2)
			Marine Superintendent	Research Vessels (4)
		Fishery Protection	Engineer Superintendent	Fishery Cruisers (8)
	Division K—	Highland Questions Electricity		
Under Secretary	Division D—	Crime Licensing	....	State Management Districts (33 hotels, etc.)
		Private Legislation Procedure	Counsel for Private Legislation	
	Division G—	Prisons	....	Prisons (9) (3 with Borstal Sections)
		Borstal Services	....	Borstal Institutions (3)
	Division H—	Probation, etc. Child Care	Chief Inspector for Child Care, etc. and Staff	
Under Secretary	Division B—	Local Government		
	Division I—	Industry and Development		
	Division L—	Highways	Chief Road Engineer and Staff	

Secretary —

—Finance Division

—Liaison and Parliamentary Office, London

Also borne on the vote of the Scottish Home Department:

Solicitor's Office*   Scottish Information Office*   Statistician to the Secretary of State†

* Serves the Scottish Departments and certain U.K. Departments in Scotland.
† Serves the Scottish Departments.

PART SIX

Other Responsibilities of the Secretary of State

Joint Ministerial Responsibilities: The Forestry Commission and the Crown Estate Commissioners

THE British approach to public administration has always been empirical rather than doctrinaire. For many of the activities of Government in Scotland, the Secretary of State is, as we have seen, himself responsible to Parliament; for others, discussed in other volumes in this Series, a United Kingdom or Great Britain Minister is responsible. But there may be a middle way, more suited to certain kinds of State activity—a condominium under which the Secretary of State and an English Minister are jointly responsible for policy in Great Britain and separately concerned with matters peculiar to their own territory. In the two examples of this arrangement discussed in the present chapter, the administration of forestry and of the Crown Estate, executive responsibility has been placed by Parliament in the hands of a body of Commissioners.

Other examples of joint ministerial responsibility have already been referred to, but it may be convenient again to mention them here. The Secretary of State's interest, shared with the Minister of Agriculture, Fisheries and Food and the Home Secretary, in the Herring Industry Board and the White Fish Authority, has been discussed in Chapter XIX and the same chapter also explains the way responsibility for steamer services in the Western Highlands and Islands is divided between him and the Minister of Transport and Civil Aviation. The scheduling of Development Areas in Scotland is a function exercised by the Secretary of State jointly with the President of the Board of Trade, and along with a number of his ministerial colleagues he is a member of Committees of the Privy Council concerned with agricultural research, nature conservation, medical research and university affairs.

THE FORESTRY COMMISSION

'Jock, when ye hae naething else to do, ye may be ay sticking in a tree; it will be growing, Jock, when ye're sleeping.' (Sir Walter Scott, *The Heart of Midlothian*.)

Before 1889, although there had been much wise and far-seeing private planting in Scotland, and a Scottish Arboricultural Society

181

(founded in 1854) had been advocating for some time a national policy of afforestation, there was little or no Government activity in forestry. In that year, forestry became one of the subjects assigned to the newly-formed Great Britain Board of Agriculture, and in 1912, when the Scottish Board of Agriculture was created, it took over responsibility for forestry in Scotland. During the 1914–18 war, so many trees were felled that it became obvious that private planting could not be relied on, or reasonably expected, to make good the losses and to undertake the necessary expansion of the industry, so in 1919 Parliament passed an Act under which forestry, which had previously been treated rather perhaps as a poor relation of agriculture, became the concern of a newly-created Forestry Commission. The Commission was given the general duty—which extended to the whole of Great Britain—of promoting afforestation and the production and supply of timber, and of encouraging, with help and advice, forestry in privately-owned woodlands. Its powers included a power to acquire and plant land. The main functions of the Commission were in fact essentially quite different from those of the agricultural departments. The difference was clearly described by a Member of Parliament during the Second Reading debate on the 1945 Forestry Act:[1]

The agricultural officials are there to regulate an industry which is under private management. Theirs is an administrative function. The Forestry Commission, on the other hand, has a great executive function of running the industry of growing trees and producing timber.

In fact, the Forestry Commission has some of the characteristics of a nationalised industry, and its creation thus raised, as early as 1919, some of the problems that are still under discussion, of the extent to which a nationalised industry should be held accountable by Parliament for its detailed actions. In 1919 no Minister was made responsible for the Commission's work, but between 1919 and 1945 there were Members of Parliament on the Commission and they spoke for it in the House of Commons—a rather vague method of providing for parliamentary representation without ministerial control, which had been used several times with administrative boards in the 1840s and 1850s. In 1945, when the inroads of a Second World War on the national stocks of timber had once again called attention to the need for an energetic policy of afforestation, and another Forestry Act was being passed, the opportunity was taken to alter the system.

As now constituted, the Forestry Commission consists of a chairman and not more than nine other members, of whom three must have special knowledge and experience of forestry, one must be a scientist with a technical knowledge of forestry, and one must have special knowledge and experience of the timber trade. There are

[1] *Hansard*, vol. 410, 1944–45, col. 1759.

always members on the Commission with special knowledge and experience of each of the three countries, England, Scotland and Wales. In carrying out their functions, the Commissioners are required by the Act of 1945 to 'comply with such directions as may be given to them by the Ministers', and the Minister of Agriculture, Fisheries and Food and the Secretary of State are jointly responsible for the Commission's general policy and answer for it in Parliament. The Secretary of State is, however, separately concerned with, and acts individually in, forestry matters affecting Scotland only, and land acquired under the Forestry Acts in Scotland is vested in him. It should be emphasised that his officers in the Department of Agriculture for Scotland give no advice to him on forestry matters; they may comment on the agricultural aspect of forestry proposals, but that is all. The unusual structure of the Scottish Office does, however, give the Secretary of State one advantage when he has forestry questions to consider; he is able to seek assistance from the two senior officers, the Permanent Under-Secretary of State and the Assistant Under-Secretary, who work outside his four departments.

The Forestry Commissioners normally meet in London, but they have National Committees for Scotland, for England and for Wales. Questions of general policy are reserved to the Commission itself and decisions on land acquisitions, finance and establishment matters are taken by it, but control of the actual work of forestry is as far as possible devolved to the National Committees. The Scottish Committee consists of those Commissioners who represent Scottish interests, and up to three outside members, and it usually meets once a month in Scotland during the week prior to the Commissioners' monthly meeting. The senior permanent officer of the Commission in Scotland, the Director of Forestry for Scotland, attends all the meetings of the Committee. The Director has his headquarters in the Scottish office of the Commission in Drumsheugh Gardens, Edinburgh, and below him, Scotland is divided into four Conservancies, each in charge of a Conservator, with the necessary technical, professional and administrative staff.

The word 'Conservancy', which the Commission uses rather than 'area' or 'division' to describe its regional organisation, carries a misleading suggestion that the Commission is content to save existing woodlands from injudicious felling. In fact, its principal aim is a much more positive one, to be 'ay sticking in a tree', and for Britain to have by the end of this century 5 million acres of productive woodlands. New plantings by the Commission and private owners have brought the total area of existing woodlands under proper management half-way to this target; Scotland's share of this is over 1 million acres. To complete the programme nearly $2\frac{1}{2}$ million acres not at present bearing trees will have to be planted, mostly by the Commission, and it is estimated that nearly half this acreage of new forest will probably be in Scotland. The acquisition of enough suitable land for a programme of this magnitude is a formidable undertaking.

At the one extreme there are large areas of barren land which the Commission could probably acquire without difficulty, but which would not grow a worthwhile crop of trees; at the other there is fertile hill grazing land which it would be delighted to acquire, but which in the national interest ought to remain in agricultural use. Between this Scylla and Charybdis, the Commission steers a difficult course. All proposals to acquire land for forestry are discussed by the Scottish Director with the Department of Agriculture in order that the agricultural point of view should be fully considered. When agreement is reached, the acquisitions proposed are reported by the National Committee to the Commissioners for their approval; in the event of disagreement, the proposals are put to the Secretary of State for decision.

Just as one may be compelled at an auction sale, in order to buy something one wants, to take a number of miscellaneous objects for which one has no use, the Forestry Commission may find that its plantable land is made up in the same lot, as it were, with rocky hills, lochs or farm land. The arrangement by which the Department of Agriculture takes over the management of farms acquired by the Commission in this way has already been described in Chapter IV: the wilder country is not wasted either, for out of the land in its ownership, much of which is open and unplanted, the Commission has established eight National Forest Parks, of which four, the Argyll, Glen Trool, Glenmore and Queen Elizabeth (Loch Ard) Parks, are in Scotland, and a fifth, the Border Park, extends across the Border into Roxburghshire.

The Forestry Commission has an important economic part to play by providing employment in rural areas, especially in the Scottish Highlands. The Report of the Committee of Enquiry into Crofting Conditions[1] emphasised very strongly the value of forestry as an auxiliary source of employment, additional to normal crofting activities. After considering the Committee's recommendations on the subject, the Secretary of State announced in the House of Commons, on 14th July, 1955, that the Government had authorised the Forestry Commission to extend its activities in the crofting areas, even although that might require the Commission to plant on land that would give a smaller return than it would normally expect. The Commission was asked to embark on a new scheme with the object of planting 25,000 to 35,000 acres in the crofting areas between 1955 and 1965. The Commission is pushing ahead with this new programme as quickly as it can obtain suitable land, and it is hoped that the result will be to bring additional employment to districts where it is very much needed.

[1] Cmd. 9081.

It would be beyond the scope of this book to describe the manifold activities of the Commission, all of which are part of its principal business of growing trees, but it would be misleading not to remind the reader that the organisation described exists to produce wood and not paper. When the Commission has acquired its plantable land, the work of afforestation falls naturally into three stages. First, the land must be prepared and planted and the forest established. It will need to be fenced to keep out rabbits, sheep and deer, and, especially where the soil is covered with peat, it will have to be drained. This is now mostly done mechanically, with crawler tractors and heavy ploughs. Young trees, grown in the Commission's own nurseries from home or imported seed, are then planted. The second stage, which begins when the trees are about 18 years old and may last for some 50 years, is one of thinning and maintenance; the thinning process produces considerable quantities of material which the Commission sells for such purposes as fencing, pitwood for the mines, or for manufacture into wallboards or sawn timber. Lastly, as each plantation reaches maturity, there is the period of felling and of regeneration, and the whole cycle begins again. Throughout the life of the trees, they must be protected by a well-organised system of fire precautions. Patient and detailed research into choice of species, rate of growth, damage by insects and fungi, and all the other problems of forestry is carried on in the field all over Scotland, as well as in the Commission's research station at Alice Holt in Surrey.

It is perhaps worth mentioning specially that the National Committees are responsible for determining what houses are needed for their workers and where they should be built; in some counties, local authorities have helped in the provision of houses. And something should be said of the Commission's work in relation to private forestry, in which its functions are not executive but more akin to the administrative functions of one of the agricultural departments in regulating and assisting an industry in private ownership. For example, the Commission promotes and encourages good forestry by such means as the Dedication Scheme, under which it makes financial grants (which may be either on an acreage basis or 25 per cent. of approved net expenditure) in return for an undertaking by the owner to manage his woodlands for the production of timber on lines approved by the Commission, and to employ skilled supervision. Private forestry is of great and increasing importance; during recent years more than one-quarter of the planting of forests has been carried out by private owners. The local Conservators also grant the licences required in accordance with the Forestry Act, 1951, for fellings by private owners. They do this in accordance with general principles laid down by the Commissioners for Great Britain as a whole.

N

THE CROWN ESTATE COMMISSIONERS

This book is published at a time when an alteration has recently been made in the administration of the Crown Estate in Great Britain and Northern Ireland. It comes too late to describe in detail the working of the old organisation. It comes, equally, too early to describe the new system in operation, for the Act which set it up, the Crown Estate Act, 1956, only came into effect on the 14th December of that year, and it is still therefore at the running-in stage.

The Crown Estate represents the ancient hereditary possessions of the Crown and includes not only a large acreage of rural land but also very valuable urban property, much of the foreshore around the coasts of the United Kingdom, some mineral and other rights, and a portfolio of Government securities. The Scottish part of the Estate consists of rural land in the counties of Banff, Caithness, Moray, Perth and Stirling extending to nearly 106,000 acres. Since 1760 the hereditary revenues of the Crown have been placed at Parliament's disposal, and the management of the Crown Estate therefore entails a dual responsibility—to the Sovereign for preserving, and if possible augmenting, the capital value of the Estate; and to Parliament for paying into the Exchequer each year the highest possible net revenue.

For many years these duties were carried out by 'Commissioners of Woods, Forests and Land Revenues', or, as they were called after a change in title in 1924, 'the Commissioners of Crown Lands'. The land revenues of Scotland were placed under their management between 1832 and 1835, when the Barons of Exchequer,[1] in whom the management had previously been vested, ceased to exist. The President of the Board of Agriculture and Fisheries—as the office then was—was made a Commissioner in 1906 and the Secretary of State for Scotland in 1943, and between that year and 1955 there were three Commissioners of Crown Lands, the two Ministers and a Permanent Commissioner who was a civil servant. A Committee under the chairmanship of Sir Malcolm Trustram Eve, Bt., G.B.E., Q.C., which had been appointed to consider the organisation for the administration of Crown Lands, made its report in 1955.[2] One of the principal recommendations of the committee was that a strong managing board was desirable, and the 1956 Act therefore provided for the setting up of a new body of not more than eight Crown Estate Commissioners to manage the Crown Estate in the United Kingdom. Sir Malcolm Trustram Eve, who became an additional Commissioner of Crown Lands in 1955, has been appointed First Crown Estate Commissioner and is chairman. A Second Commissioner, who is deputy chairman, and six other Commissioners have also been appointed. The new Commissioners took up their duties on 14th December, 1956. One of

[1] See page 198.
[2] Cmd. 9483.

the Commissioners is a Scottish Commissioner who will have special responsibilities in relation to the Scottish properties which form part of the Estate.

The Act of 1956 follows the recommendations of the Eve Committee in making other changes, perhaps the most important of which concerns responsibility to Parliament. Whereas previously there were ministerial Commissioners and the Treasury held a general power of direction over the Commissioners, the Act made the Lord Privy Seal and the Secretary of State answerable to Parliament for the Crown Estate by transferring this general power of direction to them. In recognition of the fact that the Crown Estate is the property of the Queen, the Act requires the Commissioners to make their annual report to Her Majesty, as well as to lay a copy before each House of Parliament.

CHAPTER XXII

The Smaller Scottish Departments and Offices

AN attempt to show the administration of Scotland in the form of a diagram would produce something rather like a map of the Holy Roman Empire in an historical atlas. The greater part of the territory would be divided between the four main departments—each of them, as we have seen, standing in the same relationship to the Secretary of State—but scattered among them would be the highly-coloured principalities of a number of smaller departments and offices, one or two independent of the Secretary of State and the St. Andrew's House departments, and others coming within his jurisdiction for various limited purposes. Although they do not form part of the Scottish Office proper, this book would hardly be complete without mention of these offices, some of which are of great antiquity.

We cannot examine these bodies and offices together, since there are few points of similarity in their organisation and functions. Their independence is partly at least due to this very fact, that each of them is unique in its problems and its duties. The main feature which they have in common is that they are fortunate enough to be able to go on with their work without troubling Ministers and without, as a general rule, becoming the subject of political or public controversy. If, however, any question about their operations arose in Parliament, it would fall to the Secretary of State to answer it.

THE GENERAL BOARD OF CONTROL

No specific reference was made in Chapter XIII to the position of the mentally ill or mentally defective in Scotland. Where they require care in a hospital or an institution, they receive it under the auspices of the National Health Service, and mental hospitals are administered in the same way as any other hospital in the Service. But all questions concerning the liberty of those who are detained in mental hospitals or institutions and the welfare and the interests of the individual patients are the concern not of the Department of Health but of the General Board of Control for Scotland, and the Secretary of State, in carrying out his responsibilities for this branch of the health of Scotland, is required to consult the Board. The decision to release anyone who has been placed at Her Majesty's Pleasure by the Courts is, however, taken by the Secretary of State, after the case has been considered by the Scottish Home Department.

The General Board of Control consists of a Chairman and seven other Commissioners (three of whom are medical and one legal), all of whom are appointed by the Queen on the recommendation of the Secretary of State. The Board is one of the few survivors of the old Scottish Boards referred to in Chapter II and Appendix I. It began almost a hundred years ago as the General Board of Commissioners in Lunacy in Scotland, when the care of persons of unsound mind was taken from the Board of Supervision under the Poor Law; and in 1937 it survived a particularly close scrutiny by the Gilmour Committee, who concluded that, although the treatment of mental illness must not be considered in isolation from the treatment of other forms of illness, it was right that the quasi-judicial functions which the Board exercised in relation to the liberty of the subject should remain with it instead of being transferred to the Secretary of State, where they would be exposed to all the winds of political pressure. As a result of the National Health Service (Scotland) Act, 1947, the Board's organisation has been more closely linked with that of the Department of Health; the medical Commissioners and the Secretary also hold appointments in the Department.

Besides looking into requests for the discharge of individual mental patients, the Board has the primary responsibility for considering the discharge of mental defectives. It is also responsible for sanctioning the admission of voluntary patients to mental hospitals, the transfer of patients from one hospital to another, and the liberation of patients either on probation or licence. The Board pays particular attention to any complaints of ill-treatment, and the Medical Commissioners periodically visit all mental hospitals and mental deficiency institutions, to interview patients and to satisfy themselves that they are satisfactorily treated. Patients who are boarded out in private dwellings are also visited and supervised by officers of the Board.

Defectives of dangerous or violent propensities are looked after in the State Institution at Carstairs, which is under the direct control of the Board. When—probably towards the end of 1957—the provisions of Section 63 of the Criminal Justice Act, 1949, are brought into operation, the Board will also become responsible for running the new State Mental Hospital (also to be at Carstairs) which is to take the place of the Criminal Lunatic Department of Perth Prison.

LYON KING OF ARMS

The office of Lyon King of Arms is even older than that of the King's Secretary, as in its remote origins it is derived from a pre-heraldic official who was custodian of the Royal genealogy and 'Inaugurator' of the Celtic Kings. Lyon first appeared as King of Arms about 1318, when Robert the Bruce was King of Scotland. He still uses many medieval terms in the performance of his duties, and wears on ceremonial occasions the Royal Tabard or robes of medieval beauty and splendour.

Lyon's functions are both ministerial and judicial, and he, styled 'Lord Lyon King of Arms' from the sixteenth century, can, like the former Lord Admiral, rescind his own decrees. Until 1707 a Scots Privy Councillor, he is still technically a *Conseiller du Roi* and one of the Sovereign's Lieutenants. He directed the Royal and public ceremonial of the Scottish Court, including the Coronation, and, so far as necessary, he still does.

Lyon's jurisdiction rests on both common and statute law, and covers such matters as armorial bearings, badges and cognizances; genealogy; family representation (which includes the determination of the chiefship of a family), name and change of name; and various questions of rank and title, including Nova Scotia baronetcies.[1] From his court—which is a court of record—appeal lies to the Court of Session and House of Lords, since arms, although they are in the nature of dignities, are also heritable property. In certain circumstances Lyon has power to impose substantial penalties, and can also, in Visitation or otherwise, enforce or carry out Lyon Court decrees.

Lyon takes evidence relating to questions of Scottish peerage precedence and to claims to baronetcies in the Scottish section of the roll of baronets. His certificates and extracts from the Public Registers of Arms and Genealogies are admissible as evidence in proving succession to dignities and property at home and abroad. He also enforces the Royal Warrants of Precedency in Scotland, makes Proclamations, and controls the Messengers-at-Arms. He is also Secretary of the Order of the Thistle, the Chancery of which is in Lyon Office.

Lyon's staff includes the Lyon Clerk, who is appointed by the Crown, three heralds (at present Marchmont, Rothesay and Albany), three pursuivants (at present Carrick, Kintyre and Unicorn), a herald painter and a procurator fiscal, who are all appointed by Lyon, and a small office staff. It is a testimony to the sustained interest in heraldry, genealogy and precedence that the Lyon Office earns a substantial income in fees which are paid into Her Majesty's Exchequer.

DEPARTMENT OF THE REGISTERS OF SCOTLAND

The record of the past, some of whose outward pageantry survives in the office of Lyon King of Arms, is steadily built up from the

[1] The Order of Knights Baronet of Nova Scotia was created by King James VI in 1624; those so created undertook to furnish a certain number of settlers in the Canadian territory of Nova Scotia and received a grant of land there. By an ingenious legal fiction the baronets took sasine, or formal possession, of their baronetcies, at Edinburgh Castle, by earth and stone symbolically handed over to them by a representative of the King.

present in the Department of the Registers of Scotland and in the Scottish Record Office. The task of the first of these is the registration of a wide range of legal documents—including, in particular, instruments relating to transactions in land—in 14 registers, the very names of which[1] indicate their antiquity. That of the Great Seal, extant since 1306, is the oldest; one or two others may be specially mentioned.

The General Register of Sasines provides the chief security in Scotland for rights in land and other heritable property. It was instituted by an Act passed by the Scots Parliament in 1617 and is the oldest still current record of its kind in the world. Registration is now governed by the Land Registers (Scotland) Act, 1868. Whenever heritable property in Scotland is sold, the deed recording the transaction must be presented at the Department of the Registers, where it is scrutinised and entered in the Register of Sasines. Deeds were copied in manuscript from 1617 to 1920, when typewriting was rather belatedly introduced. The Department has since proved, however, that it has no reluctance to use modern methods, for in 1934 the typewriter was in turn superseded by a photographic process of copying. The negatives are bound chronologically in volumes, from which a positive print can be readily made whenever an extract is required, and which form a continuous record of all transactions of landed property in Scotland.

In the Register of Deeds, which begins in 1554 and is by far the bulkiest of the other Registers, are entered marriage contracts, bonds and obligations of all kinds, articles of incorporation, and (since 1824) testaments, besides an infinite variety of other deeds. This Register likewise is now kept by photographing the writs presented, although most of the original warrants are also retained for preservation.

The Register of Hornings is now comparatively of trivial importance, but the origins of its name are curious. An officer of the law was given 'letters of horning' to direct him to charge a debtor to pay his debts. If this failed, the officer blew three blasts of his horn at the appropriate market-cross and the publication of this fact constituted 'denunciation at the horn'.

Today the office of Keeper of the Registers is a separate one. But it was not always so. Both the Registers and the Public Records of Scotland were once in the formal charge of the Lord Clerk Register, an Officer of State whose appointment has existed for nearly seven

---

[1] The General Register of Sasines, the Register of Hornings, the Register of Inhibitions and Adjudications, the Register of Entails, the Register of Deeds, the Register of Protests, the Register of Service of Heirs, the Registers of the Great Seal, the Quarter Seal, the Prince's Seal and the Cachet Seal, the Register of Crown Grants, the Register of Sheriffs' Commissions and the Register of English and Irish Judgments.

centuries. The officials who first assisted and then succeeded him dealt with both, and also with the registration of births, deaths and marriages, and this curious blend of duties persisted until after the 1914–18 war. In 1920 a separate Registrar-General was appointed and the divorce of the Registers and the Records was finally accomplished in 1949.

In addition to his other duties, the Keeper of the Registers is Deputy Keeper of the Seal appointed by the Treaty of Union to be used in place of the Great Seal of Scotland. He is appointed by the Secretary of State with the consent of the Lord President of the Court of Session, and has a staff of over 200.

SCOTTISH RECORD OFFICE

The record volumes steadily compiled in the Department of the Registers, and the relevant warrants deposited for preservation, are not retained there but pass in a regular flow to the Scottish Record Office. This Department receives each year about 150 volumes and 15,000 warrants of the Register of Deeds, and about 900 volumes of the Register of Sasines. The Record Office's task is to preserve these and other records—legal, departmental and historical—to arrange for their binding, cataloguing, and indexing, and to produce them for inspection by the public as required.

The records and processes of the Court of Session come here, some 10 volumes and over 6,000 bundles annually. Under certain recent Acts of Parliament, the records of several sheriff courts and of nine burghs have also been lodged here. Besides legal records, the Record Office receives those of Scottish Government departments and Royal Commissions, and the valuation rolls. It also preserves all the public records of the pre-Union kingdom, including those of Parliament, the Privy Council, and the Royal Household. Private muniments and commercial records, if of historical value, are accepted for preservation with the public records, and add considerably to the value of the national archives as a centre for historical research by scholars and students.

There are two search rooms. One is for legal searches, where the Registers of Deeds, Sasines and others are consulted every day, and the other for historical searches. The annual income in fees for searches and extracts approaches £7,000. There is a staff of 67, including the Curator of Historical Records (Deputy Keeper), and 10 Assistant Keepers.

The known history of the Record Office—or the Lord Clerk Register's Department, as it used to be—goes back to the thirteenth century. At various periods in its history, it has been lodged in Edinburgh Castle and in Parliament House, but since 1789 it has been housed in H.M. General Register House, designed by the brothers Robert and James Adam, the first building in Europe erected as a records repository.

The long association of the Record Office with the Lord Clerk Register was recognised in the Reorganisation of Offices (Scotland) Act, 1928, which specifically left with it the duty of preparing for the election of the Scottish representative peers, recording the proceedings at the election and assisting the Lord Clerk Register in making the return.

The Secretary of State appoints the Keeper of the Records, with the consent of the Lord President. He and the Lord President are advised by a body called the Scottish Records Advisory Council, of which the Keeper is Chairman, and which consists of up to 12 members appointed by the Secretary of State.

REGISTRAR-GENERAL FOR SCOTLAND

Probably the best known of the Registrar-General's duties is that of conducting the census of the population of Scotland which takes place from time to time—normally at ten-yearly intervals. The organisation of the census and the subsequent preparation and publication of voluminous reports are indeed an important part of the work of the Registrar-General's office, especially since the census is a great deal more than a mere counting of heads; the recent reports, for instance, contain information about the age and sex of the population, the size and sanitary equipment of the houses in which the people live, and so on. But in addition, the Registrar-General is responsible for controlling and guiding the local registrars of births, deaths and marriages. He receives from them periodical returns of the births, deaths and marriages in their districts, and he collates and analyses these, and publishes the resulting figures in reports. A great deal of modern planning calls for up-to-date figures of population, and the Registrar-General compiles, from the material available to him, quarterly, half-yearly and yearly estimates which are relied on for the purposes of the National Health Service and for the allocation of Treasury grants, and which meet many other statistical needs.

The early history of the Registrar-General's office has already been mentioned above, in the paragraph on the office of the Registers of Scotland. There is a community of interest between the Registrar-General's office and the Department of Health for Scotland, because the vital statistics produced by the one are of great importance to the other. This led the Gilmour Committee to suggest that the Registrar-General's office could be loosely linked to the Department of Health if the Registrar-General himself carried the rank of an assistant secretary of the Department. This recommendation was put into effect in 1939. The Registrar-General remains, however, a statutory officer in his own right and is also the accounting officer for his own separate vote.

NATIONAL GALLERIES OF SCOTLAND

So far, the offices at which we have been looking in this chapter have been rather a mixed bag, with, on the whole, the emphasis on registers and records. There follows a group of institutions concerned with the arts and learning.

The National Galleries of Scotland include the National Gallery at the Mound, Edinburgh, the Scottish National Portrait Gallery in Queen Street, and a Print Room in Ainslie Place. It would be merely tantalising to describe the collections without illustrating them, and it is perhaps enough to say that the National Gallery includes paintings by many leading artists in the European schools, including Rembrandt, Tintoretto, El Greco, Constable and Gainsborough. There is also, as might be expected, an outstanding display of the work of Allan Ramsay and Raeburn and a representative collection of other Scottish paintings, and Scottish work is strongly represented in the collection of prints and drawings by European artists in the Print Room. The water-colours include an important collection by Turner. The Portrait Gallery illustrates Scottish history through authentic contemporary portraits, and also includes a large reference section of engravings and photographs of portraits.

When the National Gallery was first opened in 1859, it was administered by the oldest of the Scottish Boards, the Board for the Improvement of Manufactures in Scotland (see Appendix I)—a body set up in 1727 to administer an annuity payable to Scotland under the Treaty of Union, whose subsequent history has to be traced along the curiously divergent paths of fisheries and the arts. In 1907, however, a new Board of Trustees, with seven members, was set up under the National Galleries of Scotland Act, 1906, to manage the National Galleries. The cost of maintaining the Galleries has since been met from public funds, and an annual grant is made for the purchase of works of art; this grant is in addition to the Treaty of Union annuity, which by the 1906 Act was payable to the new Board from the Consolidated Fund. The Board now possesses a number of private endowments, the largest of which derives from a bequest of over £55,000 made under the will of Mr. James Cowan Smith in 1919.

The Scottish National Portrait Gallery has its origin in gifts of £60,000 by Mr. J. R. Findlay of Aberlour, and the first gallery in the building was opened in 1889.

The Board of Trustees for the National Galleries is appointed by the Secretary of State, who also appoints an informal committee to advise the Board on matters relating to the National Portrait Gallery.

NATIONAL LIBRARY OF SCOTLAND

The National Library of Scotland was formed from the library presented to the nation in 1925 by the Faculty of Advocates. The Advocates' Library had been formally opened in 1689, and from 1709 had enjoyed the privilege of claiming under the Copyright Acts a copy of every book, map and piece of music printed in the United Kingdom. In this way, and by gifts and purchase, it had amassed by 1925 three-quarters of a million printed books and pamphlets and an important collection of Scottish and medieval European manuscripts. When the Faculty offered to present its library (other than the part concerned with law) to the nation, a gift of £100,000 by Sir Alexander Grant made possible the establishment of the National Library, and Sir Alexander subsequently gave a further £100,000 towards the provision of a new building.

The National Library has grown rapidly since 1925, and now contains about two million printed books. As well as continuing to receive British and Irish publications under the Copyright Act, it has bought (mainly from private benefactions) large numbers of foreign books, and has also, by gift and by purchase, acquired many collections of rare books, especially of Scottish, English, French and American interest, and several important collections of music, and augmented the collection of manuscripts.

The war and its economic consequences caused an interruption in the work of the new building on George IV Bridge, from 1940 to 1949, but the first part of it has now been completed and was opened by Her Majesty the Queen on 4th July, 1956. It contains a large reading room, a catalogue room, exhibition rooms, special collection rooms, map and microfilm reading rooms, a board room, staff rooms and nine stack-floors.

Of the Board of 33 Trustees in whose hands the management of the Library was placed by the National Library of Scotland Act, 1925, five are appointed by the Secretary of State; there are also five appointed by the Faculty of Advocates, one appointed by each of the four Scottish Universities, one by the Convention of Royal Burghs and one by the Association of County Councils in Scotland, 12 *ex officio* members (of whom the Secretary of State himself is one) and five co-opted members. If any question about the Library should be raised in Parliament or in the Cabinet, the Secretary of State would deal with it, but he has no voice—except as one of the Trustees—in the appointment of the library staff; the Librarian deals direct with the Treasury in staff matters.

NATIONAL MUSEUM OF ANTIQUITIES OF SCOTLAND

The important collection of antiquities, coins and other relics housed in the National Museum of Antiquities in Queen Street,

Edinburgh, derives from the private museum of the Society of Antiquaries, which was founded in 1780. The Society continued to be responsible for the day-to-day running of the Museum even after the collection was formally transferred to the custody, first, of the Board for the Improvement of Manufactures in 1851, and, then, of the Trustees of the National Galleries in 1906. This dual control was brought to an end as recently as 1954, by an Act which entrusted the management of the National Museum to a new Board of Trustees for the National Museum of Antiquities of Scotland. Of the 22 trustees, the chairman and 11 members are appointed by the Secretary of State; four members are appointed by the Society of Antiquaries of Scotland and the Society's President is a member *ex officio*; one member is appointed by the Senatus of each of the Scottish Universities; and the Professor of Prehistoric Archaeology in the University of Edinburgh is appointed *ex officio*.

ROYAL OBSERVATORY

The Royal Observatory is under the direction of the Astronomer Royal for Scotland, who is appointed by the Crown on the recommendation of the Secretary of State, and also holds the appointment of Regius Professor of Astronomy in the University of Edinburgh. In the words of the Psalms, 'he telleth the number of the stars; and calleth them all by their names'; or, in more precise but less pleasing language, the Observatory is concerned mainly with astrophysics (the physical study of the sun and stars) and solar and ionospheric work. Routine meteorological and seismological readings are taken, and a local time service is maintained. The principal results of the astrophysical research are published, from time to time, by H.M. Stationery Office in *Publications of the Royal Observatory*.

Since 1895, when it was moved to Blackford Hill, Edinburgh, the Royal Observatory has been maintained by public funds. The building occupied since that year was erected to accommodate the valuable astronomical instruments and library earlier presented to the nation by the Earl of Crawford.

ROYAL COMMISSION ON ANCIENT AND HISTORICAL MONUMENTS

Something has already been said in Chapter XV about the Secretary of State's duties, as Planning Minister for Scotland, in relation to our all too small store of historic buildings. He has a further interest in this work through the Royal Commission on Ancient and Historical Monuments of Scotland, whose eight members are appointed by the Crown on his recommendation.

When the Commission was appointed in 1908, its warrant gave it the comprehensive task of making 'an inventory of the ancient and historical monuments and constructions connected with or illustrative of the contemporary culture, civilisation and conditions of life of the people in Scotland from the earliest times to 1707', and of specifying those monuments which seemed most worthy of preservation. Fresh Letters Patent were issued in 1948, which gave the Commissioners power to include, at their discretion, buildings of a later date than 1707.

So far, the Commission has made 13 reports, accompanied by 15 inventory volumes. The inventories are prepared from surveys by the Commission's staff of architects and archaeologists, and extensive use is now made of air photography. In 1951 the Commissioners instituted an emergency survey of areas of 'marginal land' in which monuments are liable to be damaged by the expansion of agriculture and forestry.

The Commission's staff consists of a secretary, five investigating officers and a small office staff.

ROYAL FINE ART COMMISSION FOR SCOTLAND

The Royal Fine Art Commission for Scotland was first appointed in 1927 to consider questions of public amenity or artistic importance that might be referred to it by Government departments, or public or quasi-public bodies; it was reconstituted in 1953 and enabled to take the initiative in giving advice, instead of having to watch speechless while enormities were perpetrated on which it had not been consulted. Its nine members are appointed by the Crown on the recommendation of the Secretary of State, who also appoints the secretary —at present an officer of the Royal Scottish Museum.

ASSESSOR OF PUBLIC UNDERTAKINGS

The Assessor of Public Undertakings assesses the annual value for rating purposes of various public undertakings—for example, canals, water-works, gas-works, docks and tramway undertakings. He succeeded the Assessor of Railways and Canals, whose office was created just over a hundred years ago under the Valuation of Lands (Scotland) Act, 1854. The present title of the office dates from 1934. The functions of the office were to some extent curtailed when railways and electricity undertakings were nationalised in 1948 and a system was introduced whereby those nationalised bodies make payments of standard amounts to the Secretary of State for distribution to the local authorities. At the same time, however, the valuation of the undertakings of the Scottish Gas Board and of the British Transport Commission's road services in Scotland was entrusted to the Assessor. He is appointed by the Secretary of State, and his expenses are met by the undertakings that he values, so that no cost falls on the Exchequer from his operations.

THE ACCOUNTANT OF COURT

Quis custodet ipsos custodes? It has long been recognised in Scotland that, if someone cannot administer his own affairs for one reason or another, the person who does it for him ought to be subject to some form of supervision. At first, the Court of Session itself was formally responsible for doing this, but in 1849 an officer called the Accountant of the Court of Session was created to take over this responsibility, and in 1889 the Judicial Factors (Scotland) Act amalgamated this office and that of Accountant of Bankruptcy and gave their duties to the Accountant of Court. Since 1939 the Accountant of Court has also been Custodian of Enemy Property, and as such is responsible for the collection and disposal of 'enemy' funds, acting in this work under the directions of the Board of Trade.

The Accountant of Court is an officer of the Court of Session, but is appointed by the Secretary of State, acting on the nomination of the Lord Advocate.

THE QUEEN'S AND LORD TREASURER'S REMEMBRANCER

The officer who bears the resounding title of Queen's and Lord Treasurer's Remembrancer is an officer of the Treasury, and the Secretary of State has no functions in relation to him or his staff. In strict logic, therefore, he has no place in this book; but he has a traditional and important place in Scottish administration, and that may perhaps justify his inclusion here.

The Queen's and Lord Treasurer's Remembrancer is the twentieth-century heir of the five Barons of the Exchequer appointed under an Act of 1707, in accordance with a provision of the Treaty of Union, to act as a court of law in revenue cases and as a Treasury Board for Scotland, subordinate to the Treasury itself, for determining questions relating to customs and excise, Crown property and other matters. The most important officers of the Exchequer under the Barons were the Queen's Remembrancer, who acted as their secretary in all their multifarious duties, and the Lord Treasurer's Remembrancer; they were called Remembrancers because they had to remember all things for the Crown's service and benefit. The Barons disappeared in 1833, and in 1837 the offices of the two Remembrancers were amalgamated.

The Remembrancer's principal duties now are that he is the Treasury representative on various boards and committees in Scotland, and that he is the Accounting Officer for the Vote for Law

Charges and Courts of Law in Scotland. He makes such payments as judicial salaries from the Consolidated Fund, makes payments from the various votes of Parliament administered by the Scottish departments, and carries out many duties similar to those of the Paymaster-General in England. His banking transactions in 1956–57 amounted to £197 million. By the law of Scotland he is the administrator of estates that fall to the Crown; and he is responsible for collecting fines imposed in the High Court and the sheriff courts. By warrant of the Board of Trade, he is Registrar of Companies, Registrar of Limited Partnerships and Registrar of Business Names. He is also the Keeper of *The Edinburgh Gazette*, the Scottish counterpart of *The London Gazette*.

The Remembrancer has two less onerous but more picturesque duties; he is *ex officio* administrator of Treasure Trove, and, when it is reported, he acts in consultation with the Keeper of the National Museum of Antiquities. Any articles of antiquarian or archaeological interest are claimed on behalf of the Crown and rewards are made to the finders. He is also responsible to the Great Officers of State for the custody of the Regalia of Scotland in the Crown Room at Edinburgh Castle.

PART SEVEN

The Law Officers and
the Lord Advocate's Departments

CHAPTER XXIII

The Law Officers and
the Lord Advocate's Departments

THE LAW OFFICERS

THE law and the judicial system in Scotland are (as is well known) separate from those in England and Wales, and consequently Scotland has her own Law Officers of the Crown. These are Her Majesty's Advocate (commonly referred to as the Lord Advocate) and the Solicitor-General for Scotland. As we have seen in Chapter II, the Lord Advocate, as an Officer of State and a member of the Privy Council, took part before the Union in the political as well as the legal aspect of government. This continued after the Union, particularly during the long period in the eighteenth and nineteenth centuries when the Lord Advocate was virtually the only Scottish Minister and handled the greater part of the Scottish business in the House of Commons; and today both the Lord Advocate and the Solicitor-General are regularly consulted by the Ministers of the Scottish Office and join with them in dealing with the Government's parliamentary business. The purpose of the present chapter, however, is to describe the responsibilities of the Lord Advocate and the Solicitor-General in the sphere of their profession as lawyers.

The office of King's Advocate is a very old one. The first holder of it whose name is known was Sir John Ross of Montgrenan, who was Advocate to James III and whose loyalty to the King caused the successful rebels to charge him with treason after the Battle of Sauchieburn in 1488. Before the end of the sixteenth century, the main features of the present office had already taken shape, as the Advocate had become both public prosecutor and an Officer of State. The first Solicitor-General had also appeared before the end of the sixteenth century, in 1587, but the title of his office seems to date from about 1725. In the early years the Lord Advocate might also be a judge, and when not pleading, either as counsel for the King or for private clients, he sat on the Bench; this arrangement did not survive the seventeenth century. Up to as recent a date as 1945, he and the Solicitor-General were still entitled to engage in private practice at the Bar, provided that it did not conflict with their official duties.

The principal duties of the Lord Advocate may be summarised, in a paraphrase of a passage by an eighteenth-century writer, as follows:

to act as the chief legal adviser to the Crown in making and executing laws, to defend in all civil suits the rights and interests of the Crown and persons claiming under the Crown, and to prosecute on behalf of the Crown all criminal offences suitable for prosecution in the superior criminal courts. Much of this work must in modern times be shared with the Solicitor-General or delegated to members of a professional staff, and it is described more fully below in relation to the main divisions of that staff. Some functions, however, can be exercised only by the Lord Advocate in person—such as the duty of making recommendations to the Secretary of State (who, in turn, submits nominations to the Queen) for the appointment of all judges of the supreme courts (except the Lord Justice-General and President of the Court of Session and the Lord Justice-Clerk), sheriffs and salaried sheriffs-substitute. The Lord Advocate is also concerned personally in different degrees in the making of various other legal appointments.

THE LEGAL SECRETARIES AND PARLIAMENTARY DRAFTSMEN

It is curious that before 1885, when the Lord Advocate had, in addition to his present duties, many that now fall to the Secretary of State, he had very little permanent official assistance. During the nineteenth century it became the custom for him to appoint a member of the Scottish Bar as his legal secretary to assist him in general legal matters. Between 1877 and 1885, when the Lord Advocate was working in the 'small and dark apartment' at the Home Office,[1] this legal secretary and one clerk seem to have been his total staff in London. The legal secretary attended in London while Parliament was sitting and shared in the drafting of Scottish legislation, and in the course of time Government departments came to refer questions of Scots law to him. Up to 1919, however, the appointment was a temporary and personal one, and the holder of it retired when the Lord Advocate left office, so that the experience he had gained was lost to the public service. In that year, the post was made an established one, and there are now six members of the Scottish Bar established as civil servants and working whole time as 'legal secretaries' in the Lord Advocate's Department in Dean's Yard, Westminster.

The members of the Department are not concerned with the administration of the criminal law or with the conduct of government litigation, but, with those exceptions, they are available, as the Lord Advocate's personal staff, to provide whatever assistance he requires in carrying out his duties. In addition to this work of personal assist-

[1] See Chapter II, page 14.

ance, the members of the Department have two other main functions. First, they act as day-to-day legal advisers on Scottish matters to any Government department which has no Scottish legal adviser of its own, whether it be a department, such as the Scottish Education Department or the Scottish Home Department, which has functions in Scotland only, or a department, such as the War Office, which has functions both in Scotland and elsewhere. Secondly, they have inherited the work of the Parliamentary Draftsman for Scotland.

Prior to 1871, the drafting of Scottish Bills had been undertaken, under the direction of the Lord Advocate, partly by various individual advocates (including probably the Legal Secretary to the Lord Advocate), partly by the Crown Agent and partly by the Scottish Solicitor in London. In 1871 the Treasury sanctioned the definite appointment as Parliamentary Draftsman for Scotland of Mr. J. F. MacLennan, Advocate, who presumably continued to work under the general authority of the Lord Advocate but who was required to submit his drafts to the Parliamentary Counsel to the Treasury. After many vicissitudes the work of the Parliamentary Draftsman was transferred in 1912 to the Counsel to the Secretary of State for Private Legislation, and from him in 1925 to the Legal Secretary to the Lord Advocate.

The Lord Advocate's Department is thus now responsible for the drafting of all Government Bills applying to Scotland alone and also for the drafting of United Kingdom or Great Britain Bills in so far as they apply to Scotland. In these matters the work and status of the Parliamentary Draftsmen for Scotland are in all respects similar to those of the Parliamentary Counsel to the Treasury.

Where legislation of any importance is proposed for Great Britain, the Lord Advocate himself, as the senior Scottish Law Officer, will consider the proposals at an early stage—and in particular, such points as whether there should be separate Scottish legislation. He will be influenced in coming to a decision by such questions as whether there is already separate Scottish legislation, and whether a single measure for Great Britain, with a Scottish application clause, would be too complicated a measure—whether, in fact, the legislation for England and Scotland would start from the same point, proceed by the same route and arrive at the same destination. When the Government has decided that it wants a Scottish Bill for some purpose, the department concerned then arranges for the preparation of instructions from which the Parliamentary Draftsman will work to produce a Bill.

The Draftsman's part is by no means finished when the Bill has been introduced; he will be extremely lucky if there are not Government amendments to be drafted and he will also be required to advise Ministers and officials at all stages, both on the Bill itself and on amendments to it, whether they have been put down by Government back-benchers or by the Opposition. He will normally attend the committee and the report stages of the Bill in both Houses, and his advice on the effect of proposed amendments is at the disposal of the Chairman of the Committee, or of the Speaker of the House, as the case may be.

The Department is wholly responsible for the preparation of Scottish consolidation Bills; this is essentially the Parliamentary Draftsman's work, because it means gathering tidily in one comprehensive and logically arranged measure—but without altering the law—provisions on a given subject which are scattered through a number of Acts, passed probably over a long period.

The Lord Advocate's Department is hardly a typical Government department. In the first place, comparatively little of its work originates within the Department itself; most of it is submitted by other departments. Secondly, it is very small and its structure is the reverse of the normal broad-based pyramid; there are actually fewer executive and clerical officers on its staff than there are professional members. Lastly, it is unusual in that the work, whether the drafting of a Bill or the giving of advice on a particular point, is normally dealt with from start to finish wholly by the member of the Department to whom it has been allotted. This is not to say, however, that he is precluded from consulting the Legal Secretary or any other member of the Department, and this is indeed freely done for the purposes of co-ordination as well as for assistance on difficult or unusual points. Moreover, each member of the Department has direct access to the Lord Advocate and the Solicitor-General if he wants their views on a problem and will always consult them if he foresees political implications or possible litigation.

CRIMINAL PROCEEDINGS AND THE CROWN OFFICE

Quite separate from the Lord Advocate's duties as a Minister and as senior Law Officer of the Crown are his responsibilities for the administration of the criminal law in Scotland, and for criminal proceedings in the courts. (Indeed, it has sometimes been suggested that the two functions should be carried out by different people.) Until the latter part of the sixteenth century, the fundamental rule of Scottish criminal procedure was that prosecutions were at the instance of the person aggrieved, or his kinsmen. Two Acts of 1579 and 1583 introduced the system of Crown prosecutions in criminal cases—with the satisfactory result that a better system of justice prevailed, and that the King's revenue was substantially increased by fines levied in the courts. There are now virtually no private prosecutions, and all criminal proceedings, except for minor cases in the burgh police courts and justice of the peace courts, are taken at the instance of the Lord Advocate or his officers. Whereas in England the police and

Government departments can and do prosecute, in Scotland the police do not prosecute in any circumstances and it is only in a limited range of Customs and Excise and Factory Act cases that Government departments do so; their duty is to report any alleged infringement of the law to the Crown Office or to the procurator fiscal. The Lord Advocate has complete discretion in the prosecution of crimes, and cannot be compelled to prosecute even by the High Court of Justiciary; and even after the verdict has been pronounced, he has power to restrict the pains of law[1] or to abandon a charge.

The powers and duties of the Lord Advocate in relation to criminal proceedings—which include not only the decision whether or not to prosecute, but the conduct of cases in the courts—are exercised through the Crown Office. He is assisted in carrying them out by Crown Counsel, by the Crown Agent, a solicitor who is the permanent head of the Crown Office, and locally by the procurator fiscal at each sheriff court. Crown Counsel consist, in addition to the Lord Advocate, of the Solicitor-General and four members of the Scottish Bar, who are appointed on a part-time basis and are called the Advocates-Depute. For the purposes of criminal administration, Scotland is divided into four circuits or districts, the Home, North, South and West, and one Advocate-Depute is assigned to each, who is responsible for the various cases reported to the Crown Office from his circuit and conducts prosecutions in the High Court of Justiciary when it is on circuit within his district. (There is also an extra Advocate-Depute for the Glasgow circuit, and a Sheriff Court Advocate-Depute who conducts cases in the Sheriff Courts which the Lord Advocate regards as sufficiently important to be handled by counsel.)

In each sheriff court district, there is an official called the procurator fiscal, who is appointed by the Lord Advocate and answerable to him. There have been procurators fiscal since the seventeenth century, and in the period between 1745 and 1885, when there was no Scottish Secretary, more than one Lord Advocate explained that it was largely thanks to his network of communications with procurators fiscal all over Scotland that he was able to administer the country. Today, the procurators fiscal are able to concentrate on their duties as public prosecutors in the sheriff courts. All alleged criminal offences in his district are in the first instance investigated by the procurator fiscal and, when in his opinion the evidence warrants it, it is he who institutes proceedings in the public interest. Serious crimes will be reported to the Crown Office, so that Crown Counsel can consider them and decide whether proceedings are warranted, and, if so, whether the case should be taken in the sheriff court or in the High Court of Justiciary. The Advocate-Depute concerned may

[1] I.e. he can move the court to impose a lesser sentence than that prescribed by statute.

take the decision himself, or he may refer the case to one of the two Law Officers.

The Crown Office is, in addition to being the Lord Advocate's Edinburgh office, the headquarters of the procurator fiscal service, since all instructions to the procurators fiscal emanate from there and all establishment work for the service is done there. The posts of the Crown Agent and his principal assistant (who is also a solicitor) are regarded as interchangeable with the senior posts in the procurator fiscal service.

In all this criminal work, there are many points of difference between the Scottish way of doing things and the English. One which deserves special mention is that there are no coroners in Scotland. All inquiries into sudden and suspicious deaths are conducted, privately and confidentially, by the procurator fiscal, who reports his findings to the Crown Office. The procurator fiscal also collects and presents the material for the inquiries that are held before a Sheriff and a jury under the Fatal Accidents Inquiry Acts, and he carries out inquiries into fires. The fatal accident inquiries are required by law for industrial fatal accidents and may be held, if the Lord Advocate thinks it proper so to direct, in relation to any other fatal accident. Such a direction would usually be given because the accident occurred in circumstances that aroused public interest and concern (whether general or local) and a feeling that those circumstances would be better investigated at a public inquiry.

CIVIL PROCEEDINGS

The antiquity of the Lord Advocate's duties in relation to civil proceedings is shown by the fact that the description of them in the middle of the seventeenth century, given by Sir John Scot of Scotstarvet in *The Staggering State of the Scots Statesmen*, is still accurate today:

his business is to pursue and defend in all causes wherein the King has an interest ;

he is in fact responsible for conducting any litigation in the Scottish courts to which the Crown or any Government department is a party. In this work he is assisted by the Solicitor-General and by the standing junior counsel and the solicitor in Scotland for the department concerned. It was formerly the custom for anyone who wanted to sue the Crown to bring an action against the Officers of State, but actions by or against the Crown or by or against a Government department may, under the Crown Suits (Scotland) Act, 1857, now be brought by or against the Lord Advocate as representing the Crown or the department, and are served on him at the Crown Office. If documents which are in the hands of Government departments are demanded by litigants as being essential to the presentation of their case, the formal application is served on the Lord Advocate at the Crown Office.

It is also the duty of the Lord Advocate to intervene if necessary in certain classes of civil litigation to which no Government department is a party but in which the general public interest is involved. Examples of this are collusively contrived divorce actions and proceedings for the settlement of a scheme to regulate the administration of a public fund whose original purposes have failed. Any such intervention is conducted through the machinery of the Crown Office.

CONCLUSION

This brief account of the Lord Advocate's province is by no means complete, and either by inheritance or by statute he has gathered a variety of other functions too numerous to mention. He is *ex officio* a member of a number of public bodies, such as the Northern Lighthouse Commissioners and the committee of the Privy Council which deals with University matters for Scotland, and he has inherited the duty of the old Bible Board and issues the licences without which no Bible can be printed and published in Scotland.

CHAPTER XXIV

Conclusion

EARLY in its Report, the Royal Commission on Scottish Affairs set out what it regarded as the principles that must be observed if Scotland was to be governed effectively and acceptably. The first principle was that 'the machinery of government should be designed to dispose of Scottish business in Scotland'. The Scottish Office is in itself a recognition of this principle, and this book, while we cannot describe every detail of the work of the departments for which Scottish Ministers are responsible, may at least demonstrate just how much Scottish business is in fact disposed of in Scotland.

There is, however, more than one way of observing the Royal Commission's principle, and Great Britain Departments such as the Board of Trade, the Ministry of Labour and National Service, the Ministry of Pensions and National Insurance, the Post Office, the Ministry of Power and the Ministry of Works, none of whose work could be described in this book, also dispose of much of their Scottish business in Scotland. All of them have Scottish headquarters under the charge of experienced senior officers to whom substantial responsibilities are devolved.

Another essential principle summarised by the Royal Commission was that Scottish needs and points of view should be kept in mind 'at all stages in the formulation and execution of policy'. The importance of this, particularly at the early stages when policy is being conceived, should hardly need emphasising; a suit that is made to measure will always fit better than one originally designed for someone else and hastily altered at the last moment. To ensure that the measurements are correct when a policy is being cut out is one of the continuous preoccupations of Ministers and civil servants.

All Government departments with business in Scotland must, of course, consider Scottish needs and points of view, but the Scottish Office is in a special position in that it alone has its administrative headquarters in Scotland and is concerned solely with Scotland. It has therefore acquired—or if it has not, it has been very much at fault—a specialised knowledge and experience of the country. This knowledge and experience are at the disposal of the Secretary of State, who is Scotland's representative in the Cabinet, and they make the Scottish Office something more than the sum of its component departments. Not only is it responsible for the central administration of agriculture, education, health and home affairs in Scotland, with the duty of helping to work out for all these a policy that will both meet Scottish requirements and be fundamentally consistent with what is proposed for England and Wales; it also has to keep an eye on what other departments are doing, and to be ready to bark, and if need be to bite, when it senses danger to Scottish interests.

The administrative arrangements which this book describes are those that were in operation at the beginning of 1957, and although it should be remembered that they have recently been examined in detail by a Royal Commission and adapted to give effect to its recommendations, it is extremely unlikely that they are in any way final. Indeed, if this book has a theme, it is perhaps one of constant adaptation to changing circumstances. A living organism—and it is submitted that whatever its critics may say, the Scottish Office *is* a living organism—must continue to evolve. How it will evolve time alone will show, and it is no part of this book's purpose to attempt to see into the future. Its object has rather been to give for the first time a full and reasonably comprehensive account of what the Scottish Office has to do and how it does it. If it leads to a better understanding of the nature and duties of the Scottish Office, it will have achieved its purpose.

APPENDIX I

The Scottish Boards

THE BOARD OF MANUFACTURES

MOST of the Boards were a nineteenth-century development, but the first originated in two Acts brought forward by Lord Advocate Duncan Forbes and passed in 1726—the Linen and Hempen Manufactures (Scotland) Act and the Fisheries (Scotland) Act. The Treaty of Union had provided that £2,000 a year should be spent for seven years on the encouragement of the coarse-wool industry in Scotland, but the money had simply accumulated and—perhaps because of the '15 Rebellion—nothing had been done with it. Duncan Forbes's Acts provided for the appointment of up to 21 trustees—who were to be 'persons resident in Scotland' and not London or emigrant Scots—to utilise the funds, and an annual grant which would be made available, in 'the improvement and encouragement of fishery and manufactures in that part of Great Britain called Scotland'; the trustees were also to supervise and improve the linen industry.

Duncan Forbes—whose energy and breadth of interests would have found full scope in the post of Secretary of State for Scotland two centuries later—was one of the trustees, and his correspondence shows that he took a close personal interest in the methods by which the linen industry was developed (they included subsidies, prizes and the importation of French Protestant weavers from Picardy). As time went on and, presumably, the linen and woollen industries became well established, the trustees (who came to be known as the Board of Manufactures) widened and altered their interests. It seems to have been at their instance that the Forth and Clyde Canal was begun in 1768, but in the nineteenth century they became increasingly concerned with industrial design, the decorative arts and the encouragement of education in the fine arts. The Arts Council and the Council of Industrial Design thus had a Scottish prototype over 100 years ago. In 1906 the Board of Manufactures was succeeded under the National Galleries of Scotland Act by the Trustees for the National Galleries. They in turn in 1954 ceded to a new body of Trustees their responsibility for the National Museum of Antiquities. Thus the Boards of Trustees for the National Gallery and the National Museum of Antiquities derive in unbroken descent from the first post-Union Scottish board.

THE FISHERY BOARD

The Board of Manufactures was required to encourage Scottish fisheries as well as linen manufacture; their diverging interests were recognised by the Herring Fishery (Scotland) Act, 1808, which increased the number of trustees to 28 and turned seven of them into a separate Fishery Board. The Fishery Board at first had jurisdiction in England and the Isle of Man as well as Scotland, but lost England in 1849 and the Isle of Man in 1868. The economical Treasury directed in 1839 that the Fishery Board and the Board of Manufactures should share a Secretary and clerical staff and they did this until 1882, when the steadily accumulating powers of the former were conferred on a new Fishery Board under the Fishery Board (Scotland) Act of that year.

It is an interesting commentary on the scale of administration a century ago that the joint headquarters expenses of the Board of Manufactures and the Fishery Board in 1869—as reported to the Camperdown Commission—were £1,749 and the whole amount voted to the Fishery Board by Parliament in that year was £13,223.

The new Fishery Board established by the Act of 1882 and the Fisheries Regulation (Scotland) Act, 1895, consisted of a chairman and six members appointed by the Crown on the recommendation of the Secretary of State.[1] Four of the members were representative of sea-fishing interests, one was a sheriff and one a scientist. The Board acted under the direction of the Secretary of State; it continued until 1939, when its functions were transferred to him.

POOR LAW AND PUBLIC HEALTH

The second of the main Scottish Boards was set up a long time after the Board of Manufactures, in 1845, under the Poor Law (Scotland) Act of that year. It was called the Board of Supervision for the Relief of the Poor in Scotland, and its creation followed a common nineteenth-century pattern: first, strong public concern, in this case focused by a pamphlet by Dr. William Alison;[2] then, a Commission of Enquiry; then, in spite of the protests of those who, like the great Dr. Chalmers, favoured the local and voluntary organisation of relief, the setting up of a central administrative body. The Board consisted of the Lord Provosts of Edinburgh and Glasgow, the Solicitor-General, three sheriffs and three members (one paid) appointed by the Crown, and was subject, in some respects, to the control of the Secretary of State (i.e. the Home Secretary) and the Lord Advocate.

Later the Board acquired powers in relation to public health—under the Vaccination Act, 1863, and the Public Health (Scotland) Act, 1867—and so became the ancestor of the present Department of Health for Scotland.

In 1894 the Local Government (Scotland) Act created a new body called the Local Government Board for Scotland, which took over the functions of the old Board of Supervision, and general responsibility for the work of parish councils. The Secretary for Scotland was President and the other members were the Solicitor-General, the Permanent Under-Secretary for Scotland and three persons appointed by the Crown on the Secretary for Scotland's nomination, one of whom acted as chairman; one of the others was an advocate and one a doctor.

Two other Scottish Boards followed early this century, the Scottish Insurance Commissioners, appointed in 1911 under the National Insurance Act, and the Highlands and Islands (Medical Service) Board, set up as a result of the Highlands and Islands (Medical Service) Grant Act, 1913, to improve medical services in the Highlands. These bodies had only a short independent life, as in 1919 Parliament transferred their functions and those of the Local Government Board for Scotland to a new body called the Scottish Board of Health. This Board had the Secretary for Scotland as its President, the new Parliamentary Under-Secretary as Vice-President, and up to six members appointed on the Secretary for Scotland's nomination—of whom two were to be doctors, one a woman and one an advocate or law agent.

In 1928 the Board of Health was abolished and its work assigned to a statutory department (the Department of Health for Scotland) acting under the control and direction of the Secretary of State. The Department, like the old Board, at first had permanent staff of the executive and clerical grades only, but in 1935, in accordance with the views of the Haldane Committee, it adopted the normal civil service pattern and acquired administrative officers to deal with the policy matters that had formerly been the concern of the Board members. In 1939, under the Reorganisation of Offices Act, the functions of the Department were transferred to the Secretary of State.

LUNACY AND MENTAL DEFICIENCY

In its early days, the Board of Supervision had central responsibility for the treatment of lunatics and mental defectives in Scotland, but the arrangement did not work well, and after 'an American philanthropical lady, Miss Dix', had persuaded the Government to appoint a Royal Commission,[3] Parliament passed the Lunacy (Scotland) Act, 1857, setting up the General Board of Commissioners

---

[1] Between 1885 and 1926 the Secretary for Scotland.

[2] Observations on the Management of the Poor in Scotland, and its Effects on the Health of the Great Towns, 1840.

[3] Minutes of evidence given to the Commissioners appointed to inquire into certain Civil Departments in Scotland, 1870, Question 1,479.

in Lunacy for Scotland. The Board was composed of an unpaid Chairman and two paid Commissioners with up to three unpaid Commissioners appointed by the Crown under the warrant of the Secretary of State (the Home Secretary).

The Board survived as a separate organisation the scrutiny of Lord Camperdown's Commission in 1870, the Royal Commission on the Civil Service in 1914 and the Gilmour Committee in 1937, but was renamed the General Board of Control for Scotland in 1913. Its composition was slightly altered under the Reorganisation of Offices (Scotland) Act, 1939, and since then its organisation has been more closely integrated with that of the Department of Health for Scotland.

PRISONS

Under the Prisons Administration Act of 1840 a General Board of Directors was appointed to control the General Prison at Perth and to supervise local prisons in Scotland. The Board was replaced in 1860 under the Scottish Prisons Act of that year by Managers—a stipendiary manager (Dr. Hill Burton, the historian, who combined the appointment with that of Historiographer Royal), the inspector of local prisons, the Sheriff of Perth and the Crown Agent—responsible to the Home Secretary. The Managers lasted 17 years, but were in turn replaced under the Prisons (Scotland) Act, 1877, by the Prisons Commission for Scotland. Parliament had now made the running of local prisons a responsibility of the Government and it was the Commission's job to do it. There were three Commissioners appointed by the Crown, the Sheriff of Perth and the Crown Agent. The Commission became a Department in 1928, for the same reasons as the Board of Health,[1] and the functions of the Prisons Department were transferred to the Secretary of State in 1939 like those of the other Scottish departments and were allotted to the Scottish Home Department. By then the development of the prison system and the establishment in 1908 of borstals had considerably enlarged these functions from those of the old 'managers' who had blandly told Lord Camperdown's Commission in 1870 that 'there is no enumeration of the letters of the Department and it would be a serious work to count them'.

EDUCATION

Next in chronological sequence comes education. Curiously enough, this subject, in which the Scots have always prided themselves on their superiority, was never centrally supervised by a Board of the kind we are at present discussing.[2] From 1839 the Privy Council exercised jurisdiction in educational matters throughout Great Britain through a Committee of Council, but in 1872 the Education (Scotland) Act formed 'the Scotch Education Department' which was defined as 'the Lords of any Committee of the Privy Council appointed by Her Majesty on Education in Scotland' but was in effect a Government department working under the direction of the Vice-President of this Committee. Between 1872 and 1885 the Vice-President held a similar office in England and was in effect Minister of Education for Great Britain, but in 1885 the newly appointed Secretary for Scotland became Vice-President. The position remained unchanged (apart from the amendment of 'Scotch' to 'Scottish' in 1918) until 1939, although the Committee itself never met after 1913. In 1939 the Department's functions were vested in the Secretary of State.

AGRICULTURE

The last of the important Scottish administrative boards dealt with agriculture. A Crofters Commission consisting of three members had been formed under the Crofters Holdings (Scotland) Act, 1886, and 11 years later the Congested Districts (Scotland) Act, 1897, set up Commissioners (who included Ministers, civil servants and independent members) to administer funds for the assistance of agriculture and fisheries and the improvement of facilities generally in the Highlands and

---

[1] See Chapter II, page 18.
[2] There was a temporary Board of Education between 1872 and 1877; they acted as agents and assistants in Edinburgh for the new Department in London.

Islands. These two acts of 1886 and 1897 were in fact a sign of Parliament's recognition that the Highlands presented special problems and required special treatment.

The Lowlands of Scotland were the concern of the Great Britain Board of Agriculture between 1889 and 1912, but in 1911 Parliament passed the Small Landholders Act which created the Board of Agriculture for Scotland. The new Board not only took over the powers of the Crofters Commission and the Congested Districts Board but all the functions in Scotland of the Great Britain Board, except those relating to diseases of animals. Its main task was the development of smallholdings, but it was given the formidable and very generalised duty of promoting the interests of agriculture, forestry and other rural industries and of promoting, aiding and developing agricultural education and research and agricultural organisation and co-operation.

Like the other main Scottish Boards, the Board of Agriculture was replaced in 1928 by a statutory department whose functions were in turn transferred to the Secretary of State in 1939.

APPENDIX II

HOLDERS OF THE OFFICE OF SECRETARY OF STATE OR SECRETARY FOR SCOTLAND SINCE 1707

Secretary of State, Scottish Department

1707   The Earl of Loudoun and The Earl of Mar
1708–9 The Duke of Queensberry, till his death on 6th July, 1711
1713   The Earl of Mar, again
1714   The Duke of Montrose
1716   The Duke of Roxburghe, till August, 1725
1741–42 The Marquess of Tweeddale, till January, 1745–46

Secretary for Scotland

1885 Rt. Hon. The Duke of Richmond and Gordon, K.G.
1886 Rt. Hon. G. O. Trevelyan (later Sir G. O. Trevelyan, Bt.)
1886 Rt. Hon. The Earl of Dalhousie, K.T.
1886 Rt. Hon. A. J. Balfour (later Earl of Balfour)
1887 Rt. Hon. The Marquess of Lothian
1892 Rt. Hon. Sir G. O. Trevelyan, Bt., again
1895 Rt. Hon. Lord Balfour of Burleigh
1903 Rt. Hon. A. Graham Murray (later Viscount Dunedin)
1905 Rt. Hon. The Marquess of Linlithgow, K.T., G.C.V.O., G.C.M.G.
1905 Rt. Hon. J. Sinclair (later Lord Pentland)
1912 Rt. Hon. T. McKinnon Wood
1916 Rt. Hon. H. J. Tennant
1916 Rt. Hon. R. Munro (later Lord Alness)
1922 Rt. Hon. Viscount Novar, G.C.M.G.
1924 Rt. Hon. W. Adamson
1924 Rt. Hon. Sir John Gilmour, Bt., D.S.O.

Secretary of State for Scotland

1926 Rt. Hon. Sir John Gilmour, Bt., D.S.O.
1929 Rt. Hon. W. Adamson, again
1931 Rt. Hon. Sir Archibald Sinclair, Bt., C.M.G. (later Viscount Thurso)
1932 Rt. Hon. Sir Godfrey Collins
1936 Rt. Hon. Walter E. Elliot, M.C.
1938 Rt. Hon. D. J. Colville (later Lord Clydesmuir)
1940 Rt. Hon. Ernest Brown, M.C.
1941 Rt. Hon. Thomas Johnston
1945 Rt. Hon. The Earl of Rosebery, D.S.O., M.C.
1945 Rt. Hon. Joseph Westwood
1947 Rt. Hon. Arthur Woodburn
1950 Rt. Hon. Hector McNeil
1951 Rt. Hon. James Stuart, M.V.O., M.C.
1957 Rt. Hon. John S. Maclay, C.M.G.

MINISTERS OF STATE, SCOTTISH OFFICE, FROM 1951

1951 Rt. Hon. The Earl of Home
1955 Rt. Hon. Lord Strathclyde

PERMANENT UNDER-SECRETARIES OF STATE
(*Permanent Under-Secretaries before 1926*)

1885 Rt. Hon. Sir Francis R. Sandford, K.C.B. (later Lord Sandford)
1888 R. W. Cochran-Patrick, LL.D.
1892 Col. Sir Colin Scott Moncrieff, K.C.S.I., K.C.M.G., LL.D.
1902 Sir Reginald Macleod, K.C.B.
1909 Sir James M. Dodds, K.C.B.
1921 Sir John Lamb, K.C.B.
1933 Sir John Jeffrey, K.C.B., C.B.E., F.R.S.E.
1937 John E. Highton, C.B.
1937 Sir Horace P. Hamilton, G.C.B.
1946 Sir David Milne, K.C.B.

JOINT PARLIAMENTARY UNDER-SECRETARIES OF STATE
(*Parliamentary Under-Secretaries for Health before 1926; there was only a single Parliamentary Under-Secretary of State between 1926 and 12th February, 1941*)

1919 J. W. Pratt
1922 James Kidd
1923 Walter E. Elliot, M.C.
1924 James Stewart
1924 Walter E. Elliot, M.C., again
1929 Thomas Johnston
1931 Joseph Westwood
1931 A. N. Skelton
1935 D. J. Colville (later Lord Clydesmuir)
1936 H. J. Scrymgeour-Wedderburn (later the Earl of Dundee)
1939 Captain J. H. F. McEwen (later Sir John McEwen, Bt.)
1940–45 Joseph Westwood, again
1941–42 H. J. Scrymgeour-Wedderburn (later the Earl of Dundee), again
1942–45 A. Chapman
1945 Commander T. D. Galbraith (later Lord Strathclyde)
1945–47 George Buchanan
1945–51 T. Fraser
1947–50 J. J. Robertson
1950–51 Miss M. Herbison
1951–55 Commander T. D. Galbraith (later Lord Strathclyde), again
1951–55 W. McNair Snadden (later Sir William McNair Snadden, Bt.)
1952–57 J. Henderson Stewart (later Sir James Henderson Stewart, Bt.)
1955 J. N. Browne, C.B.E.
1955 N. M. S. Macpherson
1957 Lord John Hope

SECRETARIES OF DEPARTMENTS
Department of Agriculture for Scotland
1929–34 Sir Robert Blyth Greig, M.C., LL.D., D.SC.
1934–53 Sir Patrick R. Laird, K.B.E., C.B., F.R.S.E.
1953 Sir Alexander Glen, K.B.E., C.B., M.C.

Scottish Education Department
1873–84 Sir Francis Richard Sandford, K.C.B. (later Lord Sandford)
1884–85 Patrick Cumin, C.B.
1885–1904 Sir Henry Craik, K.C.B.
1904–22 Sir John Struthers, K.C.B.
1922–29 Sir George Macdonald, K.C.B., F.B.A.
1929–36 Sir William Wallace McKechnie, K.B.E., C.B.
1936–40 Sir James Wallace Peck, C.B., F.R.S.E.
1940–52 Sir John Mackay Thomson, C.B., F.R.S.E.
1952–57 Sir William Stuart Murrie, K.B.E., C.B.
1957 W. F. Arbuckle, C.B.

P

Department of Health for Scotland
1929–33 Sir John Jeffrey, K.C.B., C.B.E.
1933–37 J. E. Highton, C.B.
1937–39 W. S. Douglas (later Sir William Douglas, G.C.B., K.B.E.)
1939–43 W. R. Fraser, C.B. (later Sir Robert Fraser, K.C.B., K.B.E.)
1943–53 Sir George H. Henderson, K.B.E., C.B.
1953–56 H. R. Smith, C.B.
1956 J. Anderson, C.B.

Scottish Home Department
1939 Sir Norman Duke, K.B.E., C.B., D.S.O., M.C.
1942 David Milne, C.B. (later Sir David Milne, K.C.B.)
1946 Sir Norman Duke, K.B.E., C.B., D.S.O., M.C., again
1948 Sir Charles Cunningham, K.B.E., C.B., C.V.O.
1957 Sir William Stuart Murrie, K.B.E., C.B.

HOLDERS OF THE OFFICE OF LORD ADVOCATE SINCE 1692

1692 Sir James Stewart (later Bt.)
1709 Rt. Hon. Sir David Dalrymple of Hailes, Bt.
1711 Sir James Stewart, Bt., again
1714 Thomas Kennedy
1714 Rt. Hon. Sir David Dalrymple of Hailes, Bt., again
1720 Robert Dundas, yr., of Arniston (later Lord Arniston)
1725 Duncan Forbes of Culloden (later Lord Forbes)
1737 Charles Erskine of Barjarg (later Lord Tinwald)
1742 Robert Craigie of Glendoick (later Lord Craigie)
1746 William Grant of Prestongrange (later Lord Prestongrange)
1754 Robert Dundas of Arniston (later Lord Arniston)
1760 Thomas Miller of Barskimming and Glenlee (later Lord Glenlee)
1766 James Montgomery of Stanhope (later Lord Montgomery)
1775 Rt. Hon. Henry Dundas (later Viscount Melville)
1783 The Hon. Henry Erskine
1783 Ilay Campbell of Succoth (later Lord Succoth)
1789 Robert Dundas of Arniston (later Lord Dundas)
1801 Charles Hope of Granton (later Lord Granton)
1806 The Hon. Henry Erskine, again
1807 Archibald Colquhoun (later Lord Colquhoun)
1816 Alexander Maconochie (later Lord Meadowbank)
1819 Rt. Hon. Sir William Rae, Bt.
1830 Francis Jeffrey (later Lord Jeffrey)
1834 John Archibald Murray (later Lord Murray)
1834 Rt. Hon. Sir William Rae, Bt., again
1835 John Archibald Murray (later Lord Murray), again
1839 Andrew Rutherfurd (later Lord Rutherfurd)
1841 Rt. Hon. Sir William Rae, Bt., again
1842 Duncan M'Neill (later Baron Colonsay and Oronsay)
1846 Andrew Rutherfurd (later Lord Rutherfurd), again
1851 James Moncrieff (later Baron Moncrieff)
1852 Adam Anderson (later Lord Anderson)
1852 John Inglis of Glencorse (later Lord Glencorse)
1852 James Moncrieff (later Baron Moncrieff), again
1858 John Inglis of Glencorse (later Lord Glencorse), again
1858 Charles Baillie (later Lord Jerviswoode)
1859 David Mure (later Lord Mure)
1859 James Moncrieff (later Baron Moncrieff), again
1866 George Patton (later Lord Glenalmond)
1867 Edward Strathearn Gordon (later Baron Gordon)
1868 James Moncrieff (later Baron Moncrieff), again
1869 Rt. Hon. George Young (later Lord Young)

1874   Rt. Hon. Edward S. Gordon, Q.C. (later Baron Gordon), again
1876   Rt. Hon. William Watson (later Baron Watson)
1880   John M'Laren (later Lord M'Laren)
1881   Rt. Hon. J. B. Balfour (later Baron Kinross)
1885   Rt. Hon. J. H. A. Macdonald, Q.C. (later Lord Kingsburgh)
1886   Rt. Hon. J. B. Balfour, Q.C. (later Baron Kinross), again
1886   Rt. Hon. J. H. A. Macdonald, Q.C. (later Lord Kingsburgh), again
1888   Rt. Hon. J. P. B. Robertson, Q.C. (later Lord Robertson)
1891   Rt. Hon. Sir Charles J. Pearson, Q.C. (later Lord Pearson)
1892   Rt. Hon. J. B. Balfour, Q.C. (later Baron Kinross), again
1895   Rt. Hon. Sir Charles J. Pearson, Q.C. (later Lord Pearson), again
1896   Rt. Hon. A. Graham Murray, Q.C. (later Viscount Dunedin)
1903   Rt. Hon. Charles Scott Dickson, K.C. (later Lord Dickson)
1905   Rt. Hon. Thomas Shaw, K.C. (later Baron Craigmyle)
1909   Rt. Hon. Alexander Ure, K.C. (later Baron Strathclyde)
1913   Rt. Hon. Robert Munro, K.C. (later Baron Alness)
1916   Rt. Hon. James A. Clyde, K.C. (later Lord Clyde)
1920   Rt. Hon. T. B. Morison, K.C. (later Lord Morison)
1922   Rt. Hon. C. D. Murray, C.M.G., K.C. (later Lord Murray)
1922   Rt. Hon. William Watson, K.C. (later Baron Thankerton)
1924   Rt. Hon. Hugh P. Macmillan, K.C. (later Baron Macmillan)
1924   Rt. Hon. William Watson, K.C. (later Baron Thankerton), again
1929   Rt. Hon. A. M. MacRobert, K.C.
1929   Rt. Hon. C. M. Aitchison, K.C. (later Lord Aitchison)
1933   Rt. Hon. W. G. Normand, K.C. (later Baron Normand)
1935   Rt. Hon. D. Jamieson, K.C. (later Lord Jamieson)
1935   Rt. Hon. T. M. Cooper, K.C. (later Baron Cooper)
1941   Rt. Hon. J. S. C. Reid, K.C. (later Baron Reid)
1945   Rt. Hon. G. R. Thomson, K.C. (later Lord Thomson)
1947   Rt. Hon. John Wheatley, K.C. (later Lord Wheatley)
1951   Rt. Hon. J. L. M. Clyde, K.C. (later Lord Clyde)
1955   Rt. Hon. W. R. Milligan, Q.C.

HOLDERS OF THE OFFICE OF SOLICITOR-GENERAL FOR SCOTLAND SINCE 1709

1709   { Thomas Kennedy
       { Sir James Stewart, Bt.
1714   John Carnegie of Boysack
1714   Sir James Stewart, Bt., again
1717   Robert Dundas, yr., of Arniston (later Lord Arniston)
1720   Walter Stewart
1721   { John Sinclair (later Lord Murkle)
       { Charles Binning
1725   Charles Erskine (later Lord Tinwald)
1737   William Grant (later Lord Prestongrange)
1742   Robert Dundas, yr., of Arniston (later Lord Arniston)
1746   { Patrick Haldane of Gleneagles
       { Alexander Hume
1755   Andrew Pringle of Alemoor (later Lord Alemoor)
1759   Thomas Miller of Barskimming and Glenlee (later Lord Glenlee)
1760   { James Montgomery (later Lord Montgomery)
       { Francis Garden (later Lord Gardenstone)
1764   James Montgomery (later Lord Montgomery), again
1766   Henry Dundas (later Viscount Melville)
1775   Alexander Murray of Henderland (later Lord Henderland)
1783   Ilay Campbell of Succoth (later Lord Succoth)
1783   Alexander Wight
1784   Robert Dundas of Arniston (later Lord Dundas)
1789   Robert Blair of Avontoun (later Lord Blair)
1806   John Clerk of Eldin (later Lord Eldin)

1807 David Boyle of Shewalton (later Lord Boyle)
1811 David Monypenny of Pitmilly (later Lord Pitmilly)
1813 Alexander Maconochie (later Lord Meadowbank)
1816 James Wedderburn
1822 John Hope (later Lord Hope)
1830 Henry Thomas Cockburn (later Lord Cockburn)
1834 Andrew Skene
1834 Duncan M'Neill (later Baron Colonsay and Oronsay)
1835 John Cunninghame (later Lord Cunninghame)
1837 Andrew Rutherfurd (later Lord Rutherfurd)
1839 James Ivory (later Lord Ivory)
1840 Thomas Maitland of Dundrennan (later Lord Dundrennan)
1841 Duncan M'Neill (later Baron Colonsay and Oronsay), again
1842 Adam Anderson (later Lord Anderson)
1846 Thomas Maitland of Dundrennan (later Lord Dundrennan), again
1850 James Moncrieff (later Baron Moncrieff)
1851 John Cowan (later Lord Cowan)
1851 George Deas (later Lord Deas)
1852 John Inglis of Glencorse (later Lord Glencorse)
1852 Charles Neaves (later Lord Neaves)
1853 Robert Handyside (later Lord Handyside)
1853 James Craufurd (later Lord Ardmillan)
1855 Thomas Mackenzie (later Lord Mackenzie)
1855 Edward Francis Maitland (later Lord Barcaple)
1858 Charles Baillie (later Lord Jerviswoode)
1858 David Mure (later Lord Mure)
1859 George Patton (later Lord Glenalmond)
1859 Edward Francis Maitland (later Lord Barcaple), again
1862 George Young (later Lord Young)
1866 Edward Strathearn Gordon (later Baron Gordon)
1867 John Millar (later Lord Craighill)
1868 George Young (later Lord Young), again
1869 Andrew Rutherfurd Clark (later Lord Clark)
1874 John Millar (later Lord Craighill), again
1874 William Watson (later Baron Watson)
1876 John H. A. Macdonald (later Lord Kingsburgh)
1880 John Blair Balfour (later Baron Kinross)
1881 Alexander Asher, Q.C.
1885 J. P. B. Robertson, Q.C. (later Lord Robertson)
1886 Alexander Asher, Q.C., again
1886 J. P. B. Robertson, Q.C. (later Lord Robertson), again
1888 Moir T. Stormonth Darling, Q.C. (later Lord Stormonth Darling)
1890 Sir Charles John Pearson, Q.C. (later Lord Pearson)
1891 Andrew Graham Murray, Q.C. (later Viscount Dunedin)
1892 Alexander Asher, Q.C., again
1894 Thomas Shaw, Q.C. (later Baron Craigmyle)
1895 Andrew Graham Murray, Q.C. (later Viscount Dunedin), again
1896 Charles Scott Dickson, Q.C. (later Lord Dickson)
1903 David Dundas, K.C. (later Lord Dundas)
1905 Edward T. Salvesen, K.C. (later Lord Salvesen)
1905 James Avon Clyde, K.C. (later Lord Clyde)
1905 Alexander Ure, K.C. (later Baron Strathclyde)
1909 Arthur Dewar, K.C. (later Lord Dewar)
1910 William Hunter, K.C. (later Lord Hunter)
1911 Andrew M. Anderson, K.C. (later Lord Anderson)
1913 Thomas B. Morison, K.C. (later Lord Morison)
1920 Charles D. Murray, C.M.G., K.C. (later Lord Murray)
1922 A. H. B. Constable, K.C. (later Lord Constable)
1922 Hon. Wm. Watson, K.C. (later Baron Thankerton)
1922 D. P. Fleming, M.C., K.C. (later Lord Fleming)
1923 F. C. Thomson, K.C.
1924 J. C. Fenton, K.C.

1924 D. P. Fleming, M.C., K.C. (later Lord Fleming), again
1926 A. M. MacRobert, K.C.
1929 W. G. Normand, K.C. (later Baron Normand)
1929 J. C. Watson, K.C. (later Sir John)
1931 W. G. Normand, K.C. (later Baron Normand), again
1933 D. Jamieson, K.C. (later Lord Jamieson)
1935 T. M. Cooper, K.C. (later Baron Cooper)
1936 Albert Russell, K.C. (later Lord Russell)
1936 J. S. C. Reid, K.C. (later Baron Reid)
1941 Sir David King Murray, K.C. (later Lord Birnam)
1945 D. P. Blades, K.C. (later Lord Blades)
1947 John Wheatley, K.C. (later Lord Wheatley)
1947 D. H. Johnston, K.C.
1951 W. R. Milligan, K.C.
1955 William Grant, Q.C.

Index

Accountant of Court, 198
Advertisements, control of, 122, 128
Advisory Committee on Fisheries
　　Research, 168
Advisory Committee on Medical
　　Research in Scotland, 112
Advisory Council on Child Care, 160
Advisory Council on Education in
　　Scotland, 68, 82, 89
Advisory Panel on Highlands and
　　Islands, 172, 175-176
After Care Council, 152
After Care Services:
　　sick persons', 108
　　prisoners', 152
Agricultural:
　　advisory services, 53, 55
　　colleges, 52, 53-55, 92
　　deficiency payments, 60
　　drainage, 41
　　education, 53-55, 92
　　Executive Committees, 37, 38, 39,
　　　40, 42, 51-52
　　expansion programme, 59
　　guarantee system, 58-63
　　holdings, 42
　　husbandry, action against bad, 52
　　Improvement Council, 53
　　production, improvement of, 46-57
　　production grants, 61, 62, 63
　　marketing, 57, 59, 60, 63
　　Organisation Society, 57
　　research, 48, 53
　　Research Council, 54
　　seeds, control and improvement of
　　　quality, 47-48
　　statistics, 63
　　subsidies, 40, 53, 62
　　Wages Board, 56
　　wages regulation, 56
Agriculture, Departmental adminis-
　　tration of, 35-64
Agriculture in Scotland, 35, 37, 39,
　　46-47, 59
Alkali Works inspection, 133
Ambulance Services, 107
Amenities, protection and preservation
　　of, 122, 123, 127-128, 197
Ancient and Historical Monuments,
　　Royal Commission on, 196

Animal Diseases Research Association,
　　54
Animal Health, 20, 50-51
Animals, protection of, 158
Approved Schools, 68, 78-80, 150
Art Galleries, 68, 194
Arterial drainage, 41
Arts Council, representation on, 93
Assessor of Public Undertakings, 197
Association of County Councils in
　　Scotland, 31, 68
Association of Counties of Cities, 31,
　　68
Association of Directors of Education,
　　68
Association of Headmasters of
　　Secondary Schools, 68
Astronomer Royal for Scotland, 196
Atmospheric pollution, 135
Atomic Energy, 170

Bibles, licences for printing and
　　publishing, 209
Birds, protection of, 158
Births, deaths and marriages, registra-
　　tion of, 192, 193
Blind persons, welfare of, 119
Board for the Improvement of Manu-
　　factures, 194, 212
Board of Agriculture, 17, 18, 36, 215
Board of Education in Edinburgh, 72,
　　214
Board of Health, 16, 213
Board of Supervision for the Relief of
　　the Poor, 116, 169, 213
Board of Trade, 123, 124, 129, 130, 199
Borstals, 146, 150-152
Bridges, 20, 41
British Transport Commission, 197
Building byelaws, 140
Buildings:
　　development plans for, 124
　　preservation orders, 128
　　school, 73-75, 76
Byelaws, 78, 114, 140, 158

Calf subsidy scheme, 63
Camperdown Commission (1870), 14,
　　18, 214
Capital punishment, reprieve of, 153

Central Institutions for Advanced Education, 71, 87, 92, 95
Central Office of Information, 30
Ceremonial, 158, 190
Charitable collections, 158
Chemists' prescriptions, statutory charge for, 110
Child Care:
  adoption, 160
  boarded out children, 159
  children's homes, 159
  Departmental responsibilities and duties, 160
  Inspectorate, 160
  Local Authority responsibilities, 29, 159, 160
  Scottish Advisory Council on, 160
  training in, 146, 160
Child guidance centres, 78
Children Act (1948), 159
Children :
  numbers in care or under supervision, 159
  regulation of employment of, 78
  release from school for harvesting, 56
Cinemas, 158
Civil defence:
  Departmental responsibilities and duties, 156-157
  Local Authority responsibilities, 157
Civil Proceedings, 208
Clean Air Act (1956), 135
Clyde Committee, 159
Coast Protection, 29
Common grazings regulations, 43
Community centres, 164
Congested Districts Commissioners, 43
Congested Districts (Scotland) Act (1897), 43, 214
Constabulary, appointment of H.M. Inspector of, 147
Convention of Royal Burghs, 13, 31
Coronations, 190
Coroners, 208
Country Industries Development Trust, 57
County Councils, general responsibilities, 31
Court of Session, 99, 192, 198, 204
Courts of Law, 149, 198, 204, 206
Criminal Justice (Scotland) Act (1949), 151
Criminal Lunatic Department, 189
Criminal Proceedings, 154, 206-209

Croft, statutory meaning of, 42
Crofters Commission, 42, 43, 214
Crofters' holdings, 42, 43
Crofters' houses and buildings, 41
Crofters (Scotland) Act (1955), 42
Crofting:
  areas, forestry in, 184
  conditions, 42-43
Crop husbandry, schemes for improvement of, 47-49
Crop production, grants for, 62
Crops:
  destructive insects and pests, control of, 48
  diseases of, control, 48
  guaranteed prices for, 60
  inspection and certification of, 47-48
  seeds of, improvement of quality, 47-48
Crown Agent, 207, 208
Crown Estate in Scotland, 186
Crown Estate Commissioners, 7, 186
Crown Lands Act (1943), 19
Crown Office, 4, 207, 208, 209
Crown Suits (Scotland) Act (1857), 208
Curtis Committee, 159

Dairies:
  hygiene in, 114
  licensing of, 114
  Local Authority responsibilities, 114
  registration of, 114
Dairy Research Institute, 54
Deeds, registration of, 191, 192
Dental Estimates Board, 110
Dental inspection in Schools, 77
Dentists, remuneration of, 109
Department of Agriculture for Scotland:
  Accounting Officer, 5
  Administrative responsibilities and duties, 35-64, 115
  Agricultural Executive Committees, 38, 39, 40, 42, 51-52
  Farm Economics branch, 54
  history of, 214
  Inspectorate, 30, 40, 48, 49, 53, 55
  Lands Officers, 38, 43, 44, 184
  main functions of, 4, 35
  organisation of, 36, 64
  Scientific Services Station, 47, 54
  Secretaries of, 217
  staff of, 36
  stud farms, 50

Department of Health for Scotland:
Accounting Officer, 5
Administrative responsibilities and
duties, 78, 105-141, 156, 171, 189,
193
Architects, work of, 121, 138, 141
Engineers, work of, 29, 134, 167
history of, 116, 213
Inspectorate, 114, 119, 133, 141
main functions of, 4, 105
Medical Commissioners, 189
Medical Officers, 106
Organisation of, 142
Planning Officers, work of, 121
Secretaries of, 218
Staffing, 141
Department of the Registers of
Scotland, 146, 190
Destructive insects and pests, control
of, 48
Development and Industry, Scottish
Council for, 173, 174
Development Commission, 168
Development Corporations, appoint-
ment of, 130
Development Fund, grants from, 57
Development plans, preparation and
approval of, 124-126
Director of Forestry for Scotland, 183
Director of Prisons and Borstal
Services, 151
Discharged Prisoners' Aid Society,
152
Disease, prevention of, 108, 132
Diseases of animals, control of, 50
Diseases of fish, control of, 168
Diseases of plants, control of, 48
Distribution of Industry Act (1945),
133
Distribution of Industry Panel, repre-
sentation on, 124
District Wages Committees, functions
of, 56
Doctors, remuneration of, 109
Dogs and cats, supervision of quaran-
tine premises, 51
Drainage, 41, 135
Dredging of fishery harbours, 167
Drugs, 113, 114
Drugs Accounts Committee, 110
Drunkenness, 158

Economic affairs, 30, 123, 173-177
Edinburgh and East of Scotland Col-
lege of Agriculture, 54
Edinburgh Gazette, Keeper of, 199

Education:
advanced, 92
Advisory Council on, 68, 82
agricultural, 53-55, 92
bursaries, 100
byelaws, 78
Central Institutions for, 71, 87, 92, 95
Departmental administration of,
67-101
financing of, 94-100
further education, 70, 83, 91-93
grant regulations, 95
of handicapped children, 67, 70, 87
part-time education, 70
vocational, 70-71
Education Authorities:
examination of expenditure of, 96
grants regulations, 95
organisation and functions, 72-73,
74
Education (Exemptions) (Scotland)
Act (1947), 56
Education (Scotland) Act (1918), 94
Education (Scotland) Act (1945), 70,
98
Education (Scotland) Act (1946), 68,
70
Education (Scotland) Acts, regula-
tions under, 67
Education (Scotland) Fund, 86, 88,
92, 95, 97, 100
Educational Endowments, 98-100
accounts of, 96
Commissioners under, 99
Local Education Authority, 99
schemes approval orders, 99
Educational Institute of Scotland, 68
Educational system in Scotland, 68-71
Electricity Boards, 169, 170
Electricity Reorganisation (Scotland)
Act (1954), 20, 169
Electricity supply industry, 169-170
Employment and industry, 173
Employment and Training Act
(1948), 78
Epilepsy Association, Scottish, 120
Estates (see Parliament of Scotland)
Eve Committee Report on Crown
Lands, 186
Exchequer equalisation grant, 162
Executive Councils (General Practi-
tioner Service), 109, 111, 113
appeals against decisions of, 111
failure to carry out statutory
duties, 113
Export of plants, 48

Farm:
dispossession of, procedure, 42, 52
labour, 53, 56
modernisation of, 62
output, 46
price review, 50
water supplies, 40
Farming standards, improvement and
control of, 52
Fatal Accidents Inquiry Courts, 208
Fertiliser subsidies, 62
Fine Art, Royal Commission for
Scotland, 197
Fire Brigades Advisory Council for
Scotland, 156
Fire Services:
Brigades, 155
College, 156
history of, 155
Inspector of Fire Services for
Scotland, appointment of, 156
Local Authority expenditure on, 155
organisation and administration of,
154-156
Firemen:
conditions of service, 155
numbers in Scotland, 156
training of, 146, 156
Fires, inquiries into, 208
Fish diseases, control of, 168
Fisheries:
Departmental administration of,
165-168
freshwater, 168
Inspectorate, 167
International co-operation on, 168
protection of, 146, 167
salmon fisheries, 168
sea fisheries, 166-168
Fishery:
Board, 17, 19, 145, 165, 212
cruisers, 146, 167
fleet, Scottish, 167
harbours, 146, 167
officers, 146, 167
Research Stations, 146, 168
Fishing industry, subsidies to, 166
Fishing, regulation of close season
for, 168
Food:
adulteration of, 113
hygiene of, 114
pests of stored, 49
production, 37
standards, 114
supplies, 38

Food and Drugs (Adulteration) Acts,
113, 114
Forestry:
administration of, 181-185
Commission, 7, 38, 44, 181-185
Conservancies, 183
Conservators, 185
land, acquisition for, 184
land, management of, 44, 184
planting proposals, procedure, 38
Secretary of State's responsibilities
for, 20, 181
Further Education Centres, inspection of, 83
Further Education (Scotland) Code
(1952), 92

Gas Board, Scottish:
rating assessments and payment,
197
valuation of undertakings, 197
General Board of Commissioners in
Lunacy for Scotland, 189, 214
General Board of Control for Scot-
land, 19, 188-189, 214
Gilmour Committee, 7, 19, 20, 25,
173, 193, 214
Goschen formula, 94
Grass-drying, assistance for, 57
Great Britain Police Council, 148, 149

Haldane Committee on Machinery
of Government, 18
Handicapped children, education of,
67, 70, 87
Handicapped persons, welfare of,
117, 119-120
Hannah Dairy Research Institute, 54
Harbours:
grants and loans for, 167
works, 41
Harvest labour, 56
Health Centres, 110
Health Services Council, Scottish, 106,
113
Health services (see National)
Herring Industry Board, 166
Highland development programme,
176
Highlands and Islands:
Advisory Panel, 172, 175-176
employment in, 184
livestock improvement in, 50
medical service, 106
Medical Service Board, 213
remuneration of doctors in, 109-110

Highlands and Islands—*continued*
  schemes for improvement, 41, 176
  Standing Committee on Health
    services, 106
  steamer services, 171
  veterinary services, 50
  water-power resources, development
    of, 169
Highway Authorities, payment of
    grants to, 170
Hill Farming Research Organisation, 54
Hill farming:
  Advisory Committee, 40
  improvement of, 40
  livestock rearing, 40
  livestock subsidies schemes, 63
  production grants, 63
Historic buildings, 196
Historic Buildings Council for Scot-
    land, 128
Historical records, 192
Home Care services, 108
Home Office, 148, 157
Hornings, Register of, 191
Horticultural marketing, 57
Horticultural Research Institute,
    Scottish, 54
Hospital Boards of Management, 107,
    112, 113
Hospital Boards, Regional, 112, 113
Hospital Endowments Research Trust,
    Scottish, 112
Hospital services, 106-108
Hospitals:
  building programme, 108
  control and management of, 107
  teaching, 107
House-building, assistance for, 141
House-ownership, encouragement of,
    141
Houses:
  private, maintenance and improve-
    ment grants, 140
  standards of construction, 137, 140
  unfit, repairs and improvement or
    demolition of, 139, 141
Housing:
  Advisory Committee, Scottish, 138
  Associations, assistance to, 141
  Departmental administration and
    duties, 136-141
  Inspectors, 141
  land for, 38
  Local Housing Authority, responsi-
    bilities and duties, 38, 136, 140,
    141

Housing—*continued*
  New Town Corporations, responsi-
    bilities of, 138
  of special groups, 117, 118, 138,
    141, 185
  Special Housing Association, Scot-
    tish, 138-139
  subsidies, 136, 137, 138, 139
Housing (Repairs and Rents) (Scot-
    land) Act (1954), 139
Hydro-electricity, schemes for, 38, 169

Industrial Design, Council of, 93
Industrial development, 129, 174
Industrial sites, planning permission
    for, 129
Industry:
  and transport, 165-172
  distribution of, 124, 129
  encouragement of, 173-177
  Scottish Board for, 173
  Scottish Council for Development
    and, 173, 174
  Tourist Board, Scottish, 174
Information Office, Scottish, 30
Insurance Commissioners, Scottish,
    213
International Council for the Explora-
    tion of the Sea, 168

Judges, appointment of, 204
Judiciary system, 203
Justice, miscarriage of, 153
Justices of the Peace, appointment
    of, 20

Keeper of Registers, Office of, 19, 191

Labour:
  employment in rural areas, 184
  farm, 56
  wages of agricultural, 56
Land:
  acquisitions of, 38, 43, 44, 52, 122,
    123, 124, 127, 129, 171, 183
  improvement schemes, 39
  management of, 43, 184
  registration, 191
  requirements of Service Depart-
    ments, 38
  restoration, 38
  rights, 191
  settlement, 43
  tenure, 42, 43
  use of, 37-39, 44, 121-124, 126, 129,
    130, 183, 184

Land Court, Scottish, 43, 52
Lands Officers, work of, 38, 43, 44
Lands, valuation of, 197
Law and Order, maintenance of, 145-154, 157, 163
Law Charges (Scotland) Vote, 154
Law Courts, accounting officer, 199
Law Officers, 4, 25, 203
Law Society of Scotland, 154
Leaving Certificate, Scottish, 69
Leaving Certificate examination, 83, 84-85
Legal Advice, 29, 205
Legal Aid Scheme, 154
Legal Secretaries, 204
Liberty of the Subject, 153, 188, 189
Licensed premises, State management of, 146, 158
Liquor licensing, 157
Livestock:
  artificial insemination of, 49, 53
  Breeding Societies, grants to, 49
  guaranteed prices for, 60, 62
  humane slaughter of, 115
  imports and exports, administrative control of, 51
  inspection of, 49
  licensing of, 49
  production grants, 61, 63
  progeny testing stations, 49
  quarantine, 51
  subsidies for, 63
Livestock husbandry, schemes for improvement, 49-51
Local Government, 30-32, 161-164
Local Government Board for Scotland, 213
Local Registrars, 193
Lord Advocate:
  Departments of, 203-209
  Office of, 4, 9, 11, 203, 204, 218
  responsibilities of, 25, 29, 198, 203
Lord Clerk Register, 9, 191, 192
Lord Justice Clerk, 9, 149, 204
Lord Justice-General, 204
Lord President of the Court of Session, 149, 192, 204
Lord Privy Seal, joint responsibilities with, 187
Lords of the Articles, 9
Lunacy, General Board of Commissioners in, 189, 214
Lunacy and Mental Deficiency Acts, duties under, 108
Lyon Clerk, 190
Lyon King of Arms, 189

Macaulay Institute for Soil Research, 54
Marginal agricultural production schemes, 39, 63
Marketing Boards, 59, 60, 63
Marketing of agricultural produce, assistance for, 57
Meat inspection, 115
Medical:
  Commissioners, 189
  inspection in schools, 77
  Officers, work of, 106, 108
  research, 111-112
Medical Education Committee, 107
Medical Research Council, 112
Medical services:
  Highlands and Islands, 213
  Local Authority, 106
  national health, 106, 109
Mental defectives, care and treatment of, 108, 189, 214
Mental hospitals, administration of, 188
Mental institutions, detention in, 188
Mercy, Royal Prerogative of, 152
Milk:
  attested herds scheme, 50, 115
  hygiene, 114
  in schools scheme, 77
  Marketing Boards, 115
  special designations, 114
Milk and Dairies Act (1914), 114
Minister of State, 4, 16, 24
Minister of State, holders of Office of, 216
Ministry of Agriculture, Fisheries and Food, 20, 50, 58, 114, 115, 166
Ministry of Education, 75, 78
Ministry of Health, 111, 114
Ministry of Housing and Local Government, 135
Ministry of Labour, 78
Ministry of National Insurance, 20
Ministry of Power, 38, 130, 169
Ministry of Transport, 170, 171
Ministry of Works, 123, 128
Mothers and young children, care of, 108, 109
Museums, 68, 93, 195, 212

National Assistance Act (1948), 117
National Assistance Board, 116
National Coal Board, 38, 130
National Committee for the Training of Teachers, 82, 83, 86, 88
National Farmers' Union, 59

National Federation for Welfare of
the Blind, grants to, 120
National Forest Parks, 184
National Galleries, 146, 194, 212
National Health Service:
administrative organisation and re-
sponsibilities, 105-113
Executive Councils, 109, 111, 113
general practitioner service, 106, 109
hospital and special services, 106-108
Local Authority services, 108, 113
salaries and conditions of employ-
ment in, 111
National Health Service (Scotland)
Act (1947), 105, 117, 189
National Institute of Agricultural
Engineering, Scottish Station, 54
National Joint Council, 89, 90
National Library of Scotland, 195
National Museum of Antiquities of
Scotland, 195, 199, 212
National Parks, 128
National Parks Survey Committee, 128
Nationalised Industries, payment of
rates, 197
Nature Conservancy, 128
Nature reserves, development plans
for, 124
New Towns:
designation of areas, 128
Development Corporations, 122,
130
housing in, 138
Local Planning Authority responsi-
bilities, 122
North of Scotland College of Agri-
culture, 54
North of Scotland Hydro-Electric
Board, 38, 169
Northern Lighthouses Commission,
209
Noxious fumes, control of, 133
Nuclear generating stations, 170
Nuisances, Statutory, 132

Offensive trades, licensing of, 133
Old people:
homes for, 118-119
welfare services for, 117-118
Old People's Welfare Committee,
Scottish, 118
Open spaces, development plans for,
124
Opencast coal operations, 38
Ophthalmic services Committees, 109
Over-fishing, restrictions on, 168

Parliament of Scotland, 9, 191
Parliamentary:
Bills, drafting of, 205
Draftsmen, 204
records, 192
Parliamentary Private Secretaries,
duties of, 27
Parliamentary Under-Secretaries of
State:
appointment of, 16
holders of Office of, 217
responsibilities of, 24
Parliaments, Union of, 8
Peat Committee, Scottish, 41
Peat, use of, 41, 170
Permanent Under-Secretary of State,
19, 25, 217
Pharmaceutical Council, 111
Physical Training and Recreation Act
(1937), 164
Piers, 41
Planning:
administrative organisation and re-
sponsibilities, 121-131
control system, 126-127
decisions, appeals against, 37, 127
Development Corporations, 130
development plans, 37, 124
liaison, 123
Local Planning Authority responsi-
bilities, 121-124, 129, 163
new towns, 129
Officers, work of, 121
permission, 129
powers, 128-129
redevelopment, 129
restrictions, compensation for, 127
town development, 130
Planning Committee, Scottish
Physical, 124
Plant Breeding, Scottish Society for
Research in, 48, 54
Playing fields, grants for, 164
Police:
College, 147, 156
Departmental responsibilities for,
146-149
Local Police Authorities, 147
Police Council, Great Britain, 148,
149
Police Council, Scottish, 148, 149
Police Forces, organisation of, 147
Policemen:
conditions of service, 148
numbers of, in Scotland, 156
training of, 146, 147

Valuation of Lands (Scotland) Act (1854), 197
Valuation of Public undertakings, 197
Valuation Rolls, 192
Veterinary services, 50
Village halls, grants for, 164
Vocational education and training, 70-71, 91
Voluntary Boards, delegation of responsibilities to, 113

War pensioners, medical care of, 20
Warrants, 8, 154, 158
Water Advisory Committee, Scottish, 134
Water supplies:
  Departmental responsibilities and duties, 133-134
  farm, 40
  Local Authorities responsibilities, 134
  Rural Water Supplies and Sewerage Acts, 133, 134

Welfare foods, distribution of, 109
Welfare services:
  Departmental responsibilities and duties, 116-120
  for children, 159-160
  for the mentally ill, 188
  Local Authority responsibilities, 118-120
West of Scotland Agricultural College, 54
Whaling, 168
White Fish Authority, 166, 167
Whitley Councils, 109, 111
Woodlands (see also Forestry)
  Dedication Schemes, 184
  Licences for felling, 185
Women's Rural Institutes, 57

Young offenders, 150
Young persons, employment of, 78
Youth Clubs, 71
Youth and Employment service, 78, 83

Poor Law, 116, 213
Population census, 193
Population, decentralisation of, 130
Prisoners:
  after-care of, 152
  rehabilitation of, 152
  remission of sentences, 153
  treatment of, 151
Prison Visiting Committees, 152
Prisons:
  administration of, 19, 145, 146, 150-152, 214
  Criminal Lunatic Department, 189
Private Legislation Procedure, 163
Private Office, 26
Privy Council, 203, 209
Probation:
  Council, Scottish Central, 150
  Local Probation Committees, 149
  Officers, 150
  service, 149-150
Proclamations, 190
Procurators Fiscal, 207, 208
Property, heritable rights in, 191
Prosecutions, 206
Protection of birds, 158
Protection of property, 155
Provisional Orders, 163
Public Health:
  Departmental responsibilities and duties, 113-115, 132-135, 213
  Local Health Authority responsibilities, 114, 133, 134
Public libraries, 68
Public Order, 145-154, 157, 163
Public Records, 191
Public Undertakings, valuation of, 197

Queen's and Lord Treasurer's Remembrancer, 198
Queen's Peace, 147, 149, 159

Rabbit Clearance campaign, 48
Rag Flocks Acts, 133
Rating, 163
Rats and mice, control of, 49
Record Office, Scottish, 191, 192
Records Advisory Council, Scottish, 193
Regalia of Scotland, custody of, 199
Regional Hospital Boards, organisation and responsibilities of, 107-108
Registers in Scotland, 191
Registrar General for Scotland, 19, 193
Registration of Companies, business names and Partnerships, 199

Remand Homes, 150
Reorganisation of Offices (Scotland) Act (1928), 193
Reorganisation of Offices (Scotland) Act (1939), 19, 25, 213, 214
Representation of the People Acts, 158
River pollution, prevention of, 135
River Purification Boards, 135
Roads, 20, 41, 124, 125, 127, 170-171
Rowett Research Institute for Animal Nutrition, 54
Royal Commission on Ancient and Historical Monuments, 196
Royal Commission on the Civil Service (1914), 18, 214
Royal Commission on Fine Art, 197
Royal Commission on Housing in Scotland (1917), 136
Royal Commission on Scottish Affairs (1954), 20, 25, 50, 115, 161, 166, 170, 171, 210
Royal Commissions, records of, 192
Royal Fine Art Commission for Scotland, 197
Royal Observatory, Edinburgh, 146, 196
Royal Prerogative, 145, 152-154
Royal Scottish Museum, 68, 93
Rural Water Supplies and Sewerage Acts, 133, 134

St. Andrew's House, 4, 19
Salmon fisheries, 168
Saltire Society, 140
Sanitation:
  general functions concerning, 132-135
  Local Authority responsibilities, 132, 133, 134, 135
Sasines, General Register of, 191, 192
School:
  curriculum, 69
  leaving certificates, 69, 84-85
  meals service, 76, 83
  promotion schemes, 76
  Promotions Boards, 69
Schools: 72-80
  broadcasting in, 83
  building of, 73-75, 76, 125
  closing of, 75
  comprehensive, 70
  dental inspection in, 77
  fee-paying, 70
  for handicapped children, 67
  grant-aided, 69, 70, 96
  health service in, 77

Schools—*continued*
  independent, 69
  inspection of, 82
  libraries, 83
  medical inspection in, 77
  numbers of, 69
  primary, 69
  Secondary, 69
  voluntary, 95
Schools (Scotland) Code, 73, 82
Scottish Advisory Council on Child Care, 160
Scottish After Care Council, 152
Scottish Agricultural Improvement Council, 53
Scottish Agricultural Organisation Society, grants to, 57
Scottish Agricultural Wages Board, 56
Scottish Board for Industry, 173
Scottish Boards, 17-18, 188, 212-215
Scottish Central Probation Council, 150
Scottish Council for Development and Industry, 173, 174
Scottish Council of Social Service, grants to, 57
Scottish Country Industries Development Trust, financial assistance to, 57
Scottish Court Service, 149
Scottish Dental Estimates Board, 110
Scottish Departments:
  constitutional position of, 5, 19
  liaison staff, 28
  main functions of, 4, 19
  payment of Votes administered by, 199
  records of, 192
Scottish Education Department:
  Accounting Officer, 5
  administrative responsibilities and duties, 67-101, 150, 164
  approved schools, 150
  Finance and Accountant's branches, work of, 95
  history of, 19, 68, 72, 214
  Inspectorate, 68, 73, 75, 76, 80, 81-85, 92
  main functions of, 4, 67-68
  organisation of, 101
  Secretaries of, 217
  staff of, 68
Scottish educational system, 68
Scottish Epilepsy Association, grants to, 120

Scottish Gas Board, valuation of undertakings of, 197
Scottish Health Services Council, 106, 113
Scottish Home Department:
  Accounting Officer, 5
  administrative responsibilities and duties, 145-178
  history of, 19, 145
  Inspectorate, 150
  main functions of, 4, 146
  organisation of, 178
  Secretaries of, 218
  staff of, 145, 146
Scottish Horticultural Research Institute, 54
Scottish Hospitals Endowment Research Trust, 112
Scottish Housing Advisory Committee, 138
Scottish Information Office, 30
Scottish Insurance Commissioners, 213
Scottish Land Court, 43, 52
Scottish Leaving Certificate examination, 69, 84-85
'Scottish Managers', 11
Scottish Office:
  and Parliament, 27-28
  and Local Authorities, 30-32
  common services, 29-30, 141
  creation of, 8, 15-17
  Departmental functions, 4
  liaison arrangements, 26, 28-29, 30, 123
  Ministerial arrangements, 23-25
  Ministers, 4, 23, 216-217
  organisation and structure of, 4-7, 19, 22-23, 183
  Private Office, 26
  Permanent Under-Secretary of State, 25
  Solicitor's Office, 29
  Statistician, 30
Scottish Old People's Welfare Committee, grants to, 118
Scottish Peat Committee, 41
Scottish Physical Planning Committee, 124
Scottish Police College, 147, 156
Scottish Police Council, 148
Scottish Record Office, 191, 192
Scottish Records Advisory Council, 193
Scottish Representative Peers, election of, 193

Scottish Secretary, 10
Scottish Society for Research in Plant Breeding, 48, 54
Scottish Special Housing Association, 138-139
Scottish Standing Committee, 27
Scottish Tourist Board, 173
Scottish Water Advisory Committee, 134
Scottish Women's Rural Institutes, financial assistance to, 57
Sea fisheries, 166, 168
Sea transport services, 171
Seals, 8, 191, 192
Secretary for Scotland Acts (1885 and 1887), 15, 16
Secretary of State for Scotland:
  as arbiter of land use, 57
  as landowner, 43, 52
  as Scotland's Minister, 1, 3, 7, 79
  general functions and responsibilities, 1, 3-7, 18-21, 28, 67, 106, 120, 123, 134, 136, 146, 152, 155, 169, 170, 173-179
  joint responsibilities, 53, 78, 114, 123, 128, 166, 181-187
  Parliamentary responsibilities, 6, 16, 28, 187
  rights of appeal to, 37, 76, 111, 127, 132
  Seal of, 8
  transfers of functions, 15-17, 18-21, 98, 115, 116, 165, 169, 170
Secretary of State for Scotland, Office of:
  creation, 6
  development, 18-21, 98, 145
  holders of, 216
  reorganisation of, 18
Service Departments, land requirements of, 123
Sewage disposal, 133
Sheriff Clerk's Office, staffing of, 146
Sheriff Courts, 192, 199, 207
Sheriffs, appointment of, 204
Shops, legislation concerning, 158
Silo subsidies, 62
Slaughterhouses, hygiene and control of, 115
Small Landholders (Scotland) Acts, 42, 215
Smoke-control areas, designation of, 135
Social Service, Scottish Council of, 57
Society for the Vindication of Scottish Rights, 13, 15

Solicitor-General for Scotland:
  duties of, 4, 25, 203
  holders of Office of, 219
Solicitor's Office, 29
Sorn Committee, 163
South of Scotland Electricity Board, 169, 170
Special Housing Association, Scottish, 138-139
Standing Committee, Scottish, 27
State Management Districts, 146,
State Management (licensed premises), 146, 158
Steamer services, subsidies for, 171
Stud farms, 50

Teachers, 86, 90
  certificates, 86, 87
  emergency scheme, 88
  guidance of, 83
  of handicapped children, 87
  pensions, 95, 96-97
  qualifications of, 92
  recruitment of, 87-89
  salaries regulations, 89
  superannuation regulations, 95, 96-97
  Training Colleges, 86-89
  training of, 82
  training regulations, 86
  University graduates, 88, 89
Teaching hospitals, 107
Theatres, 158
Tourist Board, Scottish, 173
Town and Country Planning. (See Planning)
Town Councils, powers of, 31
Transport, 165, 170, 172, 174
Treasure Trove, 199
Treasury representative in Scotland, 198
Treaty of Union, 11, 192, 194, 195
Trees:
  licences for felling, 185
  preservation orders, 122, 128
Trunk roads, planning control,
Tuberculosis, control of, 112

University Grants Committee, 98
University matters, 209
University scholarships, 100
Universities, and teaching hospitals
University education, 67

Valuation and Rating (Scotland) Act (1956), 162, 163

Poor Law, 116, 213
Population census, 193
Population, decentralisation of, 130
Prisoners:
   after-care of, 152
   rehabilitation of, 152
   remission of sentences, 153
   treatment of, 151
Prison Visiting Committees, 152
Prisons:
   administration of, 19, 145, 146,
      150-152, 214
   Criminal Lunatic Department, 189
Private Legislation Procedure, 163
Private Office, 26
Privy Council, 203, 209
Probation:
   Council, Scottish Central, 150
   Local Probation Committees, 149
   Officers, 150
   service, 149-150
Proclamations, 190
Procurators Fiscal, 207, 208
Property, heritable rights in, 191
Prosecutions, 206
Protection of birds, 158
Protection of property, 155
Provisional Orders, 163
Public Health:
   Departmental responsibilities and
      duties, 113-115, 132-135, 213
   Local Health Authority responsi-
      bilities, 114, 133, 134
Public libraries, 68
Public Order, 145-154, 157, 163
Public Records, 191
Public Undertakings, valuation of, 197

Queen's and Lord Treasurer's Remembrancer, 198
Queen's Peace, 147, 149, 159

Rabbit Clearance campaign, 48
Rag Flocks Acts, 133
Rating, 163
Rats and mice, control of, 49
Record Office, Scottish, 191, 192
Records Advisory Council, Scottish,
   193
Regalia of Scotland, custody of, 199
Regional Hospital Boards, organisation
   and responsibilities of, 107-108
Registers in Scotland, 191
Registrar General for Scotland, 19, 193
Registration of Companies, business
   names and Partnerships, 199

Remand Homes, 150
Reorganisation of Offices (Scotland)
   Act (1928), 193
Reorganisation of Offices (Scotland)
   Act (1939), 19, 25, 213, 214
Representation of the People Acts, 158
River pollution, prevention of, 135
River Purification Boards, 135
Roads, 20, 41, 124, 125, 127, 170-171
Rowett Research Institute for Animal
   Nutrition, 54
Royal Commission on Ancient and
   Historical Monuments, 196
Royal Commission on the Civil
   Service (1914), 18, 214
Royal Commission on Fine Art, 197
Royal Commission on Housing in
   Scotland (1917), 136
Royal Commission on Scottish Affairs
   (1954), 20, 25, 50, 115, 161, 166,
   170, 171, 210
Royal Commissions, records of, 192
Royal Fine Art Commission for
   Scotland, 197
Royal Observatory, Edinburgh, 146,
   196
Royal Prerogative, 145, 152-154
Royal Scottish Museum, 68, 93
Rural Water Supplies and Sewerage
   Acts, 133, 134

St. Andrew's House, 4, 19
Salmon fisheries, 168
Saltire Society, 140
Sanitation:
   general functions concerning, 132-
      135
   Local Authority responsibilities, 132,
      133, 134, 135
Sasines, General Register of, 191, 192
School:
   curriculum, 69
   leaving certificates, 69, 84-85
   meals service, 76, 83
   promotion schemes, 76
   Promotions Boards, 69
Schools: 72-80
   broadcasting in, 83
   building of, 73-75, 76, 125
   closing of, 75
   comprehensive, 70
   dental inspection in, 77
   fee-paying, 70
   for handicapped children, 67
   grant-aided, 69, 70, 96
   health service in, 77

Schools—*continued*
  independent, 69
  inspection of, 82
  libraries, 83
  medical inspection in, 77
  numbers of, 69
  primary, 69
  Secondary, 69
  voluntary, 95
Schools (Scotland) Code, 73, 82
Scottish Advisory Council on Child
  Care, 160
Scottish After Care Council, 152
Scottish Agricultural Improvement
  Council, 53
Scottish Agricultural Organisation
  Society, grants to, 57
Scottish Agricultural Wages Board,
  56
Scottish Board for Industry, 173
Scottish Boards, 17-18, 188, 212-215
Scottish Central Probation Council,
  150
Scottish Council for Development and
  Industry, 173, 174
Scottish Council of Social Service,
  grants to, 57
Scottish Country Industries Develop-
  ment Trust, financial assistance to,
  57
Scottish Court Service, 149
Scottish Dental Estimates Board, 110
Scottish Departments:
  constitutional position of, 5, 19
  liaison staff, 28
  main functions of, 4, 19
  payment of Votes administered
    by, 199
  records of, 192
Scottish Education Department:
  Accounting Officer, 5
  administrative responsibilities and
    duties, 67-101, 150, 164
  approved schools, 150
  Finance and Accountant's branches,
    work of, 95
  history of, 19, 68, 72, 214
  Inspectorate, 68, 73, 75, 76, 80, 81-
    85, 92
  main functions of, 4, 67-68
  organisation of, 101
  Secretaries of, 217
  staff of, 68
Scottish educational system, 68
Scottish Epilepsy Association, grants
  to, 120

Scottish Gas Board, valuation of
  undertakings of, 197
Scottish Health Services Council, 106,
  113
Scottish Home Department:
  Accounting Officer, 5
  administrative responsibilities and
    duties, 145-178
  history of, 19, 145
  Inspectorate, 150
  main functions of, 4, 146
  organisation of, 178
  Secretaries of, 218
  staff of, 145, 146
Scottish Horticultural Research
  Institute, 54
Scottish Hospitals Endowment Re-
  search Trust, 112
Scottish Housing Advisory Com-
  mittee, 138
Scottish Information Office, 30
Scottish Insurance Commissioners,
  213
Scottish Land Court, 43, 52
Scottish Leaving Certificate examina-
  tion, 69, 84-85
'Scottish Managers', 11
Scottish Office:
  and Parliament, 27-28
  and Local Authorities, 30-32
  common services, 29-30, 141
  creation of, 8, 15-17
  Departmental functions, 4
  liaison arrangements, 26, 28-29, 30,
    123
  Ministerial arrangements, 23-25
  Ministers, 4, 23, 216-217
  organisation and structure of, 4-7,
    19, 22-23, 183
  Private Office, 26
  Permanent Under-Secretary of
    State, 25
  Solicitor's Office, 29
  Statistician, 30
Scottish Old People's Welfare Com-
  mittee, grants to, 118
Scottish Peat Committee, 41
Scottish Physical Planning Com-
  mittee, 124
Scottish Police College, 147, 156
Scottish Police Council, 148
Scottish Record Office, 191, 192
Scottish Records Advisory Council,
  193
Scottish Representative Peers, election
  of, 193

Scottish Secretary, 10
Scottish Society for Research in Plant
    Breeding, 48, 54
Scottish Special Housing Association,
    138-139
Scottish Standing Committee, 27
Scottish Tourist Board, 173
Scottish Water Advisory Committee,
    134
Scottish Women's Rural Institutes,
    financial assistance to, 57
Sea fisheries, 166, 168
Sea transport services, 171
Seals, 8, 191, 192
Secretary for Scotland Acts (1885 and
    1887), 15, 16
Secretary of State for Scotland:
    as arbiter of land use, 57
    as landowner, 43, 52
    as Scotland's Minister, 1, 3, 7, 79
    general functions and responsibili-
        ties, 1, 3-7, 18-21, 28, 67, 106, 120,
        123, 134, 136, 146, 152, 155, 169,
        170, 173-179
    joint responsibilities, 53, 78, 114, 123,
        128, 166, 181-187
    Parliamentary responsibilities, 6, 16,
        28, 187
    rights of appeal to, 37, 76, 111, 127,
        132
    Seal of, 8
    transfers of functions, 15-17, 18-21,
        98, 115, 116, 165, 169, 170
Secretary of State for Scotland, Office
    of:
    creation, 6
    development, 18-21, 98, 145
    holders of, 216
    reorganisation of, 18
Service Departments, land require-
    ments of, 123
Sewage disposal, 133
Sheriff Clerk's Office, staffing of, 146
Sheriff Courts, 192, 199, 207
Sheriffs, appointment of, 204
Shops, legislation concerning, 158
Silo subsidies, 62
Slaughterhouses, hygiene and control
    of, 115
Small Landholders (Scotland) Acts,
    42, 215
Smoke-control areas, designation of,
    135
Social Service, Scottish Council of, 57
Society for the Vindication of Scottish
    Rights, 13, 15

Solicitor-General for Scotland:
    duties of, 4, 25, 203
    holders of Office of, 219
Solicitor's Office, 29
Sorn Committee, 163
South of Scotland Electricity Board,
    169, 170
Special Housing Association, Scottish,
    138-139
Standing Committee, Scottish, 27
State Management Districts, 146, 158
State Management (licensed premises),
    146, 158
Steamer services, subsidies for, 171
Stud farms, 50

Teachers, 86, 90
    certificates, 86, 87
    emergency scheme, 88
    guidance of, 83
    of handicapped children, 87
    pensions, 95, 96-97
    qualifications of, 92
    recruitment of, 87-89
    salaries regulations, 89
    superannuation regulations, 95,
        96-97
    Training Colleges, 86-89
    training of, 82
    training regulations, 86
    University graduates, 88, 89
Teaching hospitals, 107
Theatres, 158
Tourist Board, Scottish, 173
Town and Country Planning. (See
    Planning)
Town Councils, powers of, 31
Transport, 165, 170, 172, 174
Treasure Trove, 199
Treasury representative in Scotland,
    198
Treaty of Union, 11, 192, 194, 198
Trees:
    licences for felling, 185
    preservation orders, 122, 128
Trunk roads, planning control, 127
Tuberculosis, control of, 112

University Grants Committee, 93
University matters, 209
University scholarships, 100
Universities, and teaching hospitals, 107
University education, 67

Valuation and Rating (Scotland) Act
    (1956), 162, 163

Valuation of Lands (Scotland) Act (1854), 197
Valuation of Public undertakings, 197
Valuation Rolls, 192
Veterinary services, 50
Village halls, grants for, 164
Vocational education and training, 70-71, 91
Voluntary Boards, delegation of responsibilities to, 113

War pensioners, medical care of, 20
Warrants, 8, 154, 158
Water Advisory Committee, Scottish, 134
Water supplies:
  Departmental responsibilities and duties, 133-134
  farm, 40
  Local Authorities responsibilities, 134
  Rural Water Supplies and Sewerage Acts, 133, 134

Welfare foods, distribution of, 109
Welfare services:
  Departmental responsibilities and duties, 116-120
  for children, 159-160
  for the mentally ill, 188
  Local Authority responsibilities, 118-120
West of Scotland Agricultural College, 54
Whaling, 168
White Fish Authority, 166, 167
Whitley Councils, 109, 111
Woodlands (see also Forestry)
  Dedication Schemes, 184
  Licences for felling, 185
Women's Rural Institutes, 57

Young offenders, 150
Young persons, employment of, 78
Youth Clubs, 71
Youth and Employment service, 78, 83